# 30Strategies

## *for High-Profit*

# INVESTMENT
# SUCCESS

Donald L. Cassidy

**Dearborn**
Financial Publis. ౩, Inc.®

This publication is designed to provide accurate and authoritative information in regard to the subject matter covered. It is sold with the understanding that the publisher is not engaged in rendering legal, accounting, or other professional service. If legal advice or other expert assistance is required, the services of a competent professional person should be sought.

Editorial Director: Cynthia A. Zigmund
Managing Editor: Jack Kiburz
Interior design: Lucy Jenkins
Cover Design: Scott Rattray, Rattray Design
Typesetting: Professional Resources & Communications, Inc.

Published by Dearborn Financial Publishing, Inc.®

Printed in the United States of America

98 99 00 10 9 8 7 6 5 4 3 2

**Library of Congress Cataloging-in-Publication Data**
Cassidy, Don.
 30 strategies for high-profit investment success / Donald L. Cassidy.
 p. cm.
 Includes index.
 ISBN 0-7931-2680-0 (pbk.)
 1. Securities. I. Title.
 HG4521.C298 1998
 332.6--dc21                                                    97-28276
                                                                    CIP

# Contents

# PREFACE

*I*ndividual investors with some experience who do not need another volume of definitions and basic concepts, but instead are seeking answers about the nuances and "potholes" in the investment markets will find this book profitable and revealing. You understand that success comes not from hitting "home runs" but from avoiding "doubleplays" and "strikeouts." You know the basics and now want an insider's edge.

This volume comprises four clusters of strategies:

1. Strategies 1 to 11 are about you, your behavior, and your investing psychology. Who you are and how you act are integral factors in how well you perform in any given market environment.
2. Strategies 12 to 20 cover often-troublesome and mystifying aspects of specific kinds of investment media— focusing on their inherent pitfalls and potentials.
3. Strategies 21 to 24 deal with asset allocation in the context of a dynamic lifelong plan.
4. Strategies 25 to 30 focus on the details of smart, efficient, effective execution. Even good investors must also execute tactics well to maximize results.

A major underlying theme is the need to be *contrarian* in your investing behavior. Among other things, this means always looking for counterintuitive possibilities. That's important because what makes you most comfortable is what already has been happening for a long time. Staying in your comfort zone gets you into trouble because it lets you keep thinking in the past, while investment markets are always changing. If you take away a single insight from reading this book, let it be: What is counterintuitive is probably less risky than what seems obvious.

Our era is one of specialization and microexpertise, often at the expense of the overall context. This book allows you to step back, take in the overall view, and interact with the markets more profitably and confidently, because you will have become more savvy about possibilities and pitfalls. Investing has become a necessary personal skill for well-being in the 1990s and beyond. Doing it better is not only more profitable but also immensely more satisfying and fun. So, enjoy the backstage tour you're about to take!

# Make a Road Map for Yourself

### It's Entirely Up to You

*You* are in charge of your own future standard of living! Your wealth will determine your degree of freedom in your later years—freedom to travel, to buy privacy and quiet if you wish, to make gifts for grandchildren's educations, to leave needed sums to your spouse and/or children. You may wish to endow a room at the library or donate to a conservation project, enable needy kids to play youth basketball, or just know you have enough for whatever might happen.

Getting there will require some effort and discipline. Time will be either your enemy or your friend: The sooner you start investing, the less you'll need to save. Sad to say, most Americans are grossly underprepared. Stanford University professor of Economics B. Douglas Bernheim concluded in a recent study that baby boomers are saving only one-third of what they must to maintain their current standard of living after retirement and that was *assuming* taxes don't rise and Social Security benefits are not cut.

Just because you reach age 65 doesn't mean you will arrive prepared. You need to do something about it, starting now! Figure out where you want to be financially, and when. Defining your needs and goals will make you more aware of what you must do to meet them. The sooner you draw your map and start on the proper road, the less difficult your trip will be, and the less you'll need to cut back on current consumption to ensure your future comfort. This is mainly an investment strategy and tactics book, not another of the many on financial planning. But drawing your road map is truly imperative.

## Figure Out Your Needs

This book is mainly about investing well to achieve your needs and goals. Articles in money-oriented magazines constantly offer planning tips for figuring your needs. This book, however, will summarize key ideas to help you develop a full road map.

Your first step is to figure out what you need to accomplish with investment efforts. This is not difficult to do, particularly when you consider the following equation:

$$\text{Needs} - \text{Resources} = \text{Deficit to cure}$$

The rough part comes in pinning down specific needs. You are estimating in future dollars, a slippery unit of account. For most of recorded history, inflation has prevailed. A dollar today buys less than it did five or twenty years ago. But we can't know just how much less a dollar will buy when we will be ready to retire.

Over the long term, average rates of return on investments tend to outrun inflation. But that doesn't necessarily apply for every move you might make. Rather, it means that interest rates (prices that owners of money charge others for its use) scale up from the expected inflation rate. Money owners would be foolish to knowingly lend their asset for a lower rate than the speed of its decline in purchasing power—and they want to be paid on top of that.

Here's how it works: Suppose a loaf of bread costs a dollar today and you expect it to cost $1.10 next year. Being smart, you'd refuse to let me borrow your dollar for less than 10 percent interest (that extra dime) to compensate you for not buying and freezing the bread now, plus some "real" interest to compensate you for "renting" that dollar rather than using it yourself.

Yet, shockingly, people leave trillions in banks or money market accounts at low rates of interest that actually guarantee loss of purchasing power. Suppose you leave money in the bank at 3.6 percent when inflation is 2.5 percent per year. Pay your taxes on 3.6 percent at about a 33 percent combined rate and you have only 2.4 percent left. You'll have lost ground and irreplaceable time, simply to get the supposed "safety" of an insured bank CD or an uninsured money market fund account. For more on this topic, see Strategy 4.

To estimate needs, many professional retirement planners say you should expect to need about two-thirds of your earned income to maintain an equivalent lifestyle in retirement (estimates range from 60 percent up to 80 percent). Why? Several major needs will be lower. Mortgage payments should be completed, a smaller retirement home bought, or the remaining balance refinanced for a lower monthly payment. Commuting expenses will disappear, as will costs of a full workplace wardrobe and lunches out. And, if you've planned well, you will not need to save any income as you did before you retired. You may also be in a lower tax bracket, meaning you'll need less income before taxes.

## Look at Your Resources

There are three major kinds of resources. For too many people, Social Security will prove their largest. You're reading this book because you're determined not to be among those unfortunates. Employer-sponsored pension or profit-sharing plans are another major source of future income and assets. Personal savings and investments must make up the rest. This is the pot over which you have most direct control (how much you put in), and also where greatest variations in results (investment returns) can occur. A major purpose of this book is to help you avoid mistakes that will shrink that pot's size below its optimal potential. (Windfall sources of assets or income are available to a few people, but I must assume you will not win the lottery or gain an inheritance or trust fund. If you do, consider it icing on the cake. What if your rich aunt should live to be 110? No inheritance would come until you're 80, and more likely it will go for her elder-care costs.)

### Social Security

While the system will come under increasing pressure around the years 2010–2020, it's a politically safe bet it will not be abandoned or deeply cut. A realistic worst-case scenario might be a freeze on benefits (which of course would be painful if there is inflation). There also is talk of changing inflation indexes to limit benefit increases! You should, perhaps every two years, visit or call a nearby Social Security Administration office and ask for booklets describing current benefits levels. You also should mail a postcard-size SSA Form 7004, available by phoning 800-772-1213, that will generate a custom report of your benefit "account" status. (No one has an actual pile of dollars at Social Security, waiting to be withdrawn; thus my quotes around that word "account." We each have an entitlement based on current law and our past earnings history; benefits also depend on your age when you choose to start drawing, and on marital status.)

### Employer-Sponsored Plans

What about pension and profit-sharing plans associated with your job? Many fewer workers than in past generations will have a pension whose amount is guaranteed. Such so-called defined-*benefit* plans are going the way of dinosaurs. They're expensive and risky for companies to fund, because most are based on a percentage of final years' earnings, which could be driven up by late inflation. Such formulas are much like those now straining Social Security. Also, pension plans are associated with the government sector and with industries where union membership is common, industries in long-term decline. The good news is that more pensions are now insured, and many benefits are portable. Ask your personnel department what your expected monthly benefit amount will be upon retirement. Start inquiring years in advance so you can do something to supplement the final amount.

Defined-contribution and profit-sharing retirement plans have grown sharply in the past 20 years and will continue to involve more of the workforce in coming decades. These are so named because they contain formulas determining how much money is put in for you but don't guarantee what your eventual benefits will be. This lack of guarantee is because no one can know what returns will be achieved on your invested assets. Employers no longer will be ultimate guarantors of investment returns. In a best-case scenario, a defined-contribution plan's assets are invested by professional money managers. This is better than having senior company officers—who may be very good at the lumber business, but not very sharp, by Wall Street standards, making investment decisions as plan trustees.

Increasingly, companies with defined-contribution plans remove themselves as much as possible from responsibility for the size of their employees' eventual retirement assets or income streams. They don't guarantee a monthly pension amount (the old defined benefit); they do cede money management to outside professionals (quite often, via mutual funds); and they also force each employee to decide how to allocate his or her assets among several or many investment options. This has some benefits, in the form of increased control and flexibility, and the ability to implement an overall asset mix across various pots of money (company and personal). However, that shifts a serious burden to individuals: to learn about and make choices that literally will determine their future standards of living.

So, like it or not, each of us is now significantly responsible for the success of our employer-sponsored retirement plan! Our population's level of economic and financial sophistication and education to date has been woefully inadequate to the task. The mutual funds industry, through the Investment Company Institute, began addressing this issue in the early 1990s and is developing good educational materials. Several large mutual fund families and insurance companies also offer various helpful free kits and booklets. Use these as means of self-education and as aids for determining your needs; bear in mind the product biases of firms providing these materials and choose your own investments according to your needs rather than being dazzled by their products being featured. One size does not fit all!

## Accumulating What You Need, When You Need It

Now, you can define your approximate retirement needs in terms of monthly or annual income; you can roughly figure your Social Security benefits; and you can get some estimate from your employer of what level of income might be available from your pension or other retirement plan. To learn what deficit you must make up, subtract those resources from the overall need per month or per year. That is the amount described in the formula as "deficit to cure." That deficit is defined in terms of annual income—a stream of cash you'll need or want for spending.

### Determining Needed Income

Here is where the figuring can get a bit more tricky. You are aiming to create a source of annual spendable money. You can do that only by amassing a pool of assets. You need to do some math and make some assumptions in order to translate the "income deficit to cure" into a sum of money (principal) that will do the job. Some of those assumptions are controlled by your own preferences; others will be determined by economic conditions at the time you retire. What rate of return will you earn on investments once you stop working? If your income deficit to cure is $12,000 a year before taxes, and if interest rates on long-term U.S. government bonds happen to be 10 percent, you'll need $120,000 in assets to provide the income. But if rates are 6 percent, you'll need $200,000. Both of those calculations assume that inflation will not make you need more than that $12,000 annually and also that you want to live off just income and never draw down principal. (They also assume you want to leave just the needed principal amount to your heirs, favorite charities, or both.)

You also could decide to amass only a smaller kitty on the assumption that you will spend not only the income but also some principal each year. Getting $12,000 to spend each year in this mode requires a smaller asset pool to start, but involves significant danger. The worst problem, and a very real risk, is that you could adopt consume-the-principal assumptions and later see medical science enable you to outlive your resources. You might assume that you will retire at 65 and live to 80, and then actually last to 92, for example. Another real problem is that this approach leaves no cushion for inflation, because you are already counting on eating up all principal. If you think you'll need $12,000 a year and create assets of $200,000 to provide it at 6 percent interest, you have a $200,000 asset cushion in case it turns out inflation makes you need $14,000 a year instead.

Tables frequently published in magazine articles will quickly tell you how many dollars will generate a given annual income without invading principal, and how many years you can live off principal and income at various draw-down rates before running out. My strong suggestion is to plan on an interest-only basis or somewhere in between, thereby leaving yourself a cushion—it's better to be safe than sorry.

### Interest or Capital Growth?

In preceding paragraphs, I have taken some liberties with the word *interest*, occasionally using it, imprecisely, as an easy conceptual means of describing total return on capital: dividends on stocks, interest on bonds, and capital gains. Especially as they soberly look ahead at the future in terms of "income" needs, most people think automatically in terms of interest on money, like interest on a bank CD or interest on municipal or government bonds. A major theme in several later chapters is that investing for interest (using the word literally) is the wrong way to achieve best results. Instead, total return, meaning the sum of current income and more importantly growth of capital, is the way to comfortable wealth. In later years, when your risk-taking ability decreases, a rising percentage of your total return should come as cash income rather than capital growth. But as long as there is a threat of inflation, interest alone will fail you unless that interest flow exceeds your spending. You need capital growth even into your 80s and 90s.

### Determining Annual Amounts to Invest

So far, you've made an estimate of your "deficit to cure": what future income rate must come from your personal savings and investments to ensure your desired standard of living. You have translated that income requirement, after making some assumptions, into an asset amount needed at an assumed age. The following tables will help you understand how much money you must set aside annually, assuming various long-term average rates of return, to reach your asset goal. What you need to save and then invest successfully is primarily determined by your retirement needs, but, fortunately, is reduced by the future value of what you already have in hand.

---

**FIGURE 1.1**    Value of Initial $10,000 Sum Invested at Various Rates

| | | Rate of Return | | |
|---|---|---|---|---|
| **Years** | **3%** | **6%** | **9%** | **12%** |
| 5 | $11,593 | $ 13,382 | $ 15,386 | $  17,623 |
| 10 | 13,439 | 17,908 | 23,674 | 31,058 |
| 12 | 14,258 | 20,122 | 28,127 | 38,960 |
| 14 | 15,126 | 22,609 | 33,417 | 48,871 |
| 16 | 16,047 | 25,404 | 39,703 | 61,304 |
| 18 | 17,024 | 28,543 | 47,171 | 76,900 |
| 20 | 18,061 | 32,071 | 56,044 | 96,463 |
| 22 | 19,161 | 36,035 | 66,586 | 121,003 |
| 24 | 20,328 | 40,489 | 79,111 | 151,786 |
| 26 | 21,566 | 45,494 | 93,992 | 190,401 |
| 28 | 22,879 | 51,117 | 111,671 | 238,839 |
| 30 | 24,273 | 57,435 | 132,677 | 299,599 |
| 35 | 28,139 | 76,861 | 204,140 | 527,996 |
| 40 | 32,620 | 102,857 | 314,094 | 930,510 |
| 45 | 37,816 | 137,646 | 483,273 | 1,639,876 |
| 50 | 43,839 | 184,202 | 743,575 | 2,890,022 |

---

Figure 1.1 shows future values, after various numbers of years, of $10,000 now in hand and left invested undisturbed at various average rates of return. You can multiply the terminal values in the table by how many $10,000 sums you already have in retirement investments. If you have $35,000, multiply the ending amount by 3.5. Then, subtract the amount you derive by using this first table from your overall principal sum needed.

Here is an example of how this works: Suppose you're 41 now and want to retire at 65. Your present money sum has 24 years to grow larger. Suppose you assumed a 9 percent return and already have $12,000 set aside (not counting money for college expenses—a whole separate need!). At 9 percent, $10,000 will grow in 24 years to $79,111. Since you start having 1.2 times $10,000, you can multiply $79,111 by 1.2, and you'll have $94,933 at age 65 from your present nest egg (let's call it $95,000 to keep the numbers easy to handle). Compound interest is a wonderful thing, especially over a long period and particularly in a tax-deferred vehicle.

Since you've already "taken care of" that first $95,000, you can now subtract it from your overall need. Suppose, as earlier, you found you'll need $200,000 at age 65. After subtracting the $95,000, you find you must accumulate another $105,000 in 24 years. Now move to the second table, keeping that $105,000 net deficit figure in mind.

**FIGURE 1.2**    Required Annual Deposits at Various Return Rates to Accumulate $10,000

| | **Rate of Return** | | | |
|---|---|---|---|---|
| **Years** | **3%** | **6%** | **9%** | **12%** |
| 5 | $1,828.69 | $1,673.55 | $1,532.96 | $1,405.44 |
| 10 | 846.90 | 715.74 | 603.85 | 508.79 |
| 12 | 684.10 | 559.22 | 455.51 | 369.97 |
| 14 | 568.22 | 448.91 | 352.60 | 275.64 |
| 16 | 481.66 | 367.47 | 277.98 | 208.84 |
| 18 | 414.65 | 305.25 | 222.13 | 160.15 |
| 20 | 361.32 | 256.46 | 179.33 | 123.92 |
| 22 | 317.94 | 217.41 | 145.92 | 96.52 |
| 24 | 282.01 | 185.65 | 119.47 | 75.57 |
| 26 | 251.83 | 159.47 | 98.31 | 59.39 |
| 28 | 226.15 | 137.67 | 81.21 | 46.82 |
| 30 | 204.07 | 119.33 | 67.31 | 37.00 |
| 35 | 160.58 | 84.66 | 42.53 | 20.68 |
| 40 | 128.76 | 60.96 | 27.15 | 11.64 |
| 45 | 104.71 | 44.34 | 17.45 | 6.57 |
| 50 | 86.07 | 32.49 | 11.26 | 3.72 |

Figure 1.2 shows how much you need to invest, once a year, at various average rates of return, and for various lengths of

time, to end up with $10,000 at a future date. Looking at the intersection of 9 percent and 24 years, you see the answer is $119.47 per year. That will get you, now age 41, $10,000 at age 65. But you just found you'll need $105,000. So you multiply $130.22 by 10.5, being the ratio of 105 to 10; your result is $1,254 per year. Think of it as just under $105 a month. (Actually, due to compounding, monthly investments a bit less than one-twelfth any annual amount will do the job. Divide your annual saving amount by 12 for a monthly rate and you'll end up with more than that $105,000 you planned on needing.)

## But Don't Forget...

One nontrivial note to all of this: As you may have guessed, the magic word is *taxes*. The $200,000 you need to cure the retirement-income deficit needs to be an after-tax sum, or it will not all be available to generate a 6 percent income. So the returns you choose to assume when using the last two tables need to be after-tax returns. The implication? Invest all you can and all you dare in tax-deferred vehicles (IRAs, Keoghs, variable annuity contracts, and your 401(k) or 403(b) plan at work). I say "dare" because of penalties, namely taxes and partial forfeitures, associated with early withdrawals from these tax-deferred vehicles. What you put into them must be serious long-term money. Figure 1.3 shows what just half the currently allowable maximum IRA contribution can become over a lifetime!

---

**FIGURE 1.3**   Table of Accumulations
(Assuming No Taxation in Period, Annual $1,000
Deposit January 1)

| End of Year Number | Rate of Return in Percent/Year | | | | |
|---|---|---|---|---|---|
| | **3%** | **5%** | **8%** | **10%** | **12%** |
| 1 | $ 1,030 | $ 1,050 | $ 1,080 | $ 1,100 | $ 1,120 |
| 2 | 2,091 | 2,153 | 2,246 | 2,310 | 2,374 |
| 3 | 3,184 | 3,310 | 3,506 | 3,641 | 3,779 |
| 4 | 4,309 | 4,526 | 4,867 | 5,105 | 5,353 |
| 5 | 5,468 | 5,802 | 6,336 | 6,716 | 7,115 |

*(continued on next page)*

**FIGURE 1.3**　(continued)

| End of Year Number | Rate of Return in Percent/Year | | | | |
|---|---|---|---|---|---|
| | **3%** | **5%** | **8%** | **10%** | **12%** |
| 6 | 6,662 | 7,142 | 7,923 | 8,487 | 9,089 |
| 7 | 7,892 | 8,549 | 9,637 | 10,436 | 11,300 |
| 8 | 9,159 | 10,027 | 11,488 | 12,579 | 13,776 |
| 9 | 10,464 | 11,578 | 13,487 | 14,937 | 16,549 |
| 10 | 11,808 | 13,207 | 15,645 | 17,531 | 19,655 |
| 11 | 13,192 | 14,917 | 17,977 | 20,384 | 23,133 |
| 12 | 14,618 | 16,713 | 20,495 | 23,523 | 27,029 |
| 13 | 16,086 | 18,599 | 23,215 | 26,975 | 31,393 |
| 14 | 17,599 | 20,579 | 26,152 | 30,772 | 36,280 |
| 15 | 19,157 | 22,657 | 29,324 | 34,950 | 41,753 |
| 16 | 20,762 | 24,840 | 32,750 | 39,545 | 47,884 |
| 17 | 22,414 | 27,132 | 36,450 | 44,599 | 54,750 |
| 18 | 24,117 | 29,539 | 40,446 | 50,159 | 62,440 |
| 19 | 25,870 | 32,066 | 44,762 | 56,275 | 71,052 |
| 20 | 27,676 | 34,719 | 49,423 | 63,002 | 80,699 |
| 21 | 29,537 | 37,505 | 54,457 | 70,403 | 91,503 |
| 22 | 31,453 | 40,430 | 59,893 | 78,543 | 103,603 |
| 23 | 33,426 | 43,502 | 65,765 | 87,497 | 117,155 |
| 24 | 35,459 | 46,727 | 72,106 | 97,347 | 132,334 |
| 25 | 37,553 | 50,113 | 78,954 | 108,182 | 149,334 |
| 26 | 39,710 | 53,669 | 86,351 | 120,100 | 168,374 |
| 27 | 41,931 | 57,403 | 94,339 | 133,210 | 189,699 |
| 28 | 44,219 | 61,323 | 102,966 | 147,631 | 213,583 |
| 29 | 46,575 | 65,439 | 112,283 | 163,494 | 240,333 |
| 30 | 49,003 | 69,761 | 122,346 | 180,943 | 270,293 |
| 31 | 51,503 | 74,299 | 133,214 | 200,138 | 303,848 |
| 32 | 54,078 | 79,064 | 144,951 | 221,252 | 341,429 |
| 33 | 56,730 | 84,067 | 157,627 | 244,477 | 383,521 |
| 34 | 59,462 | 89,320 | 171,317 | 270,024 | 430,663 |
| 35 | 62,276 | 94,836 | 186,102 | 298,127 | 483,463 |
| 36 | 65,174 | 100,628 | 202,070 | 329,039 | 542,599 |
| 37 | 68,159 | 106,710 | 219,316 | 363,043 | 608,831 |
| 38 | 71,234 | 113,095 | 237,941 | 400,448 | 683,010 |
| 39 | 74,401 | 119,800 | 258,057 | 441,593 | 766,091 |
| 40 | 77,663 | 126,840 | 279,781 | 486,852 | 859,142 |
| 41 | 81,023 | 134,232 | 303,244 | 536,637 | 963,359 |
| 42 | 84,484 | 141,993 | 328,583 | 591,401 | 1,080,083 |
| 43 | 88,048 | 150,143 | 355,950 | 651,641 | 1,210,813 |
| 44 | 91,720 | 158,700 | 385,506 | 717,905 | 1,357,230 |
| 45 | 95,501 | 167,685 | 417,426 | 790,795 | 1,521,218 |

Municipal bond brokers argue that the tax burden implies you should put all you can into municipal bonds or municipals funds. Those may have a place, but they're not a whole answer. Why? Their after-tax yields are below those to be had in stocks over the long term, and traditional bonds never provide protection from inflation (loss of purchasing power). Figure 1.4 shows how both taxes and inflation seriously reduce the real future spendable value of principal invested on a deferred taxable basis.

**FIGURE 1.4**  Savings Results
(Assuming Various Return Rates)

| Amount Saved | $40,000 | $30,000 | $20,000 |
|---|---|---|---|
| Rate (%) | Ending Sum Resulting | | |
| 0 | $ 40,000 | $ 30,000 | $20,000 |
| 1 | 48,886 | 34,785 | 22,019 |
| 1.5 | 54,268 | 37,539 | 23,124 |
| 2 | 60,402 | 40,568 | 24,297 |
| 3 | 75,401 | 47,575 | 26,870 |
| 4 | 95,025 | 56,085 | 29,778 |
| 5 | 120,800 | 66,439 | 33,066 |
| 6 | 154,762 | 79,058 | 36,785 |
| 7 | 199,635 | 94,461 | 40,995 |
| 8 | 259,057 | 113,283 | 45,762 |
| 9 | 337,882 | 136,308 | 51,160 |
| 10 | 442,592 | 164,494 | 57,275 |
| 11 | 581,826 | 199,021 | 64,203 |
| 12 | 767,091 | 241,333 | 72,052 |

After Taxes at 33% Combined

| | $40,000 | $30,000 | $20,000 |
|---|---|---|---|
| 0 | $ 40,000 | $ 30,000 | $20,000 |
| 1 | 45,954 | 33,206 | 21,353 |
| 1.5 | 49,560 | 35,051 | 22,093 |
| 2 | 53,669 | 37,081 | 22,879 |
| 3 | 63,719 | 41,775 | 24,603 |
| 4 | 76,867 | 47,477 | 26,551 |
| 5 | 94,136 | 54,414 | 28,754 |
| 6 | 116,891 | 62,869 | 31,246 |
| 7 | 146,955 | 73,189 | 34,067 |
| 8 | 186,768 | 85,800 | 37,261 |
| 9 | 239,581 | 101,226 | 40,877 |
| 10 | 309,737 | 120,111 | 44,974 |
| 11 | 403,023 | 143,244 | 49,616 |
| 12 | 527,151 | 171,593 | 54,875 |

**FIGURE 1.4**  (continued)

| Amount Saved | $40,000 | $30,000 | $20,000 |
|---|---|---|---|
| Rate (%) | Ending Sum Resulting | | |
| After Inflation at 3% | | | |
| 0 | $ 12,262 | $12,360 | $11,074 |
| 1 | 14,087 | 13,680 | 11,822 |
| 1.5 | 15,193 | 14,441 | 12,232 |
| 2 | 16,453 | 15,277 | 12,668 |
| 3 | 19,533 | 17,211 | 13,622 |
| 4 | 23,564 | 19,560 | 14,701 |
| 5 | 28,858 | 22,418 | 15,921 |
| 6 | 35,834 | 25,901 | 17,300 |
| 7 | 45,050 | 30,153 | 18,862 |
| 8 | 57,255 | 35,348 | 20,630 |
| 9 | 73,445 | 41,704 | 22,633 |
| 10 | 94,952 | 49,484 | 24,901 |
| 11 | 123,550 | 59,015 | 27,471 |
| 12 | 161,602 | 70,694 | 30,383 |
| After Inflation at 4% | | | |
| 0 | $ 8,332 | $ 9,250 | $ 9,128 |
| 1 | 9,572 | 10,238 | 9,745 |
| 1.5 | 10,323 | 10,807 | 10,083 |
| 2 | 11,179 | 11,433 | 10,442 |
| 3 | 13,272 | 12,880 | 11,228 |
| 4 | 16,011 | 14,638 | 12,118 |
| 5 | 19,608 | 16,777 | 13,123 |
| 6 | 24,347 | 19,384 | 14,260 |
| 7 | 30,609 | 22,565 | 15,548 |
| 8 | 38,902 | 26,454 | 17,005 |
| 9 | 49,902 | 31,210 | 18,656 |
| 10 | 64,515 | 37,032 | 20,526 |
| 11 | 83,945 | 44,165 | 22,644 |
| 12 | 109,800 | 52,905 | 25,044 |

Note: These tables assume a single taxation event at end of period, not in process.

## Double Magic: Compounding and Tax Deferral

Many investors know the magic of compound interest as well as the "rule of 72," which says that 72 divided by the percentage rate of return gives the number of years money takes to double.

Few, however, realize a second aspect of compounding math—
one that makes tax-deferred investing work in your favor: Total
dollars gained jump more than the difference in the rate of
return. So, better to invest tax-deferred and pay a lump-sum tax
later than to pay as you go, at the same tax rate.

Here is an example, which also is shown in brief numerical
form as Figure 1.5: Taxable investor T invests $1,000 at 9 percent
in a taxable vehicle (e.g., a bond mutual fund paying 9 percent
as current income, in her own name). Assume a combined tax

**FIGURE 1.5**   Advantages of Tax Deferral
*Assume $1,000 invested at 9 percent for 25 years, and
current or deferred at 33.33 percent combined rate.*

|  | Pay-as-You-Go Investor T | Savvy Deferral Investor D |
|---|---|---|
| Starting Investment before | $1,000 | $1,000 |
| Ending Tax | 4,292 | 8,623 |
| Ending Tax | ( 0) | (2,541) |
| Net Assets | 4,292 | 6,082 |
| Advantage | — | 1,790 |

bracket of 33.33 percent. Therefore, her net return is 6 percent
after taxes. In 25 years the sum will have grown, after paying
out its own taxes each year, to $4,292. Savvy tax-deferred
investor D invests $1,000 in an IRA using the same mutual fund.
No taxes will be due until proceeds are withdrawn in 25 years.
At 9 percent, D's IRA grows to $8,623 and all but the $1,000 contributed will be subject to tax. The one-third tax bite on $7,623 of
gain leaves $5,082 in after-tax gain, plus the $1,000 invested, or
$6,082 in total. That's nearly $1,800 better than T's result! In
terms of net dollars earned ($5,082 versus $3,292), tax deferral
provides more than a 54 percent advantage! Yes, D does take the
risk that tax rates will be higher in 25 years than along the way

(a combined rate of 56.82 percent would wipe out the advantage). But D also has the chance to time how much she will take out of her IRA each year, possibly allowing some or all gains to be taxed at a lower postretirement marginal rate (such as 20 percent, as under the current IRS code's 15 percent plus 5 percent for the state).

Each individual or couple has a somewhat different set of circumstances: its own mix of current assets, savings stream, college obligations, possible inheritances, and other such variables. Combinations are endless. A very good means of looking at a variety of scenarios has recently emerged. Several major no-load mutual fund families and some financial media have created personal computer software programs to help with financial planning. Among those you should consider, typically priced at or below $25, are:

- Dow Jones' *Plan Ahead for Your Financial Future*
- Fidelity's *Thinkware*
- T. Rowe Price's *Retirement Planning Kit*
- Price Waterhouse's *Secure Your Future,* a combination book/software package (about $37)
- *Getting Going* by *Wall Street Journal* columnist Jonathan Clements

Additional packages are likely to emerge for competitive reasons and as boomers begin to take their situations seriously. Check advertisements in popular investment-oriented magazines to learn of new offerings or ask a favorite funds company what it might have.

# Understand Whatever You Own

*T*his chapter, placed early so you'll not dare skip over it, addresses a dangerous error investors make very often and across many asset classes. For various reasons (some of which will be explored under Strategy 6), people tend to accumulate investment holdings they don't fully understand. That lack of understanding greatly raises the chance that these mystery investments will be held indeterminately. Such forever-floating holdings tend to become failures that can seriously frustrate your reaching a financially secure future. So, this strategy features a checklist of questions you should apply to each proposed idea before buying. Using these tests, you can avoid collecting mysteries that tend to decay, suddenly or slowly, into painful losses you could have avoided.

Most Americans, unfortunately, tend to be dangerously ignorant about economic, financial, business, and investment matters. We get little or no help in high school; few major in, or even expose themselves to, such subjects at the university level. Too much of education and training seems focused on passing certain qualifying examinations or on conveying certain specific facts or procedures. Grossly insufficient effort goes into teaching people how to solve problems, and how to discover information that will be useful in real adult life situations. In short, if it's not specifically covered "in the manual," too many people have no clue about how to do it.

Investments are an area where such lack of information and sophistication is rampant. People understand they must keep enough money in a checking account to prevent checks from bouncing. But nearly everyone's eyes quickly glaze over when phrases like monetary policy, currency swaps, depreciation reserves, yield to maturity, burn rates, or debt/equity ratios are used.

To be fair, financial specialists do not know how to erect a bridge, make a skyscraper stand against winds, build a personal computer, or make sure a dam keeps generating electricity. The difference is that we are not expected to do these things for ourselves. By contrast, we are essentially on our own in managing our financial affairs. The problem is that the sales staffs of Wall Street firms are paid mainly to place new investment securities and packaged investment products with the public. They are not educated in the nuances necessary to help investors decide when it would be better to sell and move on, nor do compensation structures directly encourage brokers to act as informed counselors on such questions. They get commissions when you buy and when you sell, but not when you ask probing questions and certainly not when you do nothing (except when mutual funds pay them 12b-1 fees). Their efforts are focused on current product-of-the-month selling, not on what is called "hand-holding" after the sale. The widely encouraged buy-and-hold mentality conveniently serves their position: Investors should innocently ask no tough questions, be patient, keep what they've been sold, and frequently add new assets.

Many investors spend more time investigating and planning the purchase of an auto, VCR, or vacation package than they do when buying a security whose profit or loss will directly and profoundly change their later standard of living for many years. With tangible products, we know more questions to ask; we can often push the control buttons or take a test drive. There is no practical way to do this in the investment arena, especially with so many packaged new products lacking track records. Would you buy a riding mower or auto or VCR or a home-security or sprinkler system if it had no manual, no guarantee, and no organization making a standing promise to provide help afterward? Of course not! Yet many investors make investment purchases in just such a vacuum.

The value of an owners' manual or of a toll-free telephone line is that it helps the consumer know not only how to identify and fix certain minor problems, but also when a problem is serious. Thus informed, one can decide whether to invest in repairs or to dispose of the item for a replacement—and whether never to get involved in such a type of product again. Investments come without 800 or 888 numbers, except in the case of many families of mutual funds (to their great credit!). The security owner is on his or her own once the sale is made. There definitely is no warranty! Maybe that's why so many millions of households keep virtually all their money tucked away in the most simple places: bank accounts or perhaps certificates of deposit. They pretty much understand how these accounts work. If their institution is federally insured for the account size involved, they know there will be no real surprises. They can visit the bank and see the marble columns and the big vault. Counting in terms of paper dollars, a savings account can't lose them money. There's a certain amount of comfort in such a combination of attributes.

Financial instruments, or "products" as Wall Street has come to describe them, offer no such simplicity, no guarantees, and few owners' manuals. Sure, mutual funds and individual new securities issues must supply a prospectus, but it's typically a forbidding 98 pages of legalese. The annual report is usually a collection of incomprehensible financial schedules, followed by pages of tiny-print footnotes. These numbers are preceded by a letter from the company's chairman, who assures investors that things are going along just fine and thanks them for their continued support.

Do you own a mutual fund which, to your horror, you have discovered owns complex derivative securities that performed the wrong way? Did you believe this fund was quite safe because it specialized in rock-solid government bonds? Do you own stock in a recent start-up company that makes some kind of biotechnology-based products (or at least says it is researching them)? Or in a high-technology electronics firm that makes laser-guided thingamajigs that help computers do something-or-other faster or packed at higher density—whatever that might mean? Well, then you're one of millions who own financial "stuff" you don't understand. The information in this strategy will help you to do the following:

- Never again get stuck buying such mystery investments.
- Sort out and probably weed out much of what you've already collected, so your assets will be understandable and more useful.

### What Do You Know about the Investment?

The easiest way to find this out is to examine your level of understanding of a proposed new investment, and each you already own, using a checklist. Probably very few if any items will get a 100 percent score on this understandability scale. The lower the score, the longer you should pause and think before writing a check to buy. No investment is free of what-ifs (or else it has been presented in a too-perfect sales pitch!). Don't demand 100 percent perfection, or your money will be doomed to a bank account forever. But don't be foolhardy by being too forgiving.

Figure 2.1 offers a list of 20 critical questions whose answers will help you separate mystery financial "stuff" from useful investments that you will be able to sort out and live with (or dispose of) intelligently after the initial sale.

The questions are grouped into four major clusters: overview issues, aftermarket conditions, investment fundamentals, and exit questions. With the single exception of question 1, there is no particular order of importance. The answer to 1, however, is highly important and should guide you in answering all other 19 questions.

Your personal inability to answer one or more questions instantly should not automatically disqualify the proposed investment. It might reflect your current lack of knowledge regarding a specialty area rather than reveal a bad business idea. However, information gaps must be closed: If you cannot acquire answers readily, or a number of answers leave you feeling uncomfortable, that should raise a bright red flag and make you say, "thanks anyway."

---

**FIGURE 2.1**    20 Questions to Identify Mystery Investment "Stuff"

---

## Overview Issues

1.  Rank this investment idea at one of the following four levels:
    - ☐ Was this proposed investment introduced in a one-product seminar or as the single focus of a cold sales call?
      (Red alert!)
    - ☐ Was this idea suggested in a sales call initiated by a broker or financial planner?
      (Orange flag)
    - ☐ Did this arise after other discussion (including that of my needs), but in a conversation that I initiated?
      (Mild caution)
    - ☐ Was this my own idea?
      (Lowest concern)
2.  What can I learn about this investment at the library?
3.  How does this fit into my overall asset mix and balance?
4.  Can I accomplish very nearly the same financial effect with some other, simpler investment?
5.  Do I know anyone else who has had success with this kind of an investment for a reasonable period of time (over a year or two)?

## Aftermarket Considerations

6.  Do similar things exist whose performance histories I can check out for myself? Did the salesperson offer names of any?
7.  Where will I be able to track its value regularly without contacting the original seller? (This is a very telling point!)
8.  How liquid is the aftermarket—trading volume and typical bid/asked spread? Get this information independent of the seller.
9.  How can I take physical possession? Is that easy or difficult to do? Can I sell the investment without using the original dealer from whom I bought it?

---

**FIGURE 2.1**   (continued)

---

10. Is there a blackout period during which I cannot sell it? If so, how long is the period, and why does it exist?
11. What knowledgeable independent source could help me get needed information about this in the future?

## Understanding the Fundamentals

12. What is it—a debt or an equity?
13. Does it profess to provide me with any sort of guaranteed income?
14. What business success factors will make it work as described?
15. What would be some specific danger signs of trouble coming?
16. How will it be affected by each of the following: recession, expansion, inflation, deflation, changed regulation, tax law changes, or shifts in international currency values?
17. Does its likely total return demand no change in tax laws?
18. How will it affect my taxes? Am I putting it in the right kind of account (personal, versus trust, IRA, etc.)?

## The End Game: What Happens When It's Time to Exit?

19. Does the eventual net total return depend on a balloon event? Are there substantial exit costs or technical conditions required for my exit? If so, get them in writing before buying.
20. What three-part scenario do I have in mind (quantified story, time frame, and price) for closing this out?

---

### Analyzing Your Answers

**Overview issues.**   All 20 questions are important, but the most crucial three, in order, are 1, 20, and 14. Of these, 1 is most critical: It tips you to how sharp an eye you must use in answering the other questions.

1. If an investment idea came from outside you (levels 1–3), that means you probably have a lot to research. If it was introduced in a cold sales call (level 1) or was the entire focus of any call, be especially cautious and do your homework. If told, "You must buy right now," your response should be, "Well, I cannot do that, so good-bye." If you were contacted, or attended an interesting-sounding seminar to hear about this idea, then a sales professional will be selling you that one idea whether you need it or not. The higher on the alert scale you place this investment proposal, the more wary you need to be about it and the more independent of the selling organization you need to become when getting your information. At the other end of the spectrum, you can be much more relaxed if the idea was your own: People do not high-pressure-sell themselves things they don't or can't understand.

   In any event, for every proposed investment idea, you should always have a clear answer to questions 20 and 14. If the answer to question 1 puts you on red alert or raises an orange flag, be sure you have totally understandable and acceptable answers to questions 4, 6, 10, 16, and 19, preferably from the seller and in writing.

2. What you can learn about the investment at a library will depend on your detective skills and on how well you can get a research librarian to help you. New product and new company names will of course be impossible to find in hard-copy sources. Widen your topic a bit, but not too much. For example, if the company is proposing a biotechnology compound to treat a specific cancer, don't simply look up *drugs*, but also look up the name of the disease the product is supposed to treat. Find articles that describe promising approaches versus those that have disappointed or involve long odds. How does the company look now, based on this test? Look up the names of top executives in magazine indexes and who's-who volumes and be sure they have clean records and are not lifetime promoters. Check out the reputations of the brokerage firm(s) on the prospectus cover, especially the first one listed: Is there any pattern of complaints or suits?

3. Testing how the idea fits into your overall asset mix and balance is quite revealing. It will tell you how the risk/reward nature will sit with you over time and will reveal how much its seller has your needs in mind. Without revealing your own profile, ask the seller, "What kind of an investor is this suited for?" If you get a nonfitting response or double-talk, your research is done: Say no and invest elsewhere. No investment is ideal for everyone, so that answer is a dead giveaway, too.

4. Could some other, simpler investment do just about the same job for you? Ask the broker what is very much like what is being proposed, and why those others are not just as good. Ask what the commissions are on this and those other items for a same-size purchase. Be careful of newly packaged financial products that give bigger commissions but are not really much different. Reject things a seller claims are totally and excitingly unique, unless you verify that independently. If the new idea is different in several special or detailed ways, be sure you understand and are comfortable with all of them. A good example is a U.S. government bond fund, the first of its kind to use reverse repos, currency swaps, options on futures, caps, collars, and floors. If the seller can't explain all those and if you aren't comfortable that all are right for you, hit the "reject" button. New is not necessarily good.

5. It would be very reassuring to know someone independent of the selling broker who has had success with this kind of investment for a good period of time. This person might help you understand it and tell you the parts most puzzling to them. Talk to office colleagues, substantial investors you know, and unaffiliated brokers or financial planners. Listen carefully. Give no weight to recent-only success: You may be buying a new idea that has not yet had time to unravel under stress.

**Aftermarket considerations.**

6. Finding comparable companies or investment instruments whose records you can track either will contribute to or help you deny credibility. When a seller resists

helping you check such out, that's a very bright red flag. If you do identify similar situations, watch how much their prices fluctuate in a year (look at 52-week highs and lows) and see if they actually paid interest or dividends as promised in their original prospectuses. Once started, have dividends been consistent, raised or lowered, or are they only nominal? Absence of parallel situations means you'll be flying blind if you buy.

7. Where will you be able to check current price regularly without contacting the original seller? You ideally want to see this item, and preexisting peers, quoted daily in the *Wall Street Journal* or at least weekly in *Barron's*. A plan to be Nasdaq-listed should be stated in the prospectus where a lie would be fraud, not just conveyed orally. A listing under "local stocks" in your small-town paper is of weak comfort, and may indicate trading is very local and therefore thin. You don't want the original selling brokerage firm to be your only source of quotations or be the only market maker.

8. How liquid is its aftermarket? Trading volume and typical bid/asked spreads are important. Try to get a quotation on the item as if you were trying to sell it. See what the dealers' bid is. Definitely get this information independent of the seller.

9. Excluding commodities (you probably don't want umpteen bushels of soybeans in the front yard) it is good to find out if you can actually take physical possession. Is that easy or difficult to do? Can you sell the investment without using the original dealer from whom you bought it? Any mysteries or apparently unnecessarily exclusive arrangements involving the seller should raise bright red flags. The entire idea could be a scam. Call a major brokerage firm and ask if they could take transfer of the securities or contract from the selling dealer (name that broker); see what they say. Many bonds are now issued only as book entries, not as paper certificates. In such cases, be sure the transfer agent or trustee is a major bank.

10. If there is a blackout period during which you cannot sell the investment at all, or without major penalty, be very cautious. Specifically ask why such an embargo

exists. Make sure that does not hurt the owners while shielding the brokers. Ask for specific names of other investments with similar blackout periods; look them up yourself and see how prices acted after the blackout. Compare today's price to the initial offer price. You may be shocked at what you find.

11. What knowledgeable, trustably independent source could help you with future needed information about the investment? Do you have a friend or neighbor or know of a relative of a friend who will talk to you about it? Someone who works in that industry or technology area and understands key success/failure factors? A university professor who would read prospectus language about the technology and share his or her thoughts on prospects and risks, before you buy? You may not know many folks who might know, but if you can identify no one at all who knows anything useful, you may be dealing in a mystery or a total scam. You will be totally on your own down the road! Why should you accept that?

**Understanding the fundamentals.**

12. At the most basic level, what will you be investing in— debt or equity? Does the company owe you money and interest or not? If no, you are looking at equity, so any "promises" are going to be illusory and unenforceable. Equity should be called common or capital stock, or shares of beneficial interest, or perhaps partnership units. In the latter case, you will have a more complicated tax return and may have to pay taxes on profits in years when you get little or no cash distributions. If the word *warrants* is used, you are getting a leveraged instrument that will never pay any income and that will have value only if and when the underlying instrument (usually, the common stock) rises above a certain price. Be sure the warrants are *detachable*. This means there will be a trading market for the warrants by themselves. Otherwise you will need to come up with more money to exercise them before you can cash out. If options or futures are involved, you are dealing in short-term bets

on the amount of change in the underlying item. An option on a futures contract means you are two steps removed: counting on the change in the change. These are things that will need to be monitored hourly.

13. Does it profess to provide you with a guaranteed income? Promises are only as good those who make them. How much confidence do you have, and what do you even know, about the guarantor organization? How much in guarantees are they making, compared with their own net worth? Have they done this in the past, and for how long? Have any actual claims been made and met? If an income is guaranteed on anything other than a bond, be highly wary. Income, or current yield, is what sells investment product in the post-1987-market-crash world. You need to take a look at the financial numbers and figure out whether the guarantee is credible. Are any funds segregated, or backed by T-bills, etc.? Will the business dependably throw off enough cash to make the guaranteed income actually happen? (If this is a debt obligation, what is the credit rating?) For how long is the income stream guaranteed? If it stopped then and the quotation on the investment itself dropped to 50 percent or 25 percent of its starting level once the income disappeared, what kind of total return would that give you? (Sometimes promised income is not actually income but simply a flow of cash, largely or entirely returning your own capital!)

Does the payment stream depend on raising further pools of cash later? (That smells like, and could literally be, a Ponzi scheme, where later investors pay off early ones in chain-letter form until everything collapses when new players cannot be found.) In any case, the higher the promised income (anything over 10 percent should raise a bright red flag), the less likely it is sustainable. What seems too good to be true, probably is! For example, if building and renting out storage garages could produce returns of 30 percent a year forever for investors, the world would soon be covered with them. An eventual glut of storage space would reduce rents, so returns could not remain at 30 percent. Use common sense. Examine what would happen if this investment idea were carried out on a major scale: Would it still work for anyone besides promoters and brokers? Competitors and often falling prices are likely in good businesses!

14. What business success factors will make this investment work successfully? That is a very important question, and certainly one you'd ask if starting a new business yourself or buying an existing one from someone else. When you buy stock, you actually buy a small piece of a business; when you buy a bond, you lend that business money. Key factors to understand include the following: technology and patents; size and identity of the main competitors; marketing strengths and weaknesses; expertise and depth of management; capital intensity; and the effects of changes in regulation, taxes, and international currency values. Suppose the company in question produces a chemical whose secret formula only the genius founder knows. The miracle compound can be produced in the U.S. under an applied-for but ungranted patent 20 percent less expensively than in Germany, and since it is the best technology, it is effectively required by government regulation for cleaning up stack gases in the new widget industry. That set of conditions contains at least six crucial exclusive statements, any one of which could doom the company if terminated. Can you find them?

15. What would be some specific danger signs of trouble coming? You must know these so you can spot them quickly when and if they start appearing. You'd want to make a checklist and sell out once you see action on it. So you need to know the key success ingredients as in question 14. But could there be external forces such as tight labor or tight money markets at just the wrong time, which could strangle an otherwise successful company? Suppose it is in debt to the point where an equity secondary is needed and the market is very depressed? Might the company go bankrupt?

16. How will it be affected by each of the following: recession, expansion, inflation, deflation, changed regulation, or shifts in international currency values? You ought to be able to get these answers from the person recommending you buy. If it is a new securities issue, the

prospectus should discuss such matters under such captions as "business plan" and "risks." Think beyond the current situation. Do not assume continued rosy prosperity. What would happen if a recession and high inflation came in tandem, à la the 1970s? Could a lessening or tightening of regulation make the product or service unnecessary or illegal overnight? If major political shifts occur in Washington, such risks are very real!

17. Does the likely total return hinge on no change in tax laws? Since fewer traditional tax shelters exist now than 20 years ago, this question is no longer as important as it was then. Cash flow, however, is determined very heavily by tax rates, credits, exemptions, and allowable depreciation schedules. You may not expect these things to change, but they might. In that worst-case scenario, how would the investment fare? Here's an easy example: Suppose every source of income were tracked with 1099s, there was just one simple round-dollar exemption, and everyone paid a flat 15 percent tax after that. How would an H&R Block fare? You might consider such a tax change unlikely, but you'd at least know exactly what to be on guard for if you were a shareholder.

18. How will this investment affect your taxes? If it is a partnership, you need expert tax help, because these things could get you into complex tangles and reporting things wrong could get you everyone's nightmare: an IRS audit. Are you sure the structure is appropriate for the kind of account in which you would place it? There is no need to put even the most attractive zero-coupon municipal bond into your IRA account (you'd be making otherwise nontaxable income subject to tax on withdrawal). Will there be penalties for terminating the investment before a certain date, which could have adverse tax consequences? Consult an expert. If you are not willing to read and understand the dense legalese in a prospectus, you ought to say no and look for something simpler elsewhere. Presence of that language in the document creates a legal defense: They disclosed, you read, and you accepted; case dismissed!

**The End Game: What Happens When It's Time to Exit?**

19. Will your eventual total return depend on a single, distant, "balloon" event? In other words, is there some intended far-off final event (like selling the underlying assets) whose outcome would have a major effect on your results? An example would be a term trust investing in inner-city apartment buildings. Suppose that, at the end of the term, the home-finance market is terrible due to very high interest rates, or all the properties are in one city that is suffering from riots. How will you get your money out? Are there substantial exit costs? Check this in mutual fund, unit trust, and especially variable annuity contracts! Are very technical requirements, or multiple combinations of conditions, required for exit, and could these be used to disqualify your request to exit when you need the money? The latter should alert you that there's a trick waiting for you, just when you least can afford it.

20. What three-part scenario do you have in mind (quantified story, time frame, and price) for closing this out? You *must* have an answer to this before you enter any investment, or you are doomed to failure and to holding on probably until death do you part. Investors trip themselves here much too often. Two examples: You are buying Galactic Widgetronics, Ltd., because you expect that a new patent will be granted (story) before year's end (time), which will greatly boost sales (story) and thus raise earnings per share to at least $0.75 next year (quantified); the stock in 18 months (time) should therefore sell at 20 times earnings, or $15 per share (quantified). So you are buying now at $7 for a potential double. Or, for the more conservative: You believe interest rates are now quite near a major long-term cyclical high (story), with bond prices very depressed; you plan to retire in 17 years (time frame). Therefore you will buy $100,000 (quantified) of U.S. Treasury zero-coupon bond strips discounted to 25 cents on the dollar and put them in your IRA account. They mature in 16 years (time), meaning you will have locked in a 9 percent com-

pounded yield and then be liquid in T-bills to protect your overall portfolio value a year later when you retire. You plan to hold to maturity (time), and placing the bonds in your IRA will ward off the temptation to take them out earlier.

If you do not have a detailed plan for an investment when you acquire it, you will never know whether it is working. (Of course, a cynic would argue that may actually be why some people avoid creating the plan: They really don't want to know how badly things actually will be working out in the future.) If the plan does not contain specific quantified aspects (date, prices, expected earnings per share and price-earnings ratio, for example) you can always waffle and continue holding on the fuzzy hope things will get better. Write down your plan before buying; put a tickler on your long-term planning calendar, and force yourself to evaluate then. Failure to do this will keep you from judging past investments. (Be gentle: Consider it a test of the investments and not of yourself!) If you never do diagnostic checkups on past investments, they are doomed to remain in your collection forever because you have no standard for deciding whether to hold or fold. This failure is a prime reason people have such difficulty in selling, as contrasted with their cheerful ease in buying. Nonclosure is a killer of capital. We tend to forgive ourselves our mistakes (which then typically just get worse). We also fail to retest our successes critically, to see what we've learned and to ask pointedly whether we'd again buy them for further future holding. (Key hint: If you would not buy it again today, why are you still holding it?)

# Set Realistic Expectations

*F*ew people have solid ideas of what returns to expect from investing; others have preconceived notions, unfortunately of unrealistically high returns. It's important to have informed and realistic expectations. A grounding in realism will reduce frustration: Your judgments and decisions have a better chance of success than those based on myth or wild imaginings. Even with no guarantees in the investment arena, you do have a better chance to win and to avoid bad setbacks, if you start with a true picture of how the economic and investment worlds work. This strategy gives you some factual benchmarks. First, a few basic ideas: remember them as "the three nothings."

## The Three Nothings

**1. In investing, as in other areas of life, nothing comes easily.** Sure, once in a while you will get lucky or hit a bonanza. You may have a good string of consecutive successes, but that will prove unsustainable. Investing is a highly competitive pursuit.

Thousands of highly talented and intelligent men and women devote their entire careers and nearly all their waking attention to winning in this exciting and challenging area. You can buy their expertise, you can develop your own, or you can do both. With so many others working hard in the marketplace, you should expect never to discover a secret formula that will remain yours alone.

Because so many players are in the arena, investment prices reflect their collective judgment about the future. That judgment will seldom be precisely correct, but it usually will include more dimensions than immediately strike your eye. You may develop some insights in a particular sector of the markets—perhaps that industry in which you work—but be assured that there are greater experts in other sectors as well. Our world, as the cliché notes, is changing ever more rapidly. Therefore, keeping up with it will be a demanding task, and success will require effort. Those of us in the investment business wouldn't trade it for anything else, precisely because it is so stimulating and challenging. So, although you will need to work for investment success, that effort will be worthwhile and highly educational.

Don't let the need to work and learn discourage you. Also, don't feel you must study the investment world to death before venturing in. It is more an art than a science, so you could spend a lifetime and never master it and all its changes. Take comfort in the fact that so many investors act from ignorance and raw emotion, so your achieving above-average results may require little more than old-fashioned common sense and long-term perspective. Avoiding major losses is key to successful investing. If you apply perspective and common sense to your investment program at both a macro and a tactical level, you already will have gone a long way toward accomplishing what you must. Thus, while you shouldn't expect this to be easy (if it were, everyone would be rich already!), you do have a decent chance at success by applying native intelligence and common sense. The needed "work" here is by no means impossible!

**2. Nothing is guaranteed except low returns for the timid and losses for the gullible.**   We would all like to have investments that entail zero risk and yet somehow, magically, guarantee extremely high returns. There is no way for any investment to guarantee you any particular after-tax, after-inflation return, let alone a high one. If such an investment existed, everyone would want to put their capital in it; as a result, its return would decline because people would be bidding up the price to get in and because the oversupply would cut the underlying business activity's margins. This caution on lack of guarantees will serve you well if you recall it when thinking about that "fabulous franchise opportunity" in bagel shops (available, of course, for a limited time only) and whenever you receive a sales presentation about any prospective investment. When you hear about a guarantee, raise your level of disbelief. What is too good to be true, to quote another old saw, is exactly that! Behind every so-called guarantee is a set of assumptions, most of which require that the world freeze in its current state. Only if things stay the way they were, or are right now, can any particular investment definitely work out in some now-predicted way.

What rare guarantees do exist (assuming continuance of a capitalist economy and our national integrity) come with below-average returns attached and require locking up your capital in ways that prevent your seizing other opportunities down the road. Two guaranteed investments are insured bank deposits and U.S. government bonds, assuming each is held to maturity. As discussed elsewhere, bank accounts will get you a known but definitely subpar return, probably lower than zero after inflation and taxes. New, inflation-indexed bonds introduced in 1997 build in a 3 percent real return; are you interested? While traditional government bonds will provide a higher nominal return if held to maturity (can *you* be sure you will?), their major drawback is that they fail to protect your capital's purchasing power against inflation. History shows they will give you a lower return on average over the long term than will common stocks. So, our two exceptions to the nothing-is-guaranteed rule merely cover unattractive, below-par returns you should not seek.

**3. Nothing comes from nowhere.**   Get-rich-quick schemes, or promises of high returns, usually fall apart under close, unemotional scrutiny. Even the rich and powerful fall prey to investment fantasies, as illustrated anew by the notorious New Era scheme that bilked many in the philanthropic community in 1995. Double your money in six months? That was the promise.

How was it to be done? Through matching contributions from an extremely wealthy but very private individual. Clearly those words were classic signs of a Ponzi scheme, a pyramid that eventually can't keep doubling in size.

When you are presented with any investment idea seemingly, or (worse yet!) flatly, promising a high or guaranteed return, you need to stand back and play skeptic. Look at the business fundamentals and try to understand how such a high purported rate of return (either one-time or recurring) actually can be generated from some real economic activity. There needs to be a real business employing real people, keeping books and making something real every day, and paying taxes, to create the profit you are being promised to receive. If you believe those numbers, then ask why this apparent miracle of alchemy was never before discovered. Then if you think there's a plausible answer to that mystery, figure out how it is possible to guarantee that nothing will go wrong before you get your fabulous payback.

Finally, play this mental trump card: If this is so great, why is the salesperson not begging and borrowing every cent he or she can to invest in it? Why has the salesperson, like "The Millionaire's" Michael Anthony of TV fame, decided to bestow this wondrous gift on you rather than keeping it all for close friends and family?

The key point is that some real economic activity must underlie any financial investment or the latter cannot pay off. High returns can and do occur. However, they never come with guarantees and usually involve extremely high risk or the use of leverage. You may not see or understand the risks involved, but you should know that they are present if a high return may be earned. The most palpable risk is that you are being sold a bill of goods, because nothing legal and financially rewarding comes out of nowhere!

## All or Nothing?

Billions are wagered annually on an all-or-nothing basis. You buy a ticket for a famous sweepstakes, wager on a horse in the Kentucky Derby, or buy a state lottery ticket. At a casino you put the last dollar of your weekend's limit on red or black, or drop a final five-dollar token into a slot machine. In each of these cases, you will either get something back or lose everything.

That is gambling, not investing. Gambling involves high returns or total loss. Your results are known quickly: A single event makes you a big winner or a 100 percent loser. There is nothing in between. Because people are familiar with gambling, many subconsciously project its attributes onto investing. This false impression of how investing works sets up a mental picture of investments as potentially providing either excitement and extremely high rewards, or total failure. People operating in that frame of reference gravitate to high-risk/high-reward "investment" ventures and consider it just part of the game when they occasionally lose all.

Investing, unlike gambling, usually does not produce fabulous returns and never turns on a single sudden event to drive 100 percent loss or high success. The closer any proposition you evaluate sounds to a wager (involving complete win or loss, or rapid feedback), the less of an investment aspect it contains! In investing, returns are generated gradually over time, but not necessarily on a smooth or constant basis. In investing, you have multiple times along the way to cash out and take a partial gain or a partial loss. Forget trying to get any of your two dollars back once the ponies leave the starting gate!

Even if they don't literally expect to double or triple their money quickly on Wall Street, many people have falsely high expectations. These are fed by stories heard from others about fast profits in initial public offerings, high-flying technology stocks, or big corporate takeovers. Those kinds of gains do occur, but they are not at all the daily stuff of investing. But such tales definitely color people's expectations. Profits from investing do not come easily, rapidly, or automatically. Nor are they routinely fabulously large. The following material will indicate what actual average returns have historically been.

## Actual Long-Term Average Investment Returns

Building on what was originally an academic thesis project, a Chicago-based consulting firm now maintains a gigantic database from which it calculates historical returns, and their variances, for different classes of investments. Ibbotson Associates is the company, and its annual study is called *Stocks, Bonds, Bills, and Inflation*. It measures average rates of return over periods as long as 65 years and also shows recent shorter periods' returns for comparison in that context. This book is available in the business reference collections of any good public library and at many university libraries. You may not need to refer to it, because the results over different long-period windows tend to drift up or down relatively little. And the relative rankings of different asset classes stay the same over time. Or, you may find the details fascinating and want to buy the book.

---

**FIGURE 3.1**  What the Ibbotson Numbers Say

| Asset Class | Approximate Average Rate Per Year |
|---|---|
| Small-Company Stocks | 12% |
| Overall Common Stocks | 11 |
| Long-Term Bonds | 5 |
| Treasury Bills | 4 |
| Inflation Rate | 3 |

---

The bottom line, expressed in round numbers in Figure 3.1, is widely quoted in popular financial media. These are compounded *average* annual total returns for 65 years. This means that the rates quoted are simply mathematical means; they do not mount up like interest on a CD every year. Total returns are the sums of price change, up or down, and cash income thrown off.

Again, these are averages, *not* annual guarantees. Markets move up and down at differing speeds over time. No single stock or bond performs exactly like the overall market at all times. Variations around the mean are large, although they narrow somewhat as you move down the list. Looked at over ten-year windows, each medium's distribution has a positive bias, meaning that there are more winning than losing periods.

The numbers in Figure 3.1 are shown to offer you a realistic perspective. In context of the major bull markets enjoyed in both stocks and bonds from 1982 through, and perhaps beyond, 1997, some of those numbers look surprisingly low. But that's short-term perspective playing a trick on you. Be careful never to project the recent past (either great or awful) as a future expectation!

The now legendary Peter Lynch gained 29 percent on average for 13 years—and then quit while he was ahead! If you "expect" to make 20 percent to 25 percent a year in stocks—let alone a higher rate—you are counting on the improbable. You might do that well or better some years, but you should expect to suffer setbacks in others and come back toward the pack. To accomplish above-average returns, you usually have to take above-average risks. Data like those in Figure 3.1 measure all stocks rather than a few you might own or the 100-plus that a large mutual fund might hold for a year or two. The fewer your holdings, the more likely it is that you may have returns in some years that are far above or below the mean. Getting high returns consistently over a long term is extremely rare and requires unusual skill as well as some luck. So, do not count on doing 15 percent or more over the long term! You'll only disappoint and frustrate yourself, and a frustrated investor usually makes unprofitable decisions.

Not only are returns far from the averages unlikely to be sustained, you definitely should count on having up as well as down periods. Looking at things on an arbitrary calendar-year basis, from 1926 through 1996 there were 50 up and 21 down years for stocks. While that means stocks rise about 70 percent of all years, by no means does it mean you should expect a rhythmic pattern of three or four rises followed by one fall. Stocks have risen as many as eight years running (through 1989) and have fallen as many as four in a row (1929–1932).

Curiously, long-term bonds have produced similar proportions of winning and losing years. In the same 71-year span, bonds have been ahead in 52 and down in 19 years. Their slight frequency advantage probably stems from the fact that they begin with a significant positive cash return as part of their total return; tiny rises in interest rates still allow a positive net return on bonds.

### Inflation Colors the Numbers and Sets Your Real Return

When you look at investment returns, the nominal mathematical rate earned is only the start of the story and often can be quite misleading. You must consider both taxes and inflation. Even in a tax-free world, you would need to adjust your returns for changes in purchasing power. If you made 20 percent on a particular investment in a certain period, but the dollars you received in the end purchased 30 percent fewer goods or services, you would have suffered a net loss adjusted for inflation. This is important: When you think about retirement income, it's almost certain you'll need more dollars then to purchase whatever standard of living you buy at a certain dollar cost now. Therefore, all investment returns need to be viewed in an inflation- and tax-adjusted context.

Many people (some of whom play the state lottery!) make a huge mistake by seeking total safety when investing because they cannot bear the thought of losing a dollar. Long-term history shows that approach gives very unfortunate results, as will be discussed in Strategy 4. For now, here is one piece of perspective that makes returns shown in that table above very sobering. Remember, raw nominal returns averaged 11 percent for stocks, with more variation to be sure, versus only 4 percent for T-bills. But, after adjusting for inflation, T-bills lost money (even before taxes!) in 12 years and made less than 2 percent in 28 years, or 40 percent of the time! By contrast, common stocks after adjustment for inflation made at least 10 percent in 38 years, or more than half the time.

### Blending Asset Classes

Even though you can realistically expect higher returns (remember, on average and over the long term!) in stocks than in bonds or T-bills, that doesn't mean you should always hold 100 percent of your assets in stocks. There will be down years, and they might occur at just the wrong time, such as when you need to pay tuition, sell off some holdings to carry yourself between jobs, or when retirement time or a major illness arrives. And, if you hold stocks exclusively, you might just panic and sell out near the bottom of some major future downturn; that would prevent you from realizing their favorable long-term average returns. Therefore, a blend of asset classes, shifted from time to time due to market movements and in context of your age and risk-accepting profile, is the best policy. This will be covered more deeply in Strategies 21 and 22, but it requires mentioning here so you do not plunge everything into stocks— a chance you're more likely to take right after years like 1995–1997 than at the scary bottom in late 1987.

### High Yield

This investor-killing bugaboo gets its own full treatment in Strategy 16 but still merits brief mention here too. In the table of long-term average returns, note what relatively low returns are typically produced by bonds. To whatever degree you get promised a return higher than shown here from "guaranteed" investments like bonds, you are either in a high-inflation period or must be unwittingly assuming high risk. High yield runs parallel with high risk, meaning the chance of partial or total loss of capital. So, if you expect to earn an extremely high yield with the safety you associate with bonds, you will be sorely mistaken.

To sum up accurately the supposed virtues of high yields, Arthur Zeikel, the president of Merrill Lynch Asset Management, quotes Ray DeVoe saying that more money has been lost chasing after high yield than at the point of a gun (*Financial Analysts Journal*, 51, no. 2, [March/April 1995], published by the Association for Investment Management and Research, Charlottesville, Va.). I would say so, and "many times over."

# Accept Risk to Get Attractive Returns

"**Y**ou can never be too safe," our grandmothers told us when we were kids ready to chase a ball into the street, oblivious to traffic. From our earliest days, we've been conditioned to avoid risk, to put safety first in whatever we do. In financial markets, risk and reward generally run in parallel. This doesn't mean that every high-risk venture you enter will be a bonanza; some will be, while others will fail. But keeping all your assets in the lowest-risk asset classes will absolutely doom you to low returns. In fact, after inflation and taxes, a maximum-safety strategy often produces a net loss!

The mission of these next few pages is to help you understand and confront risk usefully. Your investment portfolio should have a balance between risk and safety so your capital can grow enough to provide a financially satisfactory retirement. Maximum-safety investing, as you will see, fails that test badly.

## Defining and Understanding Risk

What is risk, in an investment context? Most people would reply that it's "a chance I might lose money." That is really the meaning of the word *danger* when considered in the context of business. Properly, risk is the chance that an outcome will be different from what is expected. Another way of saying this is that risk is a measure of uncertainty about results.

For example, when you put money into a federally insured bank's 4 percent CD for three years, you've eliminated any risk regarding your rate of pretax, preinflation return. You will indeed get 4 percent compounded, no more or less, before taxes and inflation. While a statistician or economist would define that 4 percent expected return as being free of risk (uncertainty as to result), such an investment will actually expose you to some danger: that you will suffer a negative real return after taxes and inflation. If your combined federal and state taxes were 33 percent, a 4 percent nominal return would net you only 2.68 percent in interest. But here comes the big danger: Inflation may well have exceeded 2.68 percent and in that case you would have less purchasing power than you began with. In fact, the *amount* of danger—how bad inflation turns out to be—is actually unknown so there is indeed some risk (i.e., uncertainty of result) here. The actual after-tax purchasing power resulting from your investment cannot be predicted with certainty because it hinges on an unknown inflation rate and maybe also on any chance that tax laws will change.

Avoiding losses is centrally important to amassing wealth in the financial markets. An obsessive focus on risk avoidance can actually be self-defeating in three ways:

1. Searching for that hoped-for risk-free haven where returns are high will take you time, and is likely to become an excuse to postpone your actually starting to invest.
2. A search for zero-risk investments will lead you inevitably to choices that give extremely low or negative real returns. Thus, such a search will prove bad for your financial health.
3. Heavy focus on risk avoidance could, at worst, paralyze you into doing nothing at all. In 1995–1996, the Securities

and Exchange Commission sought public comment on better ways to disclose and explain risk in mutual fund prospectuses. A. Michael Lipper, president of Lipper Analytical Services, noted that more detailed and prominent disclosure could lead investors to spook themselves by fleeing when they see short-term volatility; he believes rather that "the biggest risk for people is *not investing.*"

## Inflation Is the Enemy

The previous example exposed you to some key concepts without using highly technical terms. The main lesson is that returns are not what they seem at first, but should be thought of on an after-tax, after-inflation basis. Following are key terms for determining returns; you already understand them intuitively:

- Nominal return—a stated, raw, percentage that still needs to be adjusted for taxes and inflation
- After-tax return—the nominal return, determined after subtracting an expected combined federal/state tax bite
- Real return—the true increase in spendable wealth, expressed in either overall or per-year percentage growth of purchasing power

In the earlier example, your 4 percent nominal bank interest became a 2.68 percent after-tax return, and would turn out to be roughly zero in real terms (or worse!), since inflation of 2.7 percent a year or more is usually to be expected.

The Laffer Curve shows that when tax rates are too high, total tax revenue will decline (to zero at tax rates approaching 100 percent). This truth applies because people will refuse to expend energy for a zero payback. If taxes were nearly 100 percent and inflation ate up the rest of your paycheck, you'd have no incentive to work from now until next payday! The exact same principle applies to saving your money for whatever goal. Saving means that you are consuming less than 100 percent of your income. When you put away a dollar, you ought to be rewarded for postponing your pleasure of consumption. You might choose today between buying a car for $30,000 or leaving that amount invested for the future. If you choose the latter, you should be disappointed if you find that your ending dollar sum, after inflation and taxes, does not buy at least the same amount of new car some years hence. If it doesn't, your choice to wait will have been unrewarded: You'll have given up needlessly the pleasure of owning a nice automobile earlier or longer.

Inflation is the main, and least predictable, enemy. Taxes are a given, although they may be postponed (and thereby probably somewhat reduced) by investing in tax-sheltered vehicles. You must insist on achieving a real (true, spendable) positive return on your investments. There are two reasons for this:

1. You deserve to be paid for postponing earlier consumption.
2. Getting a low or zero *real rate* means you'll need to save a painfully high portion of your income throughout your working life in order to be able to afford to retire.

That second point is key! It can be shown by using some numbers in the tables that follow. First, here's a conceptual statement of the idea: If you get a zero real rate of return from your highly risk-averse strategy of buying loss-proof instruments like short-term CDs and T-notes, you will end up with no more purchasing power than the total you originally put away. Forty years of saving a dollar a year at zero net return will provide you with a microscopic ending asset pool of $40 of today's purchasing power. If you want to preserve the principal and live off just the interest, suppose you can invest in long-term municipal bonds at 6 percent upon retirement in year 41. Your annual income will be $2.40 from that $40 pool, or 2.4 times what you saved per year. This means that (ignoring Social Security) in order to have a retirement income of 60 percent of your present annual income, you will need to save 25 percent of this year' pretax income every year for 40 years! (Here's the math: $40 \times 25\% = 1,000\% \times 6\% = 60\%$.) That's a daunting challenge (especially in the early years), isn't it? But that's the real result of accepting low "risk-free" returns on your investments. Thus, you endanger your future financial well-being by investing with maximum safety as your first criterion. Maximum "safety" turns out to guarantee a bad result!

## Taking Some Risk Is Your Only Way to Win

Unless, from age 25 to retirement, you can save in dollars an amount equal to 25 percent of your present annual income (a feat not accomplished even in notoriously high-savings Japan!), you've got a problem if you want enough for retirement. The only alternative solution is to achieve a significant rate of real return. You cannot accomplish that goal with low-apparent-risk CDs and similar instruments.

Figure 4.1 shows what becomes of $1,000 saved per year, invested at various rates over terms of 20, 30, and 40 years. Those terms represent the realistic working lifetime of a person who starts such a program at ages 45 (pretty late), 35, or 25, respectively. Double the amounts shown if you faithfully put $2,000 annually into an IRA every January 2. These tables are based on the assumption that taxation occurs as a one-time event at the end of the period shown, rather than annually. Thus, the results shown reflect IRA, Keogh, or 401(k)/403(b) types of results. (The tax law signed in August 1997 provides a new form of IRA, discussed at greater length in Strategy 26. Nondeductible contributions and tax freedom [not deferral] imply that the after-tax, preinflation amounts in Figure 4.1 should be marked up by a factor of 50 percent.) Saving and investing in taxable accounts will produce lower results, since you would lose the benefit of a return on the tax dollars you postpone paying in a tax-deferred vehicle.

In the last two panels in Figure 4.1, which represent real wealth after inflation, you see asterisks placed after certain values. These rows tell you what nominal return will serve merely to provide you with no loss (in real terms) for all your saving effort. As an example, if inflation is 3 percent per year and you save $1,000 per year at 7 percent for 30 years (middle dollar column), you will end up merely having tread water, with just $30,153 in buying power to show for the $30,000 you have set aside.

For savers who rely on low-return, apparently very safe instruments, the examples set forth in Figure 4.1 paint a pretty ugly picture! Put away $1,000 a year for 40 years, with a nominal rate of about 6.5 percent, and after inflation at 3 percent plus normal taxes, you'll have made no progress at all, except to have accumulated $40,000 in buying power available in your later years rather than already used up. Save that same amount for 30 years at a 6 percent

**FIGURE 4.1**    Results of $1,000 Saved Annually in Tax-Deferred Vehicles

| Years of Saving | 40 | 30 | 20 |
|---|---|---|---|
| **Amount Saved** | **$40,000** | **$30,000** | **$20,000** |
| Rate (%) | Nominal Ending Sum Resulting | | |
| 0 | $ 40,000 | $ 30,000 | $20,000 |
| 1 | 48,886 | 34,785 | 22,019 |
| 2 | 60,402 | 40,568 | 24,297 |
| 3 | 75,401 | 47,575 | 26,870 |
| 4 | 95,025 | 56,085 | 29,778 |
| 5 | 120,800 | 66,439 | 33,066 |
| 6 | 154,762 | 79,058 | 36,785 |
| 7 | 199,635 | 94,461 | 40,995 |
| 8 | 259,057 | 113,283 | 45,762 |
| 9 | 337,882 | 136,308 | 51,160 |
| 10 | 442,592 | 164,494 | 57,275 |
| 11 | 581,826 | 199,021 | 64,203 |
| 12 | 767,091 | 241,333 | 72,052 |
| Rate (%) | Nominal after Taxes at 33% Combined | | |
| 0 | $ 40,000 | $ 30,000 | $20,000 |
| 1 | 45,954 | 33,206 | 21,353 |
| 2 | 53,669 | 37,081 | 22,879 |
| 3 | 63,719 | 41,775 | 24,603 |
| 4 | 76,867 | 47,477 | 26,551 |
| 5 | 94,136 | 54,414 | 28,754 |
| 6 | 116,891 | 62,869 | 31,246 |
| 7 | 146,955 | 73,189 | 34,067 |
| 8 | 186,768 | 85,800 | 37,261 |
| 9 | 239,581 | 101,226 | 40,877 |
| 10 | 309,737 | 120,111 | 44,974 |
| 11 | 403,023 | 143,244 | 49,616 |
| 12 | 527,151 | 171,593 | 54,875 |

*(continued on next page)*

**FIGURE 4.1** (continued)

| Years of Saving | 40 | 30 | 20 |
|---|---|---|---|
| **Amount Saved** | **$40,000** | **$30,000** | **$20,000** |
| Rate (%) | After-Tax Buying Power after 3% Inflation | | |
| 0 | $ 12,262 | $12,360 | $11,074 |
| 1 | 14,087 | 13,680 | 11,822 |
| 2 | 16,453 | 15,277 | 12,668 |
| 3 | 19,533 | 17,211 | 13,622 |
| 4 | 23,564 | 19,560 | 14,701 |
| 5 | 28,858 | 22,418 | 15,921 |
| 6 | 35,834* | 25,901 | 17,300 |
| 7 | 45,050* | 30,153* | 18,862 |
| 8 | 57,255 | 35,348 | 20,630* |
| 9 | 73,445 | 41,704 | 22,633 |
| 10 | 94,952 | 49,484 | 24,901 |
| 11 | 123,550 | 59,015 | 27,471 |
| 12 | 161,602 | 70,694 | 30,383 |
| Rate (%) | After-Tax Buying Power after 4% Inflation | | |
| 0 | $ 8,332 | $ 9,250 | $ 9,128 |
| 1 | 9,572 | 10,238 | 9,745 |
| 2 | 11,179 | 11,433 | 10,442 |
| 3 | 13,272 | 12,880 | 11,228 |
| 4 | 16,011 | 14,638 | 12,118 |
| 5 | 19,608 | 16,777 | 13,123 |
| 6 | 24,347 | 19,384 | 14,260 |
| 7 | 30,609 | 22,565 | 15,548 |
| 8 | 38,902* | 26,454 | 17,005 |
| 9 | 49,902 | 31,210* | 18,656 |
| 10 | 64,515 | 37,032 | 20,526* |
| 11 | 83,945 | 44,165 | 22,644 |
| 12 | 109,800 | 52,905 | 25,044 |

* Break-even figures
Any nominal rate of return lower than about 7 percent would result in a real return below zero. So, when you look at the figure, remember that lesser returns (higher rows in the far-left column) than where you see the "*" signs mean totally unacceptable returns—investment results that don't even allow you to come out even!

nominal rate (about what CDs will get you when this book was published in late 1997) and just 4 percent inflation you will chew up over one-third of the buying power of what you had set aside. (To see how this works, refer to Figure 4.1's 4 percent inflation table, 30-year column, 6 percent rate line; you'll find your real purchasing power is $19,384.)

Clearly, inflation plus taxes spell trouble for the highly risk-averse. Nominal rates in the 6.5 percent range really mean about a zero real return after 40 years with 3 percent inflation; with 4 percent declines in purchasing power per year, it takes over an 8 percent nominal return to come out even in purchasing-power terms. Your alternatives are to save a very high—and probably impossibly high—proportion of your income starting at an early age, or to invest for higher returns than you will get in perceived low-risk investment vehicles. Let's be optimistic and assume 3 percent inflation. Investments with low risk (long-term CDs at 6.5 percent or so) will net you no gain after Uncle Sam, the state tax folks, and the inflation bogeyman take their slices.

Investing for higher return, which does indeed involve taking some risk, is the solution. Watch how dramatically your results improve with moderate increases in risk: Achieve a bit under a 9.5 percent nominal return and you'll double the real purchasing power of dollars put in over 40 years ($80,000 would lie between the 9 percent and 10 percent rows). An 11 percent annual nominal average return would just more than triple your purchasing power: from $40,000 put aside, to some $123,550. Get one more percent, at 12 percent, and you quadruple the input to over $160,000.

Here are the two questions to ask:

1. Are these kinds of return achievable over the long term without my "rolling the dice" to take high risks?
2. Would I rather take some added risk, or be forced to save an impossibly high percentage of my income for 40 years?

If you are already much older than 25, you have fewer years left to make the gains needed, so risk-taking is your only viable route. (Of course, as you age you'll feel more afraid of losses, and you will want to be more cautious—again, the intuitively comfortable being wrong. It's a tight bind, and the best escape is to start early in life!) The nasty alternatives are to save a painfully high rate now, or be poor later.

**FIGURE 4.2**   Spectrum of Risk by Asset Type

| Risk | Equities | Fixed Income |
|---|---|---|
| High | Single Country<br>World Emerging<br>Single Region<br>Single Industry/Sector<br>Capital Appreciation<br>Micro-Cap<br>Small-Cap<br><br>Global<br>Large-Cap Growth<br>Growth and Income<br>Convertible | World Income<br><br><br>Domestic High-Yield<br>  Stocks<br><br>Mortgage Securities |
| Medium | Equity Income | Long Corporate Bonds<br>High-Yield Municipal<br>  Bonds<br>Long Municipal Bonds<br>Long U.S. Government<br>  Bonds |
| Low | Balanced | Short Corporate Bonds<br>Short Municipal Bonds<br>Short U.S. Government<br>  Bonds<br>Money Market<br>Bank CDs<br>Treasury Bills |

## Where to Invest for Necessary Returns

In Strategy 3 you learned about the historical long-term average returns achieved by various asset classes. When considered in light of the sobering real returns just detailed, the conclusion is inescapable: Only a major dose of common stocks will meet your need for building real purchasing power for retirement. A mix of asset classes will reduce the chance that you might suffer a major overall setback. An illustration of this diversification benefit came in the October 1987 crash, when bond prices rose while stocks briefly plummeted.

Domestic common stocks alone are not enough. Strategies 21 and 22 will explore setting, and then fine-tuning to keep, a proper asset allocation mix. The main point here, however, is to convince you that you *must* take risk to have any chance of investing success. For examples of the types of investments that fit with various risk levels, see Figure 4.2.

Investor psychology, unless managed with uncanny discipline, can confound the best-laid plans. Greed and especially fear can take hold. These powerful emotional drivers have their greatest chances of causing trouble at exactly those times when the price of any mistake is largest. Greed becomes strongest only around market tops, when staying aggressive for too long carries maximum potential for loss. Fear grips you, very predictably, at bottoms. These are facts of financial life, and they will be dealt with later in this book. For now, accept the prescription, backed by hard numbers, that you have no choice but to accept risk. This means you will be trading away a low but certain reward for a sometimes bumpy ride to greater eventual heights.

# Put Total Return before Current Income

*T*here's a great paradox in the challenge (and fun) of investing to win: While at a tactical level much depends on the level-headed application of common sense, ironically at a strategic level, what seems most plain and obvious usually isn't the right road to follow. (Strategy 9, on how to win using contrarian principles, develops the latter point.) First, here, you'll be surprised to learn why emphasizing current income, which feels right, is not the best way to build that large asset pool you'll need later in life.

## Why Young Investors Must Reject the Siren Song of Current Income

When investing for serious goals like retirement, most people instinctively think in terms of caution, loss avoidance, and guaranteed results. The gut-level driver of such attitudes is a high awareness of dealing here with "serious money"—a fact that is undeniable. Equally true is this: You'll need to grow your asset base at a rate above those sorts of returns that very cautious investment approaches will produce. In their overly conservative approach to investing for retirement, people easily fall into the trap of seeking current income too early in life. The next few pages will show why you need to avoid that mistake.

An overly strong early focus on income for retirement needs confuses the ends with the means, a mental mixing of life phases. There are times to sow and then times to reap, but those should be kept separate. When you do reach those golden years, much of your portfolio can be invested for income, but not so throughout your lifetime. Just because you eventually will need income *then* does not mean you should invest *now* for income! When tempted by the apparent safety of investing for income in your younger years, examine your motives closely and overcome this subtle confusion of ends with means.

As shown in Strategy 4, low-risk investment approaches (meaning those where uncertainty of outcome is low) are actually dangerous. Their sure negative returns after inflation and taxes actually will prevent you from accomplishing your mission during those earlier years when your primary goal should be building assets rather than drawing an income from them.

Think about the life cycles of companies or industries, which move through several predictable phases. In the embryonic or early-growth stage change is rapid, net investment of cash is required (for research and development and capital equipment), and little or no income is generated. Companies surviving that stage move into a rapid-growth phase, where real markets develop and the revenue stream ramps up. Here, too, companies soak up rather than generate cash: Their growth requires more capital to finance rising amounts of inventory, receivables, and equipment. Later, as growth slows to a moderate rate, the stronger companies become clearly identified and dominate. They set prevailing price levels based on their superior efficiencies in production and distribution. They are profitable, while weaker competitors suffer on the margin. As growth slows and profits flow dependably, mainly to industry leaders, those companies enjoy excess cash flows and can raise their dividends. The ending phase, following maturity, is decay. Here the battle centers on consolidation and survival. New investment is unnecessary and often foolhardy; harvesting cash thrown off may be the best thing for shareholders.

What kinds of companies provide significant income streams from dividends? The answer, as the life-cycle analogy demonstrates, is the mature and decaying ones. Those are not growth companies, the kinds that will help you build capital at a significant rate. True, firms in industries like oil, steel, autos, and utilities are unlikely to disappear. But these are cyclical and mature by nature, so money invested there will tend to go up and down in value rather than grow on a secular path at a superior rate. These industries offer the allure of above-average dividend yields, but they offer little possibility of asset growth. And it is growth that you must seek while younger so you will have a large asset pile from which you'll later draw a safe and secure income stream.

There is some room in your investment mix for mature companies such as those described, but they should not dominate your asset mix. The same goes for mutual funds that invest in that style, if you decide for funds over individual stocks as your preferred means of investing. While they're far from perfect for failing to give the capital growth potential you need, mature companies do provide some stability to an overall asset mix in times of falling markets. The fact that they visibly provide a current income stream cushions them from severe price decline when the fast-growth companies' shares are withering fast. But too much of this sort of safety cushion will defeat your chances of achieving needed capital growth.

One illusory factor that draws so many people toward current income too early in their investment careers is the mirage of yield as a minimum return. Because the dividend rate is highly visible and at least seems fairly assured, investors subconsciously imagine cash yield as being a minimum expectation, somehow a floor in terms of return. This is false, but is a powerful allure to those who do not think it out carefully!

If stock prices are flat, the dividend yield you see is what you get. Only if the stock price rises will your total return (the sum of cash received plus the price change) be more than the dividend yield. When stock prices fall for a year (or, occasionally longer), however, their declines are in no way limited to the amount of dividends paid out in the same period. Here, dividends serve only to reduce the size of your net overall loss. Today, with high price volatility driven by institutional impatience, a year's worth of cash dividends can be overmatched in an hour's heavy selling in a stock like IBM, Xerox, or Exxon.

Yet another reason to reject an income-first approach to investing *for* retirement—as distinguished from investing *in* retirement—is the drag of taxes. There are two separate aspects of this important point:

1. Capital gains are taxed more favorably than dividend and interest income. Rates on capital gains are lower, and you as the owner of an appreciated asset also have the important power to determine in which year or years to recognize your gain. You have no such options regarding current interest or dividend income. While in your strongest work-income years, chances are that you'll be in a higher tax bracket rather than the lowest one. Therefore, current investment income will suffer immediate and maximum reduction at the hands of tax collectors, both federal and state.

2. The seemingly paradoxical result of the mathematics of compounding greatly affects the tax drag on current income. How soon you pay a tax *does* matter. A tax postponed is actually a tax reduced, after the magical effects of compounding have operated. To see how the difference occurs, take a look at Figure 5.1.

Two investors each achieve a 10 percent pretax return per year, but one does so from income and the other from capital gains. After losing $330 of taxes paid for the first year, the income investor will have less to reinvest and thus starts a process of falling forever further behind. In a result putting the zero-sum game economists to shame, the growth investor both pays more taxes *and* ends up richer!

A more savvy neighbor keeps her entire first-year 10 percent gain of $1,000 working. Thus, the magic of compounding applies to tax not paid, legally, until later. The extra return comes from postponed taxes earning interest. (Washington, not surprisingly, gets money sooner, but less of it!)

This two-year example shows what seems just a tiny difference, less than 1 percent. But over long periods, the compounded effect is huge. Over 40 years, a typical span from early

**FIGURE 5.1**   Why Paying the Tax Collector Later Is Better

|  | Current Income Investor | Capital Gains Investor |
|---|---|---|
| Gross Annual Return | 10% | 10% |
| Total Tax Rate | 33% | 33% |
| Net Annual Return | 6.7% | 6.7% |
| Two-Year Return after Compounding Only After-Tax Returns | | |
| On $10,000 Invested: Total Earned | 13.41% | 14.07% |
| Taxes Paid | $2,067.00 | $2,100.00 |
| Net Kept | 685.67 | 693.00 |
| | $1,341.33 | $1,407.00 |

in a work life to retirement at around age 65, the advantage of growth over income is staggering. Grow a sum at 10 percent compounded for 40 years and you get more than 45 times that starting amount; tax away 33 percent of the gain and you still have $306,537 for each starting $10,000. Pay 33 percent in taxes as you go, thus compounding at 6.7 percent net, and the 40-year value of your starting $10,000 becomes $133,810. If the resulting sum were then invested entirely for interest, our gains-first investor would have a retirement 2.3 times as great as our safety-first, income-now investor. It seems pretty likely that in retirement they no longer would live in the same neighborhood!

But the news gets better fast, twice more, for the capital gains seeker, as contrasted with the income-now investor. Strategy 3 showed that stocks have returned 10 percent or more per year on average (admittedly, including some from current income) while bonds, the surest road to current income, simply do not. Therefore our example of two investors earning the same 10 percent via different routes made a wildly false assumption (generous by a factor of two on simple rate) in favor of the income-now investor. In real life, over an investment lifetime, the 6.7 percent after-tax return used for the income investor simply will not be achieved by taking current income and paying taxes along the way! If bonds or income stocks gross 5 percent, our income

**FIGURE 5.2**   Total Return versus Current Income
Comparison: 8% Current Income vs. 4% Growth + 4% Yield

|  | Stock I | | Stock G | |
|---|---|---|---|---|
|  | **Dividend** | **Price** | **Dividend** | **Price** |
| **Year-End Buy** | | | | |
| 0 | $2.00 | $25.00 | $1.25 | $25.00 |
| 1 | 2.00 | 25.00 | 1.30 | 26.00 |
| 2 | 2.00 | 25.00 | 1.35 | 27.04 |
| 3 | 2.00 | 25.00 | 1.41 | 28.12 |
| 4 | 2.00 | 25.00 | 1.46 | 29.25 |
| 5 | 2.00 | 25.00 | 1.52 | 30.42 |
| 6 | 2.00 | 25.00 | 1.58 | 31.63 |
| 7 | 2.00 | 25.00 | 1.64 | 32.90 |
| 8 | 2.00 | 25.00 | 1.71 | 34.21 |
| 9 | 2.00 | 25.00 | 1.78 | 35.58 |
| 10 | 2.00 | 25.00 | 1.85 | 37.01 |
| Income | 20.00 | | 15.61 | |
| Capital Appreciation | | - 0 - | | 12.01 |
| Total Gain | | 20.00 | | 27.61 |
| Tax on Capital Gains at 33% | | - 0 - | | 4.00 |
| Value after Sale; Taxes | | 25.00 | | 33.00 |
| After-Tax Advantage | 2.93 | | | 8.00 |

investor paying taxes en route will see an original $10,000 grow to just $36,150, or less than one-eighth of the after-tax wealth of her former neighbor who said "go for the grow" and paid taxes later.

Our examples have leveled the playing field by assuming an equal tax bracket at termination for the growth investor. Careful timing, however, will probably allow at least some of that smarter investor's return to be taxed at a lower bracket, at favorable capital-gains rates, or both. So, after real taxes, the disadvantages of investing for income as a means of building a cash pot for retirement are overwhelming.

## Invest for Growth: Stocks or Funds?

By now, all that math probably has convinced you to seek growth rather than mainly income in building your capital before retirement arrives. But, you say, you're not a financial genius; you're afraid of the ups and downs inherent in investing in individual growth stocks and you want to spend life's precious free time doing other things besides shepherding your money.

One single answer to all three of those problems comes in one attractive package: the mutual fund. Many readers will opt for this approach to lifetime investment management. It is not the only route by any means. I have actively managed a portfolio of stocks and bonds rather than funds for several decades, but investments are my full-time work, which probably is not the case for you. Professional management, moderation of fluctuations due to diversification, and removal of the need to spend a great deal of time on the process are three benefits that the mutual funds route can provide.

## Taxes Enter the Debate

One advantage of direct investment over funds is that investing directly in stocks allows you total control over when capital gains are realized and therefore taxed. The Internal Revenue Code and the Investment Company Act of 1940 interact to require that any mutual fund taking net long-term gains (by selling stocks or bonds at a profit) during a given year must pay those gains to holders, who in turn are taxed on them. That tax applies regardless of whether such gains are reinvested into more shares of the fund. Index funds, covered in Strategy 23, can take care of much of the tax problem because of their low portfolio turnover.

You can minimize the tax bite while using mutual funds if you use them in all the tax-deferred mechanisms available to you! At a minimum, you and your spouse each can put $2,000 a year under the tax umbrella of IRAs. Beyond that, if you have other ways to meet unforeseen liquidity needs, you can put unlimited amounts into mutual funds within a variable annuity contract, thereby postponing any tax on gains until you take out the assets in later years. And, if your employer offers a 401(k), 403(b), or similar qualified plan, you can invest several thousand dollars annually inside those vehicles, again postponing the inevitable chop of the tax ax. The best news of all is this: You can do all three of these, not just one!

This strategy is devoted to steering you toward growth vehicles rather than income-now investments as you build your retirement cache for use in later years. Along the way, mention of taxes could not be avoided. Fortunately, there are definite ways to minimize and postpone the negative net effects of taxes on your wealth-building process. Tax considerations will be discussed further in Strategy 26.

**FIGURE 5.3**    Pros and Cons of Stocks and Stock Funds

|  | **Pro** | **Con** |
|---|---|---|
| Stocks | Big winners can be absolutely huge. Investors can choose the few best while a big fund must hold so many it becomes average. Holder has total tax-timing control. Holder can be sure to avoid disliked products or investment themes. | Big losers can go down 90% or 100%. Bad luck even for smart person could result in subaverage result. Stocks require more intense and constant vigilance. Institutional dominance and impatience cause unnerving volatility. |
| Equity Funds | Professional manager and staff know more than you do. Diversification over 100-plus stocks reduces risk of major loss. Range of returns is narrower than for stocks. No-loads allow zero transaction costs. Funds allow the investor to avoid single-stock worries. Cannot lose 100% unless "the world ends." | "Hero" manager might leave the company. Home runs are less likely. Most funds fail to equal their benchmarks. Investor cedes tax-timing control. With stock commissions now low, funds may impose higher overall costs. Funds are so big they move the market when trading, penalizing own returns. |

## A Scoreboard on Stocks versus Funds

As this book was written, more than 9,500 different mutual funds existed and the number was growing daily—thousands more funds than the total number of stocks traded on the New York and American stock exchanges combined! Strategy 22 suggests a broad-brush approach to lifetime asset allocation, and each of those classes recommended is well represented by numerous mutual funds whose investment objectives and policies require that they stick to specific approaches. If you buy a domestic growth and income fund, you can be assured it will not invest in foreign bonds, for example. Therefore, you can allocate your assets with confidence by using funds with tightly defined investment permissions and prohibitions (read the prospectus, as the saying goes!).

Chances are, by now you are "sold" on total return, with a heavy emphasis on growth over current income. For a list of key pro and con points for both funds and individual stocks, take a look at Figure 5.3. For a discussion of some useful insights on stocks, see Strategy 13; to look at the fund scene in some detail, see Strategy 17.

# Make Your Own Decisions

*F*inancial affairs have an aura of mysterious magic to many people who are not immersed in them full time. By nature, securities investments are intangibles (you can't "test-drive" them as you can an auto or a stereo system). And you buy investments when in an upbeat frame of mind. So your favorite Latin phrase must be the consumer's dictum: *caveat emptor.* One of the best ways to become a smart investor is by being proactive, not reactive. Whether you use a full-commission broker or a no-advice discounter, you must do the thinking and make the choices, not just go along with ideas you hear or read. Put bluntly, this means buying rather than being sold.

Each investment transaction involves a buyer and a seller. Ideally, asset exchanges should involve two equally informed parties acting totally voluntarily. How well informed do you feel about the proposed investment? Figure out how urgently each party wants what they will be getting, and what long-term stake each has in the deal. A broker will be compensated immediately while you will not even know or receive your reward (or punishment!) until some time in the future. Does the broker have a commitment to an ongoing relationship with you? Will he or she "be there" if things do not work out well for you?

What the two parties get is strikingly different:

- Sellers get two or three immediate, highly tangible benefits: a significant sum of cash from you; a commission because the deal is consummated; and when acting as principal rather than as agent, a lowering of inventory about which they have considerably more detailed knowledge than you do.
- You as buyer part with cash, our society's only unquestioned means of immediately getting what you want and need. Cash is power right now. Do you feel comfortable in parting with the palpable power of a lot of cash to get that intangible package of benefits being offered in exchange? That's a tough test. But if the proposed investment doesn't pass it, something may well be wrong.

## Why You Must Be in Control of Your Investment Life

Does all that sound so scary that you're seriously considering putting all your money back into a bank savings account? Do these questions seem to paralyze you, leaving you unable to make a decision under less than 100 percent certainty? Those certainly are not my purposes. Instead, I want you to focus on quiet, unhurried, logical, informed decision making. Remember, no one else in the world has as crucial an interest in your future financial well-being as you do. For that reason, you must be in control of the process. As consumers, we learn not to be impulse buyers. Transfer your cautious attitude and inquisitive shopping skills into your retirement-preparation life. Again, that means becoming a proactive investor, a buyer rather than someone who gets sold things.

Here are four big reasons why it is so imperative that you take control:

1. *The money involved, whatever its amount, is all you have to work with.* Saving is not easy, so losses (including lost time) are difficult, if not impossible, to replace.

2. *You are fairly easily targeted by skilled sales professionals for the following reasons:*

- Your neighborhood's demographics
- The automobile you drive
- Clubs or other organizations in which you are a member
- Any news coverage of advances in your career
- Public reports of corporate mergers and downsizings
- Your credit card accounts and magazine subscriptions, which imply lifestyle and resources
- Your professional title or degree, if any

Many of these characteristics can be rented or bought from list brokers. Sales professionals who invest in screened lists rather than following a cold-calling approach also are likely to possess strong persuasion and psychological skills. They might turn out to be very skillful in investment decisions, but more likely they are skilled primarily in sales techniques. Before you invest money with them, you need to figure out correctly which is the case.

3. *Because investments are intangibles, they're easy to sell to buyers who have no good means of resistance.* One lacks any proven, concrete tests to apply when buying. Here we cannot literally kick the tires, "squeeze the Charmin," or hold the goblet up to the light. Even the familiar turns out pretty abstract: buy 100 shares of McDonald's? Well, you won't own a particular neighborhood store; instead you'll have a tiny interest in over 20,000 locations around the world, including India and Japan, where the menus are different. Dividends will be based on the directors' evaluation of cash-flow trends. Your stock's price will be driven by investor moods and overall trends in price-earnings ratios, by net funds flows into equity index mutual funds, not only by the company's presumed continued earnings growth.

   If investing in the world's most familiar and successful hamburger stand is actually not very simple, things quickly get even tougher. What if the investment is a single-premium deferred variable annuity, a tax-preferred biotechnology research-and-development limited part-nership, an artificial intelligence software start-up, or interest-only strips of GNMA (Government National Mortgage Association) pass-through securities? When considering such esoterica, most people are no match for a trained sales professional, who is armed with a sales script and a prepared list of responses to commonly asked questions. The best defense is one most of us shrink from using: simply to say "I don't understand." Lacking hard criteria on which to base a refusal, we have few other defenses available.

4. *Buying is based on optimism.* We all want to prosper and have a secure retirement. Those who sell investments are in the position to say, "We have a nice solution here for that need; this will make you wealthy." We greatly want to believe that they are right, and we at least believe that this person is more expert in such matters than we are, that they have a key to the beautiful room we wish to enter. We know we'll need to take at least some risks to get ahead in life. Buyer readiness means being willing to believe, being ready to act despite an inevitable lack of 100 percent certainty. When we are in that psychological state, anything short of the patently ridiculous would probably be acceptable. The sales professional enters our information void at just the moment when we're prepared to allow our greed to overrule our fears. Therefore you must remain in control, which means starting with your own needs and ideas.

### Seven Steps for Putting Yourself in Control of Your Investment Life

How can you assert control? Here are seven things you can do, each of which will help keep you from losing a chunk of your hard-earned capital by being too easily sold rather than thinking and buying.

1. In case you might not already have one, a telephone answering machine, left on at all times, is the best single investment you can make! This screens out pitches you have no need to even consider. It lets you evaluate the

few worthy investment suggestions on your timetable,
when you're relaxed and can think most clearly.

2. Before you agree to do investment business with anyone, thoroughly check them and their firm out and
   impose some tests on them.

3. Subject every investment idea to a macro-level test
   before even considering any details (which will always
   sound alluringly attractive). The test: Does this kind of
   investment fit my overall plan and needs? If your portfolio is presently underbalanced toward income-oriented items, decline any aggressive-growth ideas. If you
   already have some inflation protection, don't sink assets
   into gold or oil futures. If you lack a clear overall plan,
   don't start by buying things in hopes of fitting them
   together later. Instead, go back to Strategy 1 and make a
   plan. Tell the salesperson that this specific idea doesn't
   fit. Do *not* tell him or her what would fit; if you do, the
   salesperson will tailor the next hot idea with that slant in
   mind.

4. Don't buy anything unless or until you fully understand
   it. As covered in Strategy 2, insist on educating yourself
   independent of the information (if any) offered by the
   salesperson. What you do not understand could turn out
   to be an unworthy, gimmicky, faddish idea, one that
   later you'll have no way to decide intelligently about
   holding or selling.

5. Don't bite on the unlikely. It bears repeating: "What
   sounds too good to be true, probably is." In the early
   1960s, supposedly everything was going to be sold from
   vending machines. XYZ Widgetronics will corner a
   $100-billion market in ten years (always run away from
   those nice round numbers!). Also, be wary of unrealistic
   claims, such as, that you can make an average of 50 percent a year in this stock. (Right; let me first check how
   much of it is held in a couple of top growth mutual
   funds, since they have good noses for rapid growth.)
   And beware of the classic trap for investors looking
   toward retirement: high yield. Most other investments
   presently yield between 4 percent and 7 percent, but you
   are lucky enough to be offered an absolutely safe deal

with a 15 percent annual yield. Sure. Your common sense should not be suspended when a salesperson calls.

6. Refuse to be rushed. Never agree to buy during the first discussion. Following this advice will give you the time to comply with the second and fourth points discussed in this section and will allow you to decide whether the idea passes the suitability test posed in the third point. The more insistent the seller is that you must act now, the wiser you will be to insist on taking your time, or to just say no. Insist on having a prospectus mailed before you invest, or, for an existing company, the latest annual and quarterly reports. Refusal to put written documents into your hands in advance should raise a bright red flag.

7. Apply common sense to the size of this purchase proposal. Is it in accord with your overall asset mix? Could you afford to lose 50 percent of this and not be devastated? Be careful of anything available only in huge minimum chunks or increments such as only multiples of $25,000 or more. If the sales professional suggests a purchase of a particular size without knowing you and your needs well, it is because of the commission they will earn or their need to meet a quota. Ask yourself whether, if having thought of the idea yourself, you'd have contemplated that size of commitment at first.

### Ten Tests to Apply to Financial Sales Professionals

You are in greatest danger of losing significant money on the first up to the third transaction you do with a broker who is new to you. Really bad ones will knowingly sell you something on the first contact, having no hope or desire to create an ongoing client relationship. More subtle ones may provide one or two small ideas that work out well and then, having gained your confidence and knowing more about your hot buttons, will spring a wonderful-sounding bad idea for a big sale the third time around. The following rules are designed with two objectives: to slow down the purchasing decision process by putting you in control of it, and to test the virtues of the broker and his or her firm. Apply the first four tests in order, since the broker's failure at any one stage will save you the time of pursuing any of the rest.

**Test 1:**   Insist on a resume from the broker. Be very suspicious of anyone in an occupation of trust who will not show you anything reasonable that you ask for on paper. State that you never do financial business with anyone before checking references. Even if the firm is large and well known, it still could hire a bad apple or two. So check out the person no matter how prestigious the firm. If not already familiar with the firm, ask for a corporate brochure and financial statement.

**Test 2:**   Learn how long the firm has had offices in your area. Old telephone books at the public library will reveal that. Be cautious about very recent arrivals. Insist on visiting the firm's offices and meeting the person. Deliberately set an appointment during the hours when the stock market is open. Don't be met for lunch or breakfast at a neutral site. You want to see what the office and its personnel look like and what the salesperson's work area is like (does he or she own some books, or just a picture of a boat or favorite power car?). This rule will both give you a personal impression of the broker and will prevent you from doing business with a phone voice from a thousand miles away (unless he or she was introduced and recommended by a personal friend of yours).

**Test 3:**   Contact the NASD (National Association of Securities Dealers) at (800) 289-9999 or via its Web site (www.nasdr.com); ask for a record of complaints or grievance proceedings against the broker personally, and the firm. Your state government's securities regulatory commission may maintain a similar registry. The North American Securities Administration Association, at 202-737-0900, will supply your state body's address and phone number. At a good public library, check historical newspaper indexes from the last several years for cities where the broker has worked: Be sure there are no unsavory stories.

**Test 4:**   Make sure the broker provides valid references. The list of present clients should not be from his or her preferred short list of planted names. You need a name connected to you and not just to the broker, someone whose opinion you can value. Does the broker have a client who works at your company? A church member? A golf, health, or social/service club with which you are familiar or affiliated? A reputable attorney or accountant?

Actually check out the references; don't assume that willingness to supply them means a broker "must be OK."

Observe the broker's behavior to see how he or she is likely to treat you if you become a client. Here are some simple ways to test this:

**Test 5:** Without saying so, require that the salesperson find out about your financial situation, your needs, and your risk-taking attitudes. If you're being offered specific investment suggestions without those essential preliminaries, the broker has already violated the "know your client" rule and is making it clear that a prime driver will be his or her need to make quota and earn a commission as quickly as possible. If the salesperson fails this test, go no further under any circumstances! Shockingly, 45 percent of mutual fund salespeople in bank lobbies (a place you thought you should feel protected!) failed to ask about client objectives in a 1995 secret shopper survey.

**Test 6:** Refuse to be rushed through the first four tests, or into any purchase or sale decision, or into delivering your present securities (let alone cash!) into the salesperson's firm.

**Test 7:** Beware of anyone who tries to boost the order size when you do make a purchase decision. That's sure evidence of the overriding dynamic in this "relationship": getting a bigger commission out of you, faster.

If the broker fails any of these tests, start over with someone else. This will take time, but it will save you a lot of money. No one wants to protect your hard-gotten assets as much as you do!

The final three tests pertain to the investment idea being presented. They're absolutely essential where the broker is new to you or where the idea is one he or she introduced rather than one you asked the broker to research to meet your particular interests or needs.

**Test 8:** Find out where this investment animal is publicly quoted on a regular basis. Don't take someone's word that you can find it in such-and-such Sunday paper; go look it up at the public library. Past quotations will let you note performance and volatility. If it is not quoted in print independent of the selling firm, or in an accessible electronic database, do not buy it. After being told what price you can buy it for, immediately ask what you could sell it for right now. Verify that bid/ask spread with any other local brokerage firm. Is the percentage spread acceptable?

**Test 9:**   Ask the salesperson how he or she is compensated. Start with getting a complete written commission rate schedule from the firm. Do not accept a glib response like "Oh, we follow the regular NYSE table" (since there is none) or "We're very competitive" (they ought to be eager to prove that one in writing). Be very wary if the answer amounts to, "We include our commissions in the net prices of OTC stocks so I can't exactly break them out for you." That tells you it is a high-markup firm specializing in stocks where the house controls the market and sells to you from its own inventory. Ask directly what the brokerage firm's total commission will be if you buy so many shares or bonds or dollars' worth. Don't ask the person's own cut, because that is unnecessarily intrusive. Figure the answer as a percentage, and remember that 7 percent is now considered a high load for mutual funds! Big commissions are bright red flags.

**Test 10:**   Ask the broker if he or she personally owns any of this investment product. If the response is that it does not fit onto his or her investment objective, you should consider whether a person with a different objective can fully appreciate and understand your own, which is more important to you! If the answer is positive, request to see a copy of his or her own purchase confirmation as proof.

### Never Take the Big Plunge

Tragically, thousands of Americans annually use their retirement money for major single investments that fail dramatically, ideas sold them that turn out to be frauds at worst or poorly based chances taken at best. Would you fly to Las Vegas to bet half of your retirement-plan money, two for one, on a single red/black spin of the roulette wheel? I would hope not. And yet many people will make high-risk commitments because they are packaged as "investments." Heed these lessons: Don't change full-commission brokers late in life. Never make a big bet with a new broker. Don't buy a huge piece of any exotic type of investment, or of any kind you have not previously owned. Be especially cautious about ideas that are sold to you rather than thought of first by you.

A serious rule of thumb is never to invest more than 10 percent of your retirement assets in any one situation, especially if it was not of your own initiation. The only exception would be a mutual fund (which, by its nature, is highly diversified) when you are relatively young and have a limited asset pool. Then 20 percent to 25 percent would be the individual limit. Such funds should be "true no-load funds" to save you unnecessary costs and should each have a very different investment objective. (See Strategy 17 on potential mutual fund mistakes.) As your assets reach or surpass about $500,000, lower your maximum for single positions to about 5 percent rather than 10 percent. At those asset levels, you can afford diversification and don't need thrills from big single bets that could fizzle.

Always remember that you're ultimately talking about *your* serious money, your retirement standard of living. So avoid anything that could involve obligating you for more money than what cash you put in up front. That rules out playing with commodities, uncovered options, or margin accounts when dealing with retirement money. If you can't afford to pay for it all now, you surely won't want to pay for it all if it goes bad!

# Be Proactive, Not Passive or Reactive

*B*eautifully conceived ideas are useless until implemented. In an arena of uncertainty like investing, it seems much easier to sit passively in your current position than it does to take action. Investment markets are continuous, unstructured experiences where you'll wait in vain if you expect to be given a signal it's time for action. An old Wall Street saying is that "they never ring a bell to tell you when it's time to sell." (The same is true for buying.) The next few pages will help you work to overcome passivity and learn to ring your own bell rather than just wait.

## Two Kinds of People

A professor friend and I were looking out over Denver's landscape one afternoon during lunch. Like so many other cities, Denver juxtaposes a bustling downtown area with unfortunate neighborhoods whose residents would have little use for a book such as this. In our city, as elsewhere, some people put in 50 or 60 hours a week, pay their taxes, make time for their kids' needs, and help in community activities, all while also taking night courses. Others pass many of their days beer in hand, on the front steps, bewailing their unfortunate lot in life. The professor put it crisply: she sees a world of two kinds of people— some for whom life is a series of things that *happen to you,* and others for whom life is a series of *decisions you make.* Moral of the story: By sitting passively in any part of life including investing, you're setting yourself up for victimhood. Passivity does not make good things happen.

## (Bad) Reasons Why Doing Nothing Feels Right

Investing requires work; inertia is an enemy. Any work uses energy, and you have plenty else to do. For deep psychological reasons, most people dislike handling money matters. They'd prefer to do it once and then leave it alone. These folks allow bank certificates of deposit to roll over automatically; leave IRA accounts in one mutual fund seemingly forever; allocate 401(k) assets once (or, even worse, consign them to that too-convenient and safe-appearing money-market fund pending a later decision), never again to be reexamined or adjusted.

Working on your investments takes time and mental energy. Every decision carries with it a nagging discomfort that you might be making a mistake. These hurt not only your wealth but also your ego. Investment decisions, by their very nature, are made in hopes of positive future results, but are always made with less than 100 percent certainty, leading to the very real chance of undesired results. Uncertainty is uncomfortable for us, especially when dollars are on the line.

Busyness, discomfort with uncertainty, and attempts to protect your ego from avoidable assault are common reasons for doing nothing that operate each time you consider purchasing a stock, bond, or mutual fund. When it's time to consider selling versus holding on, you may go through a whole raft of reasons why you should do nothing: you dislike paying taxes on your gains; you dislike taking losses, because they are direct hits on your ego; you resent paying commissions; and selling represents a radical, 180-degree about-face from the thinking that originally led you to buy or to hold. Might you make a double mistake by selling too soon and using the proceeds to buy something else that could then decline? And, as you recall from past experience, you'll never be happy after a sale, since getting out at the exact top is impossible. So you refuse to put yourself through that pain; by holding on, you postpone expending the energy used in making a decision while shielding yourself from possibly being wrong. (Of course, this is pretending that taking no action is not a potentially wrong action in itself.)

Selling well is extremely important, because good selling lets you take advantage of unjustifiably high prices; it helps you to avoid lengthy holding of essentially dead positions that will produce low, zero, or worse future returns; and good selling gets you out of bad stocks before they turn into major, disastrous losses. This whole question of selling is so big and complex, it could easily fill an entire separate book. In fact, it does. (See my book *It's When You Sell That Counts: Understanding and Overcoming Your Self-Imposed Barriers to Investment Success,* McGraw-Hill, 1997.)

## Why You Need to Ring Your Own Bell

Not only do markets frustratingly come without easy instructions for profitable handling, you will also find few people totally committed to your retirement financial success. Even a competent professional investment manager, charging about 1 percent annually and probably doing a credible job, cannot possibly care as much about your dollars as you do! Only you have the overriding interest in building wealth for retirement (those in the financial helping professions have an interest in earning commissions and fees by taking little slices *out of* your life-supporting assets).

And your retirement assets must command serious attention. Not spending the necessary time and intellectual energy on them is something no responsible business owner would do. Who would invest a few hundred thousand dollars in a small business and then walk away to let it run on its own, as if on automatic pilot? Your dollars must be thought of as a business with assets to be allocated and reallocated from time to time. Those assets can sit and do nothing, they can be used successfully and create profit, or they can become misapplied and incur losses. It's all up to management, which, in the case of your retirement assets, is you! As in any business, not every decision is guaranteed to produce favorable results; however, inattention and failure to make decisions are sure paths to failure.

Many money managers prefer to invest in companies where management has a large stockholder position rather than where top managers are just highly paid hired hands. Their preference is based on an obvious reason—those with strong incentives are more likely to be most attentive. So make managing your retirement assets, a business inherently vastly more important to you than to anyone else, one where you are in active control.

Don't expect or allow a broker to take charge. Using a discount broker not only saves you money but also carries a certain elegant simplicity: Clearly you are your sole asset manager and nothing happens without your initiation. You know you must manage. And if you do choose a relationship with a full-commission brokerage firm, you still must remain fully in charge of events and be the decision-maker. Being the actor rather than a reactor with your broker protects you from a chance he or she will suggest ideas mainly for the commission benefits.

But let's assume your broker is too reputable to stoop to such tactics. You still need to be the initiator, because brokerage firms have changed significantly over time. Unfortunately their so-called customers' men of bygone days are now a distinct minority. All too many of today's account executives are more skilled at asset gathering and in professional sales techniques than in choosing individual stocks and watching them closely until they appear ripe for later sale. Wall Street has nurtured a generation of brokers taught to specialize in the product of the month. Registered reps are actually discouraged from doing their own homework lest they get their firm into legal trouble because they were not qualified to do their own research.

By concentrating attention on this month's featured product, a broker focuses on one-decision investments—things they sell you and that neither you nor they are supposed to worry about ever disposing of. Life insurance, variable annuities, and your IRA assets all fall into this mold. Other manufactured products have convenient built-in maturity dates when, without any further effort by you or your broker, a pile of cash will again be available for deployment (into the then-featured product). Certificates of deposit, unit investment trusts, and closed-end term trusts investing in short-maturity bonds all include their own predictable ending dates. Short-term government bonds, while not manufactured by Wall Street, have similar benefits from a brokerage firm's perspective. With these assets, the broker also can say, "And besides, what could be safer?"

Mutual funds fall into a middle ground. They're much less burdensome to watch than individual stocks and bonds but might require a proactive decision to switch at some future date. You'll very likely be advised to expect to hold these for the long term. That actually might turn out to be good advice, but in any event it definitely serves the interests of your broker (since the investment sounds conservative and demands only extremely light maintenance—while it provides the broker with possibly trailing commissions) and the fund's management company (which collects an annual fee for multiple years until some intruding force triggers a sale).

I readily confess that I am not an adherent of the buy-and-hold philosophy. Strategy 8 will explore reasons buying and holding forever isn't always a great idea. In support here of the proposition you must be active rather than passive, remember:

- The world economy changes.
- Financial markets shift and thereby present modified risk/reward profiles over time.
- The company in which you bought shares is an evolving organism; its competitors are not sleeping either.
- You, your financial responsibilities, your risk tolerance, and your asset mix never stand still.

Another important reason you must "ring your own bell" is that financial markets, by the nature and rhythm of their process, tend to lull you into complacency. They never come to closure or render a final verdict, as a horse race does. The unending investment markets merely suspend action until the next session opens in the morning. What fell today could as easily rebound tomorrow; what rose nicely could after all extend its pleasant trend (or, if you're unlucky, give back those paper gains). We'll just watch and see—and watch, and wait, and watch some more. Getting into a frame of mind where you view investing as an active, ongoing process will help you guard against inertia that so easily creeps in due to the always-flowing, never-ending, and often frankly entertaining nature of the investment markets. You must make yourself an actor on stage, not a member of an audience to the play.

## How to Ring Your Own Bell

Following are approaches that will help keep you in a proactive position, where you are on watch at all times, ready to ring the action bell.

**Always keep P-S-T tests in place.**  Think of that "pssst!" sound one makes to pass along a secret or a reminder. Here, the mnemonic stands for price, story, and time frame. For every investment position, particularly individual common stocks, you ought to have a three-part thesis for holding. Key elements in that thesis are the driving reason for owning (a story of what is expected to happen); an expected price result of that fundamental story; and a time frame in which this is expected to transpire. All three elements are essential and tend to interact. Failure of any element implies a mistake in judgment. Mistakes must be addressed (usually by selling the investment, since most shifts in expectations are usually primarily ego-soothing rationalizations).

Here is an example of a P-S-T scenario: You have bought common shares in XYZ Wonderdrug Development at $12 each despite the company's lack of present earnings or dividends. Your reasoning was that its research department has created a unique chemical formulation designed to kill human fat cells safely, and a patent is pending while FDA effectiveness approval is also under consideration. You expect approval of both within 24 months, followed by a $300-million expansion of sales in two quarters, leading to a jump in earnings to $1 per share that same year, which other investors will capitalize at 30 times earnings. That will enable you to sell at $30 per share for a 150 percent profit. You have your three P-S-T elements: new product (story); events, earnings growth and probable EPS multiple, leading to a specific price target (price); and a specific 30-month window of time related to both the news and its expected effect on price (time). If these things do not happen, something is wrong.

Failure should trigger action, and should discourage you from waiting patiently. In this example, a specific prediction by management that an FDA approval will take X months longer than first expected (for a specific reason) would be an acceptable modification; your merely hoping that everything is OK and will eventually work out is not a good reason to stay put. Having a P-S-T scenario for each holding (and changing these only seldom and for solid reasons) creates a discipline designed to make you uncomfortable if you find yourself floating indecisively.

**Conduct periodic total reviews.** Think of these as scheduled preventive maintenance on your car, as required for keeping its warranty intact. These reviews will include both micro- and macrolevel tests. The microlevel tests will require you to look at each security position and decide whether it merits continued holding. Following are two great acid-test questions, one applying at each end of the scale:

1. If I were forced by financial need (or a pending total cut-off from all financial information for a year) to sell just one item because its prospects seem subpar looking forward, which one would I choose to sell?
2. Which among my holdings has performed so outstandingly well to date that I should realistically conclude it's due for a rest before making further gains, or might even be fully (or over-) priced?

These questions impose a dispassionate look at each holding, thus producing judgments about relative forward prospects. Our first question hunts out weakened fundamentals, while our second looks for overly generous valuation. Both seek to avoid risk (from bad news and from price vulnerability, respectively).

**Ask this hold-versus-sell question often.** Knowing all I now do (not based on what I earlier knew, expected, or hoped), and if I had cash available, and if such a purchase would not violate portfolio balance, would I buy this stock today at today's price? If the answer is not a firm "yes," you are playing a greater-fool game in which your continued holding is based on hopes that other investors will buy, and thereby prop up the price of, what you are unwilling to buy at current prices. If you would not buy it here, why hold it? Holding is merely recommitting your capital to this stock (rather than to any of thousands of alternatives) for another day without calling your broker or incurring a commission. What you would not buy now, you should not hold now. So sell it now!

The other part of your total periodic checkup, at a more macro level, involves asset allocation. Here, cluster your assets at present value (totally ignore your cost!) and compare the resulting subtotals against goals for asset balance that are appropriate to your age and risk tolerance. Perhaps you note that your domestic stocks position has pleasingly become a larger percentage than planned, bonds are a bit on the thin side of target, or maybe your international equity holdings have fallen below present targets. Meanwhile, dividend and interest receipts for your money market fund have built up too much cash in your money market fund. As a result, you trim domestic stocks and cash, and add to both bonds and overseas stocks and funds. Your selling choices in domestic stocks are dictated by the three questions that test fundamental deterioration, overly generous pricing, and which stocks you really would not buy today if starting out with cash.

Such exercises will keep you ringing your own bell rather than waiting for some outside force to trigger action. And you'll get an unexpected, second-level benefit. Having done your homework on a regular and recent basis, you'll be less prone to a product pitch from a securities sales professional. You will be confident about your present portfolio tidiness and the amount of attention you've recently given your holdings. Today's new sales face will not catch you with accidentally ready cash reserves to invest in his or her preferred way. You can legitimately say, "Thanks, but no; I've just done a complete portfolio review and everything is in good order. I don't need that." This keeps you on track with Strategy 6, buying rather than allowing yourself to be sold.

Regular reviews of your overall situation and individual holdings are like periodic general physical exams. You may detect disturbing conditions early and will then take action because you have rung your own bell. Many investors purchase individual investments without a specific P-S-T goal or scenario in mind, and then tend to hold them more or less interminably. Because a lack of control characterizes their mode of investment operation, another deadly force becomes a threat to their wealth: Such investors have become passive, "hold-unless" reactors. They hold their collection of once-promising ideas until and unless a disaster strikes. In effect, they are hoping for each holding to act like a long-term lottery ticket and eventually pay off (but, sadly, they actually have no P-S-T plan that would trigger taking such a profit when or if it becomes available). They hold on, their money adrift, until disaster strikes. Then they sell, accepting a bad price that could have been avoided if they had looked for developing fundamental weaknesses before they ballooned into an obvious disaster. Bad, low prices could have been avoided if one had accepted earlier, unjustifiably high prices as and when they developed.

Doing regular, disciplined checkups will also help you avoid selling in a panic. If you have good updated reasons to hold everything you own, you will be less likely to lose emotional control and allow the market to tweak you to the point of irrational action at exactly the worst time. Staying in control, meaning constantly holding the rope that would ring your own bell, is your best defense. On those relatively infrequent occasions (every several years) when a panic occurs, you must have the mental preparation and self-control to do what feels unnatural by stretching your comfort zone and the historical and psychological perspective to know that your reaction must be to oppose rather than blindly follow the mass or the crowd (Strategy 9 deals with contrarian analysis and behavior). Market panics are times when you must prevent general market forces from ringing your bell and prompting you to do exactly the wrong thing. Practice being in charge and ringing your own bell as a regular mode of operation. That will help build resistance to letting a market panic ring a wrong bell for you at just a critical time.

# Know When to Sell and Be Able to Do It

*M*any things formerly important in our lives may become less functional or even harmful if kept too long. As we mature and change, our needs shift. Our first tricycle, first car, wardrobes, early apartments, and jobs—we replace them all as circumstances and times change. But for many complex reasons, we have an excessively strong tendency to hold onto investments once bought. That behavior pattern is often counterproductive. With this strategy, you will learn ways to overcome this important but subtle barrier to successful lifetime investment results.

## Why Holding Forever Is a Mistake

Unless you've been a do-it-yourself, take-charge kind of personal investor for many years already, you may feel that even questioning the concept of buying and holding forever is a bit shocking. A recurring theme plays throughout this book—that you must be actively willing to challenge conventional wisdom and depart from "the way everyone always does it" to be successful in investing. Buying and holding forever will not prove wrong every time, but it is far from a perfect approach in most cases. It is based on false assumptions (either stated or unconscious) and proceeds from laziness and inertia. It also flows naturally from having no plan.

Buying and holding forever is based on four assumptions, all of them false:

1. The world will not change for the rest of my lifetime.
2. I and my needs will never change as the years pass.
3. I always make good buying decisions.
4. Stocks, bonds, and funds will rise at a steady pace forever.

Few people would make such assertions and follow them with "and therefore I plan to do such and such." And yet, making investment purchase decisions that turn into lifetime holdings implies confidence that change will no longer occur—or requires incredible good fortune. In actuality, we seldom make a buy-to-hold-forever investment decision up front; that holding-forever syndrome creeps up on us afterward.

## Why We Nevertheless Tend to Make This Mistake

Inertia and the desire to avoid pain are the main reasons investors fall into a buy-and-hold-forever mode. Except for professionals who are immersed all the time in the investment process and who thrive on it, most people spend little time dealing with investment matters. They feel inadequately prepared, they see the mountain of information as unconquerable, and they frankly dislike making decisions when surrounded by uncertainty. Some link investment decisions with negative feelings about dealing with salespeople—they don't like the pushy feeling, or they have been burned and remember that pain. Also, some psychologists espouse the theory that we subconsciously associate money with filth and therefore dislike dealing with it. Could that be a reason why it is so taboo to discuss one's personal money matters?

For such reasons, most people seek to avoid engaging in the investment decision-making process (the mutual fund industry derives a great benefit from this psychological fact, since buying a fund brings relief by turning things over to the professionals). Whatever the particular investment purchase might be, we feel great relief once we have made a choice: "It's finally done with: I don't have to agonize over that any more!" We happily tuck all that paperwork into the back of our file drawer on money matters, able now to pursue less distressing life activities.

While enduring the pain, discomfort, uncertainty, and perceived helplessness in the buying precess, we build a strong antipathy to returning to that area of decision making. Consciously or otherwise, we do not want any part of unmaking that choice previously taken under such duress. We prefer to "leave well enough alone." The trouble is, just buying it does not guarantee it will always remain "well enough." Since change is inevitable, chances are that investments, once made, will not do the job for us forever afterward. We readily trade in our first car, first job, and first home when they stop meeting our new needs—perhaps many times in the course of a lifetime. (Unfortunately, for many people the choice of a first marriage partner does not last a lifetime, either. In American culture, we find it easier to undo such choices than to replace dysfunctional financial investments chosen years ago!)

Once we've bought an investment, either of the two things most likely to happen manipulates our ego so as to discourage further action: The investment works well...or it works badly. If you make money, either in a spectacular amount or over an extended period, you build a comfort zone around your investment: it becomes a sacred cow, untouchable. In those extremely rare cases when one stock endures as a continuing winner for several decades, buying and holding it forever is of course an ideal strategy when seen in 20/20 hindsight. More commonly and realistically, however, the economy and every company goes through major changes. The world is transformed: international trade, technology, demographics, tastes, laws, health concerns, marketing evolution, substitutions by competitors, or a dozen other major types of change refuse to stand still. Rare is even a good management that will foresee and adapt to every nuance and remain atop its heap for decades at a time. So we can't reasonably assume our choice, once made, will remain the best, or even acceptable, indefinitely. If that choice does well early, our ego enjoys having it around to remind us of our wisdom, so we adopt it as a family friend.

If our investment purchase does not work out very well, its presence is a blow to our ego. We have two choices (aside from the neurotic option of wallowing in our pain): terminate this painful relationship or pretend it does not exist (or at least not at a level worth worrying about). Ending an investment gone bad is a very unpleasant experience. Selling at a loss ends any remaining hope for recovery, reminding us of "pulling the plug." Actually implementing a decision to cut our loss hurts, and the confirmation arrives in the mail, recounting both then and again at tax time the official final score: We lost. We dislike losing and feeling inadequate, dumb, outsmarted, or whatever may have caused us to make an error that cost money. Facing such feelings, we strongly prefer flight. We push away any further thought of the pain-creating investment. We hold on—on and on!

One of the few positive aspects of racetrack gambling is how it brings frequent automatic closure. Each race is swiftly completed, and its final result is clear. Tomorrow, you must actively choose whether to bet on that same pony or switch to another. Stock markets suspend action overnight; the race for riches resumes with you still riding yesterday's horse, no matter how many lengths behind you might be. Without automatic closure, whether ahead or behind we float from day to day, and then year to year. Our most comfortable action is inaction. Whether to keep our proud attachment with a winner or to submerge pain over a loser, doing nothing is our easiest path. By default, inertia rules. Is this any way to run a lifetime investment program?

Another subtle but strong factor prompting us to do nothing is a piece of ostensibly friendly and often-repeated advice: "Be a long-term investor." Friends and colleagues who've lost at trading tell us that buying for the long term is best. Brokers, wanting to sound conservative, repeat the refrain—"of course" you want to be a long-term investor. Mutual fund managements, prospectuses, and marketing literature reinforce that theme: buy and hold, and invest long term (which will lower their expenses and keep them earning a 1 percent annual fee on your money for a long time). If most investments were destined to work extremely well, buying and holding on would indeed be the plan of choice. But with the world changing, not to mention your needs, holding forever is unlikely to work. Faithfully standing pat reminds me of a bumper sticker seen on a ram-shackle pickup truck: "Hitchhikers: get in, sit down, shut up, and hang on."

This is not to say that I advocate a life of hyperactive trading. But cool logic says buy and hold forever, at the spectrum's opposite end, is far from a panacea in a life filled with financial uncertainties and change. Growth mutual funds, while urging you to hold long term, typically turn over 50 percent to 75 percent of their positions annually! Thinking strategically with a long-term horizon in mind, but executing tactics in real time as inevitably changing situations dictate, is a realistic course. Except late in life, we seldom acquire an investment position in the expectation of retaining it forever. Until then, always battle the inertia that tends to swallow you into a lazy, hold-forever trap.

## Preventing Injury from Buy-and-Hold Inertia

Following are seven rules to save you from the hold-forever trap. Rule 1 is about getting your investment head together; rules 2 through 4 apply to buying well; and rules 5 through 7 guide you when and how to sell well.

**Rule 1:**    Unburden yourself of any self-imposed standard of perfection. (For a complete discussion of this rule, read Strategy 10.) Even while making every buy decision carefully and with a long-term view, know that a time will come to reverse field and close out what you are now opening up. Accept reality: A 100 percent success rate is impossible. Be prepared to take losses as well as profits.

**Rule 2:**    Buy with both a scenario and a grand plan in mind. Every investment ought to point toward a defined purpose, or you should pass. Never buy just because "it sure sounds good." Always insist that this particular commitment of assets works toward some specific objective. For example, does it help provide (the right amount of) international diversification, a protection against inflation, an exposure to promising technology, or a fairly stable ballast in case of bad times? Have P-S-T, discussed in Strategy 7, firmly in mind, or else your money will be floating aimlessly starting on day one. Such discipline will make it uncomfortable to slide over lazily to "being a long-term investor" as your reason never to reassess and move on.

**Rule 3:** Be a proactive purchaser rather than a passive victim who is sold investments. As discussed in Strategy 6, each individual purchase is a tactic supporting your inviolable strategy. Insisting on being in charge will save you money and stress, and will help you avoid destructive relationships with sales professionals peddling their products of the month irrespective of your needs. Finally, being proactive will make you feel better about yourself for having done your homework and added to your expertise. Your odds of financial success and your self-confidence will both rise.

**Rule 4:** Know in advance how to get out. This is as basic as reading that fire-evacuation chart in your hotel room. Insisting before you buy on knowing exactly how you can exit will prevent losses from illiquid investments and will steer you away from buying things sold by sales sharpies who leave town once you have acquired worthless paper. Never venture in where you cannot clearly see a way out. Before buying, find out where this thing trades in the aftermarket, how you can get a truthful current price quotation from someone outside of the selling firm, and how wide the buy-sell price spread is. If the answers leave you at all uncomfortable, your decision about buying is mercifully made easy: Just say no.

**Rule 5:** Assume that change, rather than lack of change, will definitely occur once you own any investment. Assume that anything that can go wrong, even things you have not envisioned in advance, might well happen during your ownership. Therefore, have a plan of constant vigilance. If you do not understand what makes your investment tick or what might make it fall apart, your chance for a successful outcome is near zero. Not anticipating change dooms your dollars in advance.

**Rule 6:** Even when things go along well and seemingly according to plan, set a schedule for periodic appropriateness reviews. This is a strategic asset reassessment. Are your investments designed to do the things that you need done? It is best to do this about every 24 months, at a time of year that will not be compromised by other pressing tasks in life (income tax season, etc.). The purpose of this fitness review is not to judge performance. Here your question is, given the total of my available assets, and given my long-term goals and present situation, would I enter this investment or one very similar to it today if I had 100 percent cash? How does each investment fit an important part of the total picture?

**Rule 7:**    Ask, "Knowing all I do today, would I buy this asset at today's price?" Yes, that's a tough test, but a necessary and good one. There are thousands of alternative places to invest your money. Even if you have nothing else attractive currently in mind, holding what you have may not be as good a decision as selling and moving aside into a money market fund for a while. Avoiding loss is often easier than making profit, and it's at least as important!

Regularly asking this question about each of your holdings will discipline you to seek concrete reasons for continued holding. It will ask if there's trouble brewing that could easily get worse if you hang on longer. It also will notify you that you've done better than you'd hoped and therefore should nail down an unreasonable profit before it melts away. Apply this key test to each holding as often as monthly, probably about quarterly, absolutely at least annually.

# Adopt Contrarian
# Principles and Discipline

*M*arkets move to excesses: to extremes of optimism and of pessimism. Success in investing requires that you avoid being a part of the crowd when it acts foolishly during those times of extreme market behavior. To stand against the majority at these times, you'll need to have cultivated in advance a willingness to think and act independently. In short, you will need to have a contrarian mind-set. You need to be alert to fads and be constantly considering unpopular, unconventional possibilities. Opening up to such ideas is an important first step toward practicing contrarianism consistently in your investing.

## What, or Who, Is a Contrarian?

A contrarian is not an obnoxious full-time cynic, nor does he or she practice knee-jerk oppositism to whatever others might say. The American father of contrarian investment thinking, Humphrey B. Neill, said that to be a contrarian means you must "ruminate in directions opposite to general public opinions; but weigh your conclusions in the light of current events and current manifestations of human behavior." (Humphrey B. Neill, *The Art of Contrary Thinking* [Caldwell, Idaho: Caxton Printers, Ltd., 1967]).

Rumination, an old-fashioned word, is a process of turning something over in one's mind repeatedly—quite the opposite of making a snap judgment or an automatic, preprogrammed decision. For ruminators, thoughtful questioning, rather than immediately ready acceptance, is the natural mode of approach. Add to these qualities a predisposition to independence of thought, and you have a thoughtful contrarian, who likely will be able to withstand the emotional upheavals of unsteady financial markets.

An investing contrarian is one who looks beyond what seems obvious in the day's or the moment's news. He or she does not deny the accuracy of facts or the existence of present events and clearly established trends. Rather, the contrarian investor tries to escape the noise and step back away from any stampede of the crowd. He or she seeks to discern how important a current news item is; what (particularly what is different) could happen next or has been overlooked; and to what degree current opinion has become a blind consensus.

Being contrarian is not easy, nor is it an attitude of mind that can simply be flipped on like a light switch when needed. This way of looking at the world, especially the emotionally charged world of investments, requires enough discipline to endure loneliness, and means making decisions in conditions of considerable discomfort. This attitude is practiced by only a distinct minority of investors. Part of their distinction is in their high levels of investing success.

## Why It Pays to Be a Contrarian

Over the long term, investment prices are driven by true value. Putting that another way, fundamentals *will* prevail—Stock prices of great companies will rise, and those of weak companies will decline. Bond yields will inevitably reflect inflation, since lenders will refuse to lend unless they receive a positive real rate of return. But daily news events, short-term price fluctuations, and emotions drive immediate behavior more than logic does. Psychological forces carry prices of securities above, and then below, their underlying fundamental values (see Figure 9.1).

**FIGURE 9.1**   Fundamentals/Emotions

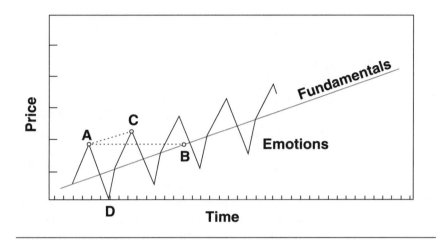

Contrarian investors attempt to identify and take advantage of periodic imbalances in behavior that push prices unrealistically far out of balance with reality. Doing so is the ultimate in buying low and selling high. Admittedly, contrarian investing is an art rather than a science. It's impossible to predict in the heat of a moment exactly how long an upside mania or a downside panic will last. Contrarians try to identify phases of crowd thinking and then take action in the opposite direction. Doing so, we contrarians willingly accept that catching an exact top or bottom is close to impossible, but being in the area is plenty close enough for financial success. Successful execution of this strategy helps contrarians accumulate wealth by capturing large upside percentage moves and then taking money off the table when leaving it there would put it at greatest risk of loss.

Buy-and-holders will sneer that this approach is "market timing." It is not; rather it is a disciplined way of reacting to the foolishness of the crowd and thereby of achieving returns exceeding the average. Those who refuse to try to capture available market swings to their benefit have doomed themselves to buying and holding forever and thereby passively accepting whatever long-term average return the market provides.

Consider this example: Anywhere you might live has its own mean annual temperature. But you dress and act according to actual conditions rather than passively pretending every day is just average! Practicing a contrarian investment approach employs similar thinking. You say, "I'm not sure exactly how far or how long this will go on, but it now feels abnormal, so I am going to refuse to remain part of this craziness."

In deliberately acting contrary to the crowd's extreme movement, you indeed sell high and buy low. Not at the exact highs or the precise bottoms, to be sure. But, when you and the world look back in a cooler period of reflection, it will be clear that your independent thinking gave you a strong chance of being in the right general area when you sold or bought. You will have gotten in close to the lows and out pretty near the highs, rather than the opposite. Always wanting to feel comfortable, the crowd will have rushed in to buy much too late (near the top) and then later in the cycle of emotional extremes will have panicked and sold much too late (at a bottom they themselves created). You will have accepted their cash when it was about to hold value better than stocks would, and you will have taken their stocks when those were soon to become much better choices than cash.

Here's the bottom line, the reason why contrarian investing works: When "everyone" has already come to believe something in common and has acted upon that conviction, literally no one remains to continue pushing prices in their recently prevailing direction. For that reason, at that very point when virtual unanimity of opinion prevails, "everyone" (those in the prevailing crowd) will be wrong and therefore will lose money. Joseph Kennedy, Sr., father of the late president, said he sidestepped the 1929 crash by selling when he noted that even every cabby and bootblack was in the stock market and talking about it. No other buyers remained to be found, so a major top had to be in the making.

You can do this. You have it inside you to act in ways counter to the trend. Being a sharp consumer is one proof you could become a smart, contrarian investor. When was the last time you rushed to the supermarket in great excitement to buy tomatoes because they had risen to $2.79 a pound? "No one is that stupid," you're thinking. If a car you had carefully researched and decided was a solid choice suddenly went on sale for 30 percent off, would you hold back in fear of its possibly going down another 5 percent or 10 percent? Of course not! You'd take advantage of the tremendous opportunity and seize today's bargain now, not worrying that it might possibly become slightly better. And you'd smile wryly while leaving those tomatoes on the shelf for someone who doesn't care about value. Your behaviors as a value-conscious consumer prove you have the raw intellectual material to become a successful investment contrarian! You buy things on sale and refuse to buy at high prices, since you know from experience that a postponable purchase will almost certainly go on sale sooner or later.

## How to Be a Contrarian

Successful investing, contrarian-style, requires observation, understanding, and finally action. First, you must see facts: events, trends, rates of growth or decline, and the early stages of decay or healing. But it is not enough to merely observe. You must develop a sense of history, an ability to put things together in context, and a knack for feeling when a trend is moving to an extreme. But all of that will do you no good if you take no resulting action. Acting will prove the most difficult skill to master.

Taking action contrary to the crowd will always feel uncomfortable. At the time you must decide and act, you will never have all the information you'll want, because gauging market psychology is more of an art than a precise science. Furthermore, your countertrend decision will make you feel lonely, and we humans are social animals who seek comfort and approval from others. Always remain tight-lipped about your investment moves. If you're a talking contrarian, people hearing of your heretical views and behavior will exert immense pressure and may possibly convince you to abandon your aberrant thinking—at precisely the wrong times.

Acting as a contrarian requires that you identify the market's situation—whether that be broad averages or the market of opinion regarding a single group or investing concept. The factual and emotional states of the economy and the market can be observed at any time. Successful investment behavior requires patience so that you don't pull the trigger at the very first observation of important elements; you need to wait for an accumulation of evidence that an extreme is developing. Trying to play contrarian on a short-term basis creates what Wall Street professionals call whipsawed traders. Humphrey B. Neill observed with characteristic clarity that "in the stock market the public is right during the trends but wrong at both ends." Therefore you should not be impatient at the first sign of overboard behavior in others. Let a trend run for a while and watch the evidence accumulate. Figure 9.2 includes some signs that, when they cluster, are historically repeating indications of tops and bottoms.

One cluster of evidence on market status that you readily can identify is that of celebration behavior. You can see this in yourself, in your friends and work colleagues, and in stockbrokers. Here are some telltale signs that a bull market has entered its old age:

- Hyperactivity—You trade more often than usual; you spend extra time doing library research; you add database, advisory, and newsletter subscriptions.

---

**FIGURE 9.2**   Signs of Turning-Point Extremes

|  | **At Tops** | **At Bottoms** |
|---|---|---|
| Economy and Profits | Clearly strong | Obviously weak |
| Employment Picture | Unemployment rate low and falling | Layoffs and plant closures |
| Press Coverage | Market on page one of local papers | Bleak cover stories by general-news magazines |
| Whom TV Interviews | Gushing optimists | Dour doomsayers |
| Attitude Toward Stock Market | Everybody in the pool: This is fun! | Fear and loathing; stocks in doghouse |
| Outlook on Risk | Risk? What risk? | I want total safety |
| Emotional Climate | Celebration | Fear, withdrawal |
| Reaction to Any Contrary Ideas | "It's different this time!" | Disbelief that any recovery will come |

---

- Risk taking—You "invest" in initial public offerings (if you can get any stock at all); you open a margin account or use margin to the maximum; you try options trading; you take money out of the money funds, bonds, or safe mutual funds to add to hot individual stocks.
- Personal—You're talking and bragging; stocks are again a common topic of conversation; you "count the chips" (tote up your portfolio value) more often than customarily— something you'd never do when the market is depressed.
- Ego—This isn't so tough after all; after all these years, you've finally figured out a winning system. You might even consider retiring early to manage your money full time.

Such are evidences of a top. Greed is dominant in this market phase. At market bottoms fear rules behavior. A similar list of symptoms and behaviors could be recited for a depressed market with the contrasts reflecting swings demonstrated by a manic depressive individual: hyperactivity occurs in the manic ("up") times and depressed inactivity dominates at panic ("down") ends of the spectrum. Extremes, those times and levels in the market when meaningful reversals occur, are defined by a maximum amount of discord between reality and expectation: Prices are most "out of whack" with true values. Tops and bottoms occur when emotions are running rampant. Being volatile, emotions cannot be measured with reliable precision so as to identify exact tops and bottoms. Therefore, do not frustrate yourself in that search for perfect execution. Settle, instead, for a preponderance of strong evidence and be content to enter *near* the bottoms and to exit *near* the eventual peaks.

Unless you have spent many years actively investing, you may find it difficult to calibrate your behavior for lack of repeated past experiences as standards. Here are four conditions you should be able to observe readily in your external environment:

1. *Length of trend (This is necessary but not sufficient in and of itself.)*—Bull markets average about 50 months and bears about 11, so don't be too quick in calling much shorter moves too long.
2. *Severity of angle on a chart*—Go to a source providing good charts of past market history, and note what angles of ascent and decline typify moves shortly before major

reversals. Sharp angles of price change are difficult to sustain over the long term, since they would take prices to zero or to ridiculous multiples of earnings with outrageous and unbelievable speed.

3. *Acceleration*—Near tops, this is often called a blow-off; at bottoms, it is the classic bottomless-pit panic stage. These are shaped like parabolic curves or waterfalls. Such movement represents an unsustainably severe emotional condition that simply *cannot* last very long and therefore must quickly reverse.

4. *Virtual universality of opinion*—There will always be a few perennial naysayers or perpetual optimists. Like broken clocks, they're right occasionally but unworthy of attention. When all market participants who are talking (other than these few full-time extremists) are in either bullish or bearish agreement, that condition creates an inescapable calculus making a move to the opposite direction imminent. Put simply, when all the buyers have already acted, prices stop rising; when all those wanting to sell have been accommodated, prices rebound.

The first three points are easily visible, charted in the financial sections of newspapers that always include such information. Prominent examples are the *Wall Street Journal* and the *New York Times*. Major stock-chart services and Internet Web sites also are valuable. The fourth condition is not something so discrete that you can look it up on a specific page; however, even a relatively inexperienced investor can use Figure 9.2 as a detective's checklist for key evidence. If you are a bit unsure about how to do such investigative work, you might refer to John Naisbitt's best-seller *Megatrends* (New York: Warner Books, Inc., 1984). The basis of his technique is news content analysis: charting changes in the number and frequency of ideas and words appearing in published and broadcast media. Regardless of whether you apply that technique in such detail, this fact bears repeating: Financial market psychology is an art, not a precise science. So never paralyze yourself into inaction by waiting for that elusive final piece of perfect information. Why? Because it doesn't carry an identification label and therefore, for practical purposes, exists only in hindsight. And you'll always know there is more to know.

# Resist Paralyzed Perfectionism

*B*ased on considerable evidence, we human beings must expect to make mistakes. We may not like it, but that's reality. Being a perfectionist in one's investment life is counterproductive. By exploring and adopting this strategy, you will be able to more clearly understand, identify, and overcome perfectionist tendencies so you can be more successful in accumulating and then holding wealth.

## The Impossible Mission

In the unlikely event that you actually need convincing, I'll state flatly that it's impossible to invest without making mistakes. These mistakes come in two forms: actual losses and opportunity losses. Anyone would readily settle for never having a loss, although that goal is unrealistic. To avoid any risk of loss requires taking no risk in nominal terms, which means burying cash under a mattress at worst or maybe putting cash into a fully insured bank account or into short-term U.S. Treasury bills.

Both approaches will prevent loss in stated dollar terms but, after taxes and inflation, will produce depreciated buying power—in fact a loss.

Even somehow defying all odds by never buying a stock, bond, or mutual fund that went down would still leave you short of the perfectionist's standard. Prices of securities constantly fluctuate, even from moment to moment. To maximize growth in your capital, meaning never to miss the most ideal opportunity available, would require that you constantly switch from one asset to another just before it experienced the fastest available price movement. Doing that would require total prescience and 100 percent of your time, 24 hours a day (markets do trade around the globe!).

Your real mission should be to do the best you can. Set realistic goals and work on extending your skills and knowledge so your results will improve over time. Do not allow perfectionism to get in your way. It is a needless distraction to worry about falling short of an impossible goal. Concentrate your energies on doing the best you reasonably can!

## Why Does Perfectionism Tempt Us?

Our culture stresses achievement. Olympic athletes establish new world records; factory production quality reaches ever closer to true "zero defects"; medical advances help to predict more diseases sooner; and autos, appliances, and workplaces are engineered for increasing safety and more nearly perfect performance. Thus our daily experience is rife with pressures to be better, faster, more accurate.

For many of us, the ultimate achievement would be to attain total perfection. The logical extension of better is best, and the ultimate best is perfect. We carry this burden of impossible expectations into our investment lives, where it only harms us.

From our earliest days, we're conditioned to seek higher standards (which are not bad in themselves until they make us crazy). Singing the least bit off tune, we are noted as spoiling the show. In school, grades of 100 percent are visible, achievable standards, as proven every day by someone in class. Children and grandchildren simply must be admitted to the best preschool program or all is lost—they'll never get into *the* best college, preventing them from becoming president of the best company, which will exclude residence in the ideal neighborhood and membership in that prestigious social or sports club, and so on. Unfortunately, these are real worries. For some, perfectionist goals are so overwhelming that suicide is the only remedy for failure. Keep a better perspective: Learn to loosen up a little and live.

A combination of nasty ingredients tempts us to seek unreachable perfection. Knowing and understanding them might not banish your temptation to seek unrealistic goals, but awareness of forces working on you can help you develop emotional steadiness. Some of the forces are external influences, while others are self-imposed burdens:

| **External Influences** | **Self-Imposed Problems** |
|---|---|
| Living in an age of science | Other-directedness |
| The exactitude of numbers | Discomfort with uncertainty |
| Media focus on extremes | Envy |
| Demands at work | Greed |
| The illusion of safety | Ego |

Let's examine these briefly.

### External Influences

**The age of science.**   We live in an age of highly visible, frequent, and amazing scientific advances. In just the final quarter of the century, immense computer power has become inexpensive, portable, and user-friendly. Medical science and biotechnology seem to be on the verge of conquering major scourges such as cancer, Alzheimer's disease, and maybe paralyzing strokes and injuries. Sheep and monkeys are cloned. Holes in space capsules are fixed on live TV. So observing, we hope and suspect that almost any problem can be mastered by applying sufficient doses of science.

**Numbers, and more numbers.**   A short step from science is the world of numbers, which bring a level of exactness.

Investing involves ubiquitous numbers: facts, ratios, trends, and projections. Seeing so many precise facts, we want to believe that any pile of data can be sorted and rearranged so as to reveal a secret formula, an answer that should have been obvious if only we'd applied enough energy sooner. Hogwash! The financial future is based on unknown future events and human emotions, elements that can't be predicted with a formula.

**Broadcast and print media's focus on extremes.**  The bizarre and the extreme sell newspapers: the welfare cheat who used the most fake identities the longest until being caught; the most opulent home, measured in bathrooms or acres, owned by a Hollywood personality; the biggest lottery winner ever—all grace news racks at supermarket checkouts. Even in investing, scorecards chronicle which mutual fund or stock or stock picker was number one—quarterly, weekly, even daily.

**Work pressures.**  At work, we see evidence that perfection is the right standard. Competition for job security raises productivity and accuracy standards. Someone else, or even a machine, might work longer or more perfectly and displace us, so we strive for machinelike precision. Such perfectionist thinking makes us expect machinelike precision in investing, which is to our detriment since it's unrealistic.

**The illusion of safety.**  Since the New Deal, politicians have been trying to create a world where all risks are anticipated, preferably prevented, or at least compensated for. Those whom we elect and whom they appoint strive to outlaw or regulate hunger, poverty, disease, hate, injury, illiteracy, an imperfect environment, unfavorable economic cycles, and whatever else could conceivably bother a voter. Again, we hope that by throwing enough effort at it, we can make a perfect world. Anyone injured or aggrieved by failure to have this imaginary ideal life sues everyone in sight for their alleged failures to be perfect on behalf of the plaintiff. We absorb such thinking and then apply it to ourselves in our investment lives.

### Self-Imposed Problems

**Worrying about what others think.** Many people allow others to define their expectations and goals. Keeping up with the Joneses rather than setting our own set of goals dominates people who act this way. "What would so-and-so say?" is an ever-present driver for such tortured souls. Did this start when our parents reminded us that Santa Claus was always watching how we behaved? Was it reinforced at school when any misdeed brought an admonishment that "This will go on your permanent record!"? The Central Intelligence Agency does exist, despite its attempts at self-camouflage, but there's no evidence that somewhere there really is a huge central "Permanent Records Repository" employing people whose occupation is Keeper of Everybody's Permanent Record. Yet we worry about what others (spouses, accountants, or brokers) may think of our investment results. Don't. Spend your time instead determining your personal financial goals. Investing is challenging enough without our loading it up with other-directed baggage.

**Discomfort with uncertainty.** For reasons I cannot explain fully, people have widely differing levels of comfort with uncertainty. Some seemingly fearless folks will try just about anything. (Some research suggests that many are more willing to risk physical harm than financial loss. This indicates how deeply our fears affect us in the realm of investing!) At an opposite pole are folks for whom making decisions without 100 percent certainty is an unspeakable torture. What a miserable self-constructed prison! Overwhelming self-doubt becomes a self-fulfilling prophecy, since inability to make any decision results in lack of any progress, which brings failure and victimhood, which only proves in the eyes of this poor soul that the world was impossibly challenging. Investment decisions are made emotionally difficult because we are highly aware of the chancy surroundings, because we accurately predict that waiting will afford us some added information, and because our precision-dominated world makes us believe a perfect answer might actually exist. So we recoil from decisions in the realization that our odds of less-than-ideal results are high. We must fight our aversion to uncertainty and get on with our investment lives as best we can.

**Envy.** This major enemy is constantly poised to defeat your investment endeavors. We see the rich and famous and read of the fabulous successes of a very few investors, but we fail to focus on their status as exceptions to the norm. Even short of 100 percent perfection, in any comparison of results only one of many will turn out to be best. By allowing envy to define the exceptional performance of others as our own standard, we help to defeat ourselves. Such self-imposed frustration leaves us concentrating on the difficulty of our task rather than on the task itself. Batting slumps in baseball occur when a player thinks more about how awful it will be to make yet another out rather than focusing on watching and then hitting the next pitch.

**Greed.** For countless investors, for whom no amount of gain is enough, greed is a success killer. Whether by long actual experience or merely by considering Wall Street's mathematical odds, we know that we will not sell at *the* highest price. And yet we hold on, for what brokers sneeringly refer to as "the extra eighth" or "one more point." Greed defeats us, as we forget writer William Saroyan's simple but profound observation that enough is plenty. Are we greedy in our investing because we know that an even bigger gain will stroke our egos even more? Do we hold on because this particular stock has treated us well and we are willing to ride with it rather than risk the unknowns of choosing a new horse? Do we act greedily because being able to brag about our home run will impress us and others more than a series of singles—even though the latter can more likely be achieved with a lower risk of striking out? Or does greed take over because in our hearts we all hope against hope for the bonanza, the lottery, the short detour to Easy Street and early and bountiful riches and retirement? Professional psychologists might be able to answer these questions, although if they could they would all quit their clinical practices to become wealthy investors. Whatever the reasons for and operating dynamics of our greed, it will defeat us. And greed is merely another way of expressing a driving need for the ultimate "more," namely perfectionism.

**Ego.** Finally and simply, ego sums up all those other self-imposed barriers to investment success. We want to be right, the best, the center of some universe, even if there are no other observers. Ego feels better when we're right and worse when we're wrong. So, in thinking about buying, we become frozen into indecision by realizing we might make a mistake, which would injure our tender egos. And, when looking at holding versus selling, we subconsciously provide our egos with more chance for stroking and forestall the known immediate pain of an ego injury by doing nothing. That way, our possibilities—for further gain, for reducing or fully recovering a loss, and for avoiding the pain of not selling at the top—are left open. Again perfectionism, now in the form of making our ego feel good, urges us to do nothing. Knowing our ego's tendency to get in the way, and observing in real time our own behaviors that indicate this is happening, can help us. It probably is not a curable disease, but can be managed by constant attention.

## Ways to Counteract Investment Perfectionism

Awareness of imperfection, overlaid by an overwhelmingly large set of information and opinion sources, sets us up for potential defeat. Investment databases are numerous and very inexpensive. Software makes it possible to analyze all that information. We can watch the stock tickers run across our TV screens on CNN. Bloomberg on the radio and "Wall Street Week" can mesmerize us. Magazines and advisory letters seem to promise wisdom and clues to what we really want: the ultimate answer. Just some (perfect) system that will always work. We see roughly 3,000 stocks trade on the New York Stock Exchange, and thousands of others on Nasdaq. We have over 9,500 mutual funds from which to choose. Correctly, we deduce that our chances of picking *the* best one are nil.

What you do with that reality is key. Your choices are to permit yourself to wallow in defeatism and paralysis, or to dive in and get on with your investment life.

Following are some investment elements you can use either to learn as much you can and proceed to trying your reasonably best, or ultimately defeat yourself with perfectionist pursuits.

### Multiple Information and Opinion Sources

Databases and experts are wonderful sources of financial information. But with more sources, their likelihood of being in conflict rises geometrically. Such conflicts will confuse you, allowing information-overload anxiety to take over. You'll see a vast array of information and ideas and will believe you should absorb it all before proceeding. After all, you don't want to make foolish mistakes for lack of adequate preparation. Actors call this performance anxiety.

Voluntarily imposed darkness is no solution. Don't cut yourself off from all facts for fear of having too much to absorb and master. Instead, use as much information as you can easily handle. Develop an investment approach that feels comfortable and stick to it; then execute your strategy. For example, if you're more attracted to value than to growth investing, go for it! If fundamentals make more intuitive sense to you than technical analysis, so be it (or the reverse, if that is the case for you). Go with what you can handle and ignore sunspot theory, the great K-cycles, six-year sugar price swings, the trends of gold and sliver, and changes in pound versus yen.

### Asset Allocation

Sure, there's going to be some optimal mix of assets (dismissing no diversification in favor of seeking a single best-performing asset). But that ideal mix will be known only in hindsight, so beating yourself up over having missed it will do you no good. Complete hindsight will never be available until your life is over, at which point it will be of no practical value. Strategies 21 and 22 develop the idea of diversification and urge that no matter what your age you always should own some equities, or equity mutual funds. No one can tell you in advance whether the most ideal answer will be 15 percent or 20 percent in international. This is fine-tuning at the margin rather than order-of-magnitude rights and wrongs. So dive in and get on with it. If one asset class does fabulously well after a few years, pare back those holdings in favor of the underperformers and let the historically proven tendency toward economic and psychological rotation work in your favor. Tinker a bit; don't demand perfection or you'll spend your whole future in the false comfort of a money market fund while trying to find a perfect answer.

### Specific Stock and Fund Choices

Again, here is a place where perfectionism will make you crazy, paralyzed, poor, or all of the above. Resign yourself to the inevitable truth: You simply will not own the best single ones. Odds are literally several thousand to one against your picking the top fund of the year, or the best-acting NYSE-listed or Nasdaq stock. Settle for good, strive for above average, and use some common sense to help you avoid the dogs.

### Ultimate Tops and Bottoms

If a medium-priced stock trades in a 25-point range over a year's time, the odds against your buying at its low price are about 201:1 (25 dollars times eight eights per dollar). Ditto for selling out at the top. Logically, then, stop focusing your attention on getting the absolutely best price for individual stocks or mutual funds. Try to buy good value when most other investors are discouraged, and try to sell what's become overpriced when the crowd is excited, celebrating recent successes, and paying too much for hot ideas. If you come even reasonably close, repeatedly, to buying below average and selling somewhat above average, rather than following the crowd, which does it just backwards, you'll become quite wealthy. You'll have had no need to worry about absolute high and low prices. Figure 10.1 shows that perfect or near-perfect timing has added little profit in the past 30 years.

### Timing

Again, forget about scoring 100 percent or anything even fairly close to it. Not all asset classes will move up and down at the same time. Nor will anything go up forever, although you'll become most willing to believe it's possible at just the wrong times: the tops of long bull markets. Domestic stocks go up roughly about 70 percent of all years, but unfortunately not exactly three out of every four years! We have not seen three consecutive down years in major stock averages since the 1930s. That doesn't make a recurrence impossible, but the odds are in your favor. One disciplined, albeit mechanical, approach to

---

**FIGURE 10.1**    Best Timing versus Regular Deposits
                    Annual Investment in Dow Jones Industrials

---

Period: 12/31/67 to 12/31/96
Annual Investment: $1,000
Total Invested: $29,000
Dow at Start: 905.11
Dow at End: 6448.27

Results of Two Methods

| **Dec 31 Every Year** | **At Best Friday Every Year** |
|---|---|
| $167,084 | $172,744 |
| Difference: | $5,660 |
| Difference in Return/Year: | 1.30%* |

\* On average amount invested.

---

good timing is to set your asset mix targets, which will gradually shift as your age rises, and then shift assets back toward those targets every couple of years. This will "time" various markets with some success, since you will be selling off things that have performed best lately and buying into others that have lagged for awhile. So, you can "time" markets without becoming obsessed about doing it perfectly.

### Time Value versus Procrastination

Especially if you are young, this is exceedingly important. A young colleague once asked me about choosing a good mutual fund or two to start her IRA account. I recommended a few that seemed appropriate. A first-time investor, she seemed somewhat more fearful than average about possibly taking a loss. I explained dollar-cost averaging. I even emphasized that the dollar losses involved from starting at the wrong time (meaning a high price in the market) were quite small when a monthly investment of $150 was involved. That seemed to help. But, as I learned later, perfectionism, or its flip side (fear of failure) unfortunately ruled the day. My friend could not select the ideal fund nor could she define any particular month as the perfect time to start, so she did nothing. The IRA papers lay uncompleted, unsigned, and unmailed. The $2,000 for that year was spent rather than put aside, and a $560 tax savings (an instant 28 percent return, if you will) was foregone, all for the fear of possibly making an imperfect choice. After just the initial year, her combined wealth loss plus tax loss was 128 percent, far worse than any conceivable investment result in a mutual fund chosen randomly. This story offers yet another reason to overcome the potentially paralyzing force of perfectionism and to get on with investing.

# Don't Panic!

*B*uy low and sell high—anyone will say that's your key to investing success. In real life, neither end of that admonition is easily implemented. Selling low, specifically during a sharp general market panic, is an especially common and brutally costly trap. By implementing the ideas in the next several pages, you will be able to escape the panic monster, which lives on dollars it devours while chewing up millions of investors when it visits every several years.

### First, Some Reality Checks

Prices of stocks, bonds, and commodities will always fluctuate because they trade in a market where human beings make decisions. Fluctuation includes both upward and downward movements in price (lest the great bull market that started in 1982 blur your memory). Mutual funds' net asset values (NAVs) change daily. Their shifts are direct mathematical results of changes in closing prices of whatever securities (stocks and bonds) each fund holds. (Funds' daily values wiggle less sharply than do those of individual stocks because on any given day some of a fund's holdings will gain while others will fall.)

By departing the sheltered but profitless world of bank CDs and U.S. Savings Bonds, you took on one certainty: Your invested wealth will fluctuate every trading day. Underlying fundamentals (earnings, dividends, cash flows, asset values, growth rates) determine security prices over the longer term. But in the short term, emotions drive prices higher or lower— and differences between price and underlying fair value sometimes become extreme. Greed and fantasy create fads that produce overpricing. Fear, a stronger emotion, creates very sharp but shorter-lived periods of undervaluation.

## Emotional Capitulation Costs You Money

Your investment lifetime will include a number of market panics. How you act during those extraordinary periods will exert a major influence on your eventual total wealth. Although brief, price panics have lasting financial effect: Ego usually prevents people from reversing themselves rapidly. Once you sell in a panic, it is very unlikely you'll think clearly enough, very shortly thereafter, to buy back in near the lows. Instead, you'll be on the sidelines a fairly long while, recovering your courage to be able to buy again. Your emotional healing process will be enhanced by a return of rising prices, which gradually will win you over. Most who sell near a bottom fail to reenter until well toward the next top.

Selling during a panic costs you money in two ways:

1. What you sell will be sold low, possibly below its cost and certainly at a loss compared with its earlier prices.
2. You'll be in cash during much of the market's ensuing rise, thus missing significant gains during that bull phase.

The first kind of loss, from selling into a panic, is an actual dollar loss visible on your tax return; the second, every bit as real and important, is an opportunity loss—a gain not taken.

## Quantifying Stock Market Panics

Understanding a panic's typical dimensions can serve to help you. By knowing how deep and how lengthy the pain is likely to be (fully realizing that past averages do not hold each time), you have a better chance than if you lack perspective and can conceive of only an endless fall.

Historians use differing terms to describe sharp and rapid stockprice declines. Here I avoid the term "crash," which properly applies only to very infrequent and economically catastrophic drops that virtually anyone can date. By that standard, since 1900 only the October 1929 crash measures up, since it ushered in eight years of economic depression. October 1987, which saw a 23 percent one-day drop in the Dow Jones Industrial Average (DJIA), did not even cause a recession. Some, however, would still designate that event a crash because of its unusual size.

The term *panic* is commonly used to label sharp market breaks caused by specific events such as commodity shocks, bank closures, assassinations, or failures by well-known institutions or individuals. Another useful and descriptive term is a market "smash," since this describes a sudden and painful experience but does not carry the historical weight of a crash. Market smashes occur fairly frequently, and in some cases they become severe enough to cause at least a bit of fleeting panic among investors and the general public (in the latter case triggered by media coverage). For purposes of discussion here, we will use the term *panic,* since it captures the emotional-content aspect of a mathematically measurable decline in prices. When stocks fall 9 percent over six or twelve months, that is not noted as a memorable event. But a one-day or one-week 9 percent decline would be felt as a severe experience; it would be called a panic or a smash.

Thus, the two essential elements in a smash or panic are severity combined with limited duration. You mentally quantify these by annualizing the damage pace. Divide the percentage price drop by the number of weeks it takes, and multiply that by 50 to approximate how much would be wiped out if such a decline persisted for a year. Most investors and market tacticians would call severe any events that last a few weeks and which, if annualized, would wipe out 75 percent or more of total market prices in a year. Such extensive declines, far out of proportion to underlying fundamentals, cannot persist precisely because they would offer incredible bargains quickly: Buyers' arrival would stop the carnage.

Since 1970, only four actual recessions and no true depressions occurred in the U.S., and unemployment peaked at about 9 percent. Yet within these 28 years there were 17 market smashes, or on average about one per 19 months, as shown in Figure 11.1. These smashes averaged just over five weeks in duration, and their lengths ranged from two to nine weeks (the longest being in autumn 1987). Fourteen lasted six weeks or less. Their declines averaged 12.1 percent, or about 11.1 percent if the single largest (1987) is put aside. Eight declines (just less than half) were of less than 10 percent. Another six, however, extended to 15 percent or

**FIGURE 11.1**  28 Years of Market Smashes...and Recoveries

| Decline Dates | Percent Change | # of Weeks | Percent Drop Per Week | Percent Rally After | | |
|---|---|---|---|---|---|---|
| | | | | 6 months | 9 months | 12 months |
| Apr-May 70 | -16 | 6 | -2.7 | 14 | 33 | 39 |
| Oct-Nov 71 | -10 | 5 | -1.9 | 15 | 17 | 21 |
| Oct-Dec 73 | -18 | 7 | -2.6 | 6 | -20 | -25 |
| Aug-Oct 84 | -25 | 8 | -3.1 | 28 | 48 | 35 |
| Oct-Nov 78 | -11 | 5 | -2.3 | 6 | 11 | 3 |
| Oct-Nov 79 | -10 | 5 | -2.1 | 2 | 19 | 17 |
| Feb-Mar 80 | -15 | 6 | -2.5 | 26 | 26 | 32 |
| Nov-Dec 80 | -9 | 3 | -3.1 | 11 | -5 | -2 |
| Jan-Feb 84 | -11 | 6 | -1.9 | 9 | 6 | 13 |
| Jul-Aug 86 | -3 | 4 | -0.8 | 22 | 29 | 45 |
| Aug-Sep 86 | -7 | 3 | -2.2 | 30 | 36 | 42 |
| Aug-Oct 87 | -28 | 9 | -3.1 | 2 | 7 | 12 |
| October 89 | -5 | 3 | -1.8 | 2 | 12 | -5 |
| January 90 | -8 | 3 | -2.8 | 14 | -3 | 3 |
| Jul-Aug 90 | -17 | 5 | -3.4 | 16 | 17 | 21 |
| Feb-Mar 94 | -5 | 6 | -0.9 | 6 | 5 | 15 |
| Jul-Jul 96 | -7 | 2 | -3.4 | 28 | N/A | N/A |
| Averages: | -12.1 | 5.1 | -2.4 | 13.9 | 14.9 | 16.6 |
| | | | | 0 downs 17 ups | 3 downs 13 ups | 3 downs 13 ups |

more. On average, these 17 smashes proceeded at a rate of 2.4 percent per week, clearly unsustainable if annualized. The 1987 decline averaged 3.1 percent per week, although vastly most of its damage took just two days. Five of our 17 smashes (including that in July 1996) involved declines of over 3 percent per week; another four saw rapid price erosion averaging over 2.5 percent per week. These were unpleasant experiences for market participants. You should expect to live through several similar downdrafts in your remaining investing lifetime.

The key issue is what you do during a market smash. Having some historical perspective should give you a better chance of acting profitably than if you are ignorant of the facts.

Figure 11.1 also shows what happened following the smashes detailed earlier. Six months later, in every single case, stocks had rallied from their smash-end levels. On average, these gains were 13.9 percent (well over 14 percent when excluding 1987's cautious aftermath). Looking out to 9 or 12 months later (1997 data were not available as this was written), gains from the smash bottoms were slightly larger on average but not quite universal. Rises in the 9-month and 12-month periods averaged 15 percent and nearly 17 percent, respectively (again, a bit better if post-1987 is excluded). Just three of the post-smash 9-month periods and three of the 12-month periods saw declines in the DJIA from its smash-phase low—three out of sixteen! Interestingly, in all of those cases of renewed decline, an actual recession followed. In other words, 9-month or 12-month losses following market smashes accurately and uniquely predicted three of the four total recessions in that quarter century. Except during the nasty, grinding bear market of 1973–1974, further losses in the post-smash phase were of 5 percent or less. Granted, not all recovery periods after the smashes brought quick full restoration of former market highs. In eight (almost half) of the post-smash periods, six-month percentage gains were smaller than the percentage losses in their preceding smashes. But still, all 17 smashes were followed by rises, which averaged nearly 14 percent; eight of those rises exceeded 20 percent within 12 months. In only three of the 17 events was there no percentage recovery at 6, 9, or 12 months that equaled the smash's percentage drop (two of those forewarned actual recessions, while the third was a highly skittish post-1987 period).

Summarizing, post-smash periods in the 1970-to-early-1997 period always provided some degree of bounce if one waited at least six months rather than selling out during the panic. Odds of gains were greater than 80 percent after nine and twelve months. Periods following smashes actually produced average rises notably greater (14 percent at six months and nearly 17 percent at twelve months) than long-term average yearly gains in stock prices (about 11 percent)! The bottom line is that selling in a smash has consistently proved to be a mistake during the past quarter century. While complete recovery did not occur absolutely every time in as little as twelve months, some recovery always happened fairly quickly. Therefore, selling in a panic or smash was a mistake; in fact, buying after a smash produced above-slope upside gains on average.

It helps to know that selling in a smash is a mistake, but you also must know how to withstand fear. Working against your fear in a conscious way will take guts and discipline. Remember, most of these smashes lasted six weeks or less. Few took as long as nine weeks. So mark your calendar and steel yourself against the pain!

## Different Holdings Mean Different Actions

In the previous section, I used data from overall market results measured by the Dow Jones Industrial Average. Diversified domestic equity mutual funds invested would have acted similarly. But individual stocks show wide variance in performance. Few act much like any average or index. Thus, a key question is whether you should hold all stocks through a smash.

While I generally would advise holding mutual funds and most stocks, some identifiable kinds of stocks should be tossed overboard in a smash. Not everything will recover with equal likelihood or equal vigor. You must identify those kinds of stocks whose likelihood of early recovery is below par. These should be abandoned during a smash (if not already weeded out during earlier periods of higher prices), to be replaced by higher-quality items, and quite promptly.

What kinds of stocks recover least well in the first advance following a market smash? Stocks that require greatest courage to buy or hold: small-capitalization, low-priced, or declining-earnings stocks. Fear being a stronger emotion than greed, prices fall sharply more readily than they rise. A market smash is followed by caution at best and pessimism at worst. As in physics, stocks fall of their own weight if they lack support. Buying pressure is needed for any stock to recover after a smash. When millions of individual and thousands of professional investors are cautious at best and worried at worst, they are least likely to buy stocks with obvious problems or lack of sponsorship.

**Small capitalization is a problem.**    If the total value of a company's shares is relatively small (say, under $500 million), its stock is unlikely to trade actively enough for huge mutual funds to be able to buy (and sell) large enough blocks to be meaningful in their portfolios. After a smash, caution rules and so liquidity is a major consideration. Fund managers are thinking about how easily they could exit if necessary. Small-cap stocks will fail that test. Funds may gradually keep selling out existing small-cap holdings as the market rises, to provide added liquidity. That selling will hurt price performance by even the most healthy of small companies' stocks.

**Low-priced stocks stay out of favor.**    Brokerage firms will wish to appear prudent, matching investors' post-smash mood. So low-priced stocks, which would appear to be risky, will be shunned. Market leaders such as GE, McDonald's, or Xerox are more likely as buy recommendations than are truly undervalued but low-priced stocks. Shares trading below $10 are especially vulnerable to this price discrimination. At many firms, stocks quoted below $5 are worthless as margin collateral, so a future market drop would accelerate such stocks' declines if they pierced the $5 barrier. Awareness of such rules keeps professional investors away in a post-smash environment.

**Companies with visible problems will be left behind.**    When caution rules, only high quality or proven growth will suffice. Companies with recent earnings problems therefore will be absent from "buy" lists. Such companies may be perfectly healthy, and may right then be correcting their fundamental problems, implying strong future earnings growth. Professional investors, however, will be seeking perceived safe havens after a smash. They will be more willing to risk loss in a well regarded stock (in case the market should fall further) than to be courageous and risk explaining why they bought into a company with known questions. Such herd thinking creates unusual values later, but in the short term it holds back troubled stocks.

**Recession-vulnerable industries will be strongly avoided.** While few smashes are actually followed by recessions, investors fear the worst from the economy when stock prices decline. So big investors will think in terms of vulnerability to recession, just in case one should follow. Stocks in cyclical industries and companies that carry heavy financial leverage will be identified and avoided. Even if no recession does materialize, such stocks will be laggards early. Eventually, absence of a recession will make them bargains, but that process takes many months. Other stocks will do sharply better right after a smash.

**Stocks in smash-related industries will lag.** Sometimes a panic is triggered by negative events in one particular industry. Bank or savings-and-loan failures are a good example. Deterioration in a high price-earnings group such as computer technology (sometimes due to no more than a quarterly earnings disappointment in one or two key companies) can stop a market advance. When such a correction turns into a painful smash, bad overall action will be blamed on and associated with the triggering group. During the early months of recovery, investors will retain their distaste for that offending group. Its stocks will trail popular averages until an extended general rise makes them appear to be bargains.

**Recent IPOs will be hurt.** For lack of established reputation, recent new issues are unlikely to be market leaders in a post-smash environment. Some such companies might even prove destined to become great growth stories, but will have no champions. Many recent IPOs will have been sold to the public during the final, frothy, phase before the smash and will be held in weak hands, by nervous (but greedy) investors. These stocks will be down sharply, and that shock will serve as a warning more than a bargain signal in the post-smash caution phase.

**High price-earnings ratios will be avoided.**    Again, a need to look and feel prudent will drive investors to names with apparent safe characteristics. Stocks with high PE ratios fail this test. Institutions will pursue risk reduction rather than potential profit maximization after a smash has injured confidence. So stocks with value characteristics will outrun fast-growth ones trading at high multiples.

Beyond thinking in terms of categories, look at your stocks individually. When your stock is falling, is it doing so because something is wrong with the company, or is it just being dragged down by traders spooked by an overall market decline? (This question bears answering as well in small declines that never even reach true "smash" proportions.) Read news and commentaries carefully. Your company may not be named as experiencing any problems, but watch for others in its industry or in its suppliers' groups. Those hints are early warnings of fundamental trouble, which should have you moving out regardless of whether an overall market decline might occur.

At a macro level, you should diagnose overall market weakness. Is a decline happening because chances of an economic setback are real? If so, you should step aside because prices probably will fall more seriously, and for longer, than if nothing fundamental is wrong. Tightened credit, a drop in consumer confidence, rising inventories, weak leading indicators, and flat retail sales accompanied by high consumer debt ratios are solid hints of recession to come. Absent these economic items, a price decline may be no more than a needed correction of a temporarily overdone rally. You should sell not because the market is going down, but rather when there is some other reason for your stock to decline. Selling in a market smash because it happens is falling into the crowd; you'll be in the poor company of many victims. To help you discern what is really happening in a market smash, review Strategy 9 on contrarian behavior.

Develop perspective! As if you could peer back from ten years into the future, ask whether today's smash will be viewed in historians' long view as significant. Was it the start of a recession, the end of some great industry's growth, the start of rapid inflation (with rising interest rates), or just another of those periodic little smashes? Some good and some bad news is always visible. Is whatever bad news you now see likely to prove fundamentally important stuff? If no, selling is not warranted in a long-term context.

# Choose Securities Over Illiquid Investments

$S$ecurities are not the only investment media—you might make substantial money in other ways. For charting a course toward a secure retirement at a time of your personal choosing, however, those other less liquid kinds of investments can pose serious problems and raise major uncertainties.

## Separating Your Assets

For many, a major feature of the American dream is running their own business. Earning a living from self-employment brings many satisfactions and can have unlimited upside profit potential. And, while I do not wish to discourage entrepreneurship, personal independence, or creativity, I do want to highlight the importance of clearly distinguishing and actually separating your business assets from your retirement assets.

A major risk of having your own business is that it could consume all your assets. If your business proves immensely successful and pays back your sizable investment in royal fashion, that will be good; otherwise, it could doom you to a subsistence-level old age and the need always to keep working. In other words, running your own business is a high-stakes endeavor.

But another, more subtle, problem is involved. A personal business tends to absorb and hold assets. If times are a little lean, you reduce or forgo your salary or fringes; a spouse gives up another paying job to "pitch in for a while." When things are going well, your ego and appetite for greater success and profit lead you to plow in everything available to help grow your business: for more inventory, to carry receivables, to open an added location, or move to a better spot. Your business can become a 900-pound gorilla that keeps saying "feed me!" You will do so rather than scale down growth plans, risk failure, or sell out. In the process, you easily succumb by putting everything you have in that labor of love you've built—unfortunately, including your retirement money.

So the crucial first admonition is that you keep your retirement money and your business forever separated. To do otherwise is to bet everything on one investment. When your ego gets involved, and it will, try hard to remember that you are not in full control of your success. Economic, demographic, regulatory, technology, and mere taste/preference/fad changes can determine long-run survival and success potentials in ways no amount of personal effort can overcome. You should have a life after work. If you plow every asset and borrowable dollar at your command into your business, you run the risk that your business may destroy your future security, or that you'll need to work forever to get your assets back.

The only choice, if security in your senior years is a concern, is to keep your retirement and business assets separate. Such separation is now required in federal statutes designed to safeguard workers' pensions and is built into restrictions on eligible investments for IRA plans. Washington may not understand all it imagines it does, but at least here our lawmakers got it right: Too many eggs in one basket is a prescription for trouble.

Another huge reason for investing your retirement assets in marketable securities is tax-driven. With planning and savvy asset allocation, you can postpone paying taxes on much of the buildup of retirement-plan money. But you pay taxes annually, either as a corporation or as an individual, on all profits from your business.

## Investment Choices for Retirement Assets

Where might you choose to invest retirement money in ways unconnected to your job or business? Many outlets are available, but their single common and critical differentiating feature is simple: liquidity or lack of it. My definition of liquidity is your ability to get out completely in no more than one business day at a predictable monetary value very close to what a (nondealer) buyer would pay. Securities investments (stocks, mutual funds, most bonds) pass this test, but other commonly owned investments do not. Collectibles, real estate, franchises, and part-time businesses all fail the liquidity test.

**FIGURE 12.1**   Spectrum of Liquidity
*Investment Media in Declining Order of Liquidity*

| Medium | Market Breadth | Spread or Price Cut |
|---|---|---|
| | **Nature of Problem(s)** | |
| Money Market Funds | | |
| Mutual Funds* | | |
| Treasury Bills | | |
| Government Bonds | | |
| Listed Stocks (Including REITs, MLPs, Closed-End Funds) | | |
| Corporate Bonds | | x |
| Municipal Bonds | | x |
| Foreign Bonds | x | xx |
| Small OTC Stocks | x | x |
| Local Company Stocks | xx | xx |
| Penny Stocks | xx | xxx |
| Residential Realty | x | |
| Untraded Limited Partnerships | xx | x |
| Untraded Tax Shelters | xxx | x |
| Raw Land | x | x |
| Operating Business | xx | x |
| Franchise | xxx | xx |
| Commercial Realty | x | |
| Industrial Realty | xx | |

* No price concession assuming absence of redemption fees.

For a list of investment media and their respective liquidity levels, see Figure 12.1.

**Collectibles.** I enjoy collectibles; they sustain wonderful connections to the past, providing a precious personal link to history. Whether your favorite items are paintings, coins, dolls, baseball cards, Franklin Mint Christmas plates, military memorabilia, or old books, they provide enjoyment and relaxation. And they *might* appreciate in value. Do not count on financial reward as part of the collectibles equation; if it comes, that's icing on the cake. Three things could foil a retirement plan based on collectibles: physical loss (due to aging, theft, or calamity); shifts in tastes; and wide buy/sell price spreads.

Be especially wary of collecting, with profit in mind, anything created specifically to become a collectible. Marketing experts take advantage of any new interest, but they cannot guarantee its long-term persistence. That means, for example, that Cabbage Patch dolls, after once commanding hundreds of dollars in a speculative market, could be just old toys when pulled from the attic a generation later. Ditto 1997's Beanie Babies! Advertising muscle deliberately changes public tastes so new things become popular and get sold in large quantity; that works against sustainable popularity for what was created for collection earlier! Enjoy it as much as you will, but do not count on it paying for a comfortable retirement.

**Real estate.** Owning a piece of ground can provide great psychological security. Acres in the Maine woods or a mountain cabin will soothe the harried soul. Others prefer real estate, such as a duplex or small commercial building, that generates a stream of income or tax benefits. In the 1970s and early 1980s, real estate and other tangibles were perceived as one-way streets to wealth. Then high inflation stopped and our lending industry shriveled, cutting off the money spigot that had fed price run-ups. Ask a friend from California or Boston how safe an investment in real estate can be, especially if financed on a low down payment. Real estate is notoriously illiquid: it usually can't be sold immediately, and its price gyrates.

For all its virtues, real estate can also become a stern master of its supposed owner: upkeep, tenant demands, and changes in law may consume your time and resources and also can dictate value or total lack thereof. Sites of old neighborhood filling stations are now unmarketable because potentially unlimited liabilities for underground remediation costs pass with title to the ground. Land within so many feet of water is worthless in Vermont because of recent wetlands-related building code changes. In short, rules can change after you own the property, possibly wiping out your investment. Real estate could demand expensive renovation just at the time you had hoped to sell it, turning a presumed cash source into a cash sink.

So direct ownership of real estate is a poor choice for retirement dollars. If you believe strongly in the long-term importance of owning real estate, hold some high-quality real estate investment trusts (REITs) and let the professionals handle it for you. These are discussed in Strategy 19.

**Franchises.**  Your local library, Sunday newspaper, and the informational-seminar circuit are replete with information on franchising "opportunities." Undeniably, many savvy and hard-working entrepreneurs have become wealthy as franchisees. Ask someone who has a small collection of successful McDonald's locations and you'll hear the fabulous upside of franchising. For every successful concept, many others range from marginal also-rans to unmitigated financial disasters.

Many franchisors require their franchisees to engage in full-time, active personal management. That rule would keep you from investing your retirement assets in such a franchise situation and still keeping your regular job. Other franchisors do allow absentee investors. This, of course, requires the local owner to hire, train, and pay an active operator, upping operating expenses and cutting profits. Franchised operations always involve controls by the concept owner, which might be impossible in your situation. What if you were forced to change outside signs or interior decor costing $25,000 amidst a tough recession, when interest rates are high, or exactly when you want to retire? You could build a great local operation but be unable to sell it at a fair price, because the franchise agreement might give your franchisor first-refusal or veto rights over any sale, effectively letting the franchisor and not you name your selling price.

The truth is, the experience of franchising includes the above considerations and problems, despite what you read in franchise-boosting magazines. No legal businesses allow effortless profit, where you just open the door and leave a magical money-gathering machine unattended with no risk. If such things existed, everyone would be operating one, and then excess supply would depress prices and erase those supposedly unlimited profits. Regardless of whether the franchise agreement requires your full-time physical presence, you need to be prepared to commit your time and energy to the care and nurturing of your investment, or it may wither and die. The bottom line is this: A franchise can come to own that person who holds legal title. That is not appropriate for retirement dollars, which are supposed to buy rather than prevent your freedom in later years.

## Tests for Appropriate Retirement Investments

To summarize, some very intriguing and otherwise attractive things make for bad retirement investments. Two major issues to consider when choosing a retirement investment are who or what is truly in control (you or the asset), and whether it is liquid. Following are a few important tests you should impose on any proposed investment of your retirement money:

- *Are you sure that you can always control it, and not the other way around?*
- *Is it liquid?* No matter how much you love it, can you in fact get out at a fair price and quickly? Will the asset be of greatly reduced value in your spouse's, or other heirs', hands? Is there actually a market in which you can sell it, or merely the illusion of one created by weekend dealer gatherings?
- *Does it have ascertainable value?* You need to be able to know, with a high certainty, what your retirement assets are worth. Only then can you know when you already have enough to be comfortable, or just how much more you need to amass to reach your financial goals. Estimates of value in magazines, or even an appraisal, will not guarantee your asset can truly be sold at the stated price. Securities, with minute-to-minute quotations, do offer that assurance of knowable price.

Illiquid investments carry a hidden danger by conditioning you to live with lack of information about actual value. You become unprepared to make follow-up evaluative choices (whether to fix, hold, or bail), precisely because you always function without full information. This is not a prudent way to have your retirement assets held.

- *Does it provide diversification?* If it consumes all your assets or exposes them to events in one part of the economy, and if something goes wrong, it will be too late in life to fix your problem except by working forever.
- *Is it divisible?* This concept is central to monetary units. It should also apply to your retirement assets. You may wish to redeploy your assets over time into a more desirable balance. If everything is tied up in one business or one piece of artwork, divisibility is out of the question. Or, your retirement may require not only living off your income but also dipping into principal. In that case, you will need divisibility. Traded securities and mutual funds carry this as a major benefit.
- *Does it allow risk taperability?* In other words, can you gradually tune down your assets over time toward greater certainty of value and returns? A mix of mutual funds, which can be shifted from aggressive growth toward short-term government bonds, offers risk taperability. No hair-cutting salon franchise or apartment building can give you that assurance.

# Understand Stocks' Subtleties

*Y*ou've noted that this book is not another starting-investor's primer providing definitions of what you already know. We are at a second level, working to expand your chances for success by revealing subtleties of how things work in the investing world, particularly in the crucial psychological and perception areas. These next few pages do not define stocks or differentiate them from bonds. Instead, they delve into what makes the stock market move and how you need to prepare for and interact with that environment.

## Long- and Short-Term Influences

Fundamentals such as earnings, revenue growth, cash flow, and asset values determine stock prices over the long term. But you must function today and every day in the short term, where emotions and expectations ride herd on prices, often suddenly and violently. Institutional involvement in the stock market is at a record level, meaning that individuals are easily trampled underfoot if and when the huge beasts become restless. Your participation in stocks and, by inference, equity mutual funds, must deal with institutional dominance effectively, lest you allow temporary nonfundamental factors such as price volatility to undo your best-laid plans.

Fundamental analysis is required for investment success: You must know whether a company is a winner or loser, because odds favor you when you focus on winners. However, your identifying a good company does not mean you will make automatic profits. Fundamental strength and stock-price progress are not linked automatically. You must find ways in your mind to separate "good fundamentals" from presumed "good value," since momentum and expectations in the market are what drive prices in the short to medium term. This requires submerging your ego, to figure out what the market most likely will do rather than assuming it will perform as you think it ought to.

## Eight Ways to Lose Money in Good Companies' Stocks

If getting rich on Wall Street were easy, fewer people would commute to day jobs, being able instead to trade handsomely for a living from their PCs or being already comfortably retired young. A great irony of investing is that there are so many ways to be wrong even after picking a good strong company. One of the most unfortunate chances is that you might choose a long-great stock just as its fundamental fortunes begin to wane. Putting such bad luck aside, here are eight other tactical and timing mistakes that can make you lose money:

1.  You can believe you're smarter than all the rest of Wall Street. Do you think you have discovered something they have missed? It could turn out they already had seen what you now do and have bid the company up to a price reflecting all of its conceivable pluses. True gem discoveries can occur, but are rare, since many excellent brains are searching the same territory.
2.  You make a good, but late, choice and jump in during market enthusiasm. For example, you buy as part of a crowd right after a positive story in *Barron's* or a clever ad campaign during the World Series, allowing you no particular room for gain.

3. You fall in love with the company or concept. By doing this, you allow yourself to overpay even for its strong growth. You are buying from earlier entrants who now see this stock as fully priced.
4. While earnings have been rising and are expected to be up in the next quarter, you buy in while totally unaware of the huge EPS rise being counted on by institutional momentum players in the upcoming report. The company indeed has a good quarter but one that misses the hallowed "analysts' consensus" by a few pennies and you find yourself with a quick 30 percent paper loss.
5. The company and its story itself are unblemished, but some widely played momentum stock in this or a closely related field issues a subpar sales or earnings report, pulling down the entire group and moving hot money away from your stock's industry to others.
6. You may have taken so long to learn of, and believe in, and become comfortable paying a high price-earnings ratio for this company's earnings that you finally buy just as Wall Street momentum players, for no special reason, are about to shift their hot money into another industry group or concept. You have bought a good company high, just before it loses sponsorship and price altitude, which will be difficult to restore without better fundamentals than have already been paid for once.
7. Impressed with the company's fundamental merit, you overlook the crucial price importance of institutional investors' already-large positions. You believe so much in the story that you overlook the fact that when 80 percent to 85 percent of a stock is held in big blocks, there are no new big sponsors to be found. The stock is already fully priced.
8. As amazing bad luck would have it, you buy at the top of a major bull swing. Your company's fundamentals remain wonderful, but its stock cannot withstand a bear market that now begins and runs for a year.

## The Good News

You might feel discouraged after reading about the many ways you can lose money by buying stock in a good company.

---

**FIGURE 13.1**    Where Selling Agility Is Most Critical

>      High Technology
> +    High Growth Rate
> +    High Expectations
> +    High Price-Earnings Ratio
> +    High Institutional Ownership
> =    High Risk Exposure!

---

Instead, just be appropriately notified that Wall Street does not go up forever. The rise of about 900 percent by the Dow Jones Industrial Average (from 780 in August 1982 to over 7,800 in July 1997) seems to have dulled memories and clearly has spawned a generation of new investors enthralled with what appears to be an alchemist money machine: Buy stocks and aggressive equity mutual funds and enjoy getting rich quick, they expect.

It is hardly that easy, but long history (recall the rates of return discussed in Strategy 3) does show that stocks outperform bonds, which in turn outperform T-bills or CDs, which barely outrun inflation.

## You Must Be Nimble in the Stock Market

In investing, nothing is forever except lost money or lost time. Companies, industries, and entire nations gain or lose prominence. Investing in individual stocks can provide extremely high rewards if you do it well, but it cannot be approached on a buy-forever basis. In early 1996, computer maker Digital Equipment Corp. ran TV ads about its ability to serve needs in a fast-changing environment. The voice intoned, "There are many visions of the future; unfortunately most of them will turn out to have been wrong." I find profound investment wisdom in remembering that unhappy truth. The world is neither simple nor stationary. Blindly intending to hold a stock for the indeterminate long term back-

---

**FIGURE 13.2**   Market-Leading Concepts of Yesteryear

---

Vending Machines
Discount Retailing
Conglomerates (2 + 2 > 4)
The Pill
Airlines
Mobile Homes
Labor Force Participation
     Restaurants
     Convenience Stores, etc.
Computers
Gaming
Biotechnology Start-ups
Rust Belt Survivors
Exporters
Gold, Resources
Oil
Cable TV
Software

## And of 1997...

Internet
Bank Mergers
Outsourcing Beneficiaries

---

handedly assumes there will be no change from the past into the future. Common sense for those who have witnessed the final quarter of the 20th century says that will not be a good bet! Technology sectors' product cycles are extremely short, but this is only one example of a reason why you must be very nimble. Several factors besides technology make the equation shown in Figure 13.1 inescapable.

Short-term agility is important, but a perspective on long-term trends is also necessary. As major shifts occur slowly, we sometimes fail to notice and therefore can fall behind the curve. Figure 13.2 shows a list of market-leading concepts and groups of the period 1957 through 1997. Going back deeper into history, leading industries in the U.S. economy were steel, cement, electric light trusts, railroads, and canal companies.

Because the world is moving rather than standing still, it's important that your portfolio of common stocks not become a collection of formerly hot ideas. We tend to become comfortable with our longer-term winners, willing to forgive problems. The key issue is whether a company's downturn is cyclical or fundamental. Nostalgia will not revive a company fading into financial has-been status. Accept the fact that you will have some losers, not all winners. In just the final third of the 20th century, fully half the 30 stocks in the revered Dow Jones Industrial Average were replaced, a few due to mergers but mainly due to obsolescence or pending failure. Of the 11 original stocks used by Charles Dow in the 1880s, all were railroads!

One of the most important decisions you will make in equities investing is whether you truly are prepared to sell as readily as you buy. If this proves impossible for you, owning individual stocks will be financially unrewarding; you then should definitely cede this management responsibility to mutual fund professionals. To illustrate the way markets change, typical growth funds average 50 percent or slightly higher turnover ratios, meaning their average holding period is barely two years for all stocks—some longer and many shorter.

## You Must Learn to Sell!

Much is made of the virtues of long-term buy-and-hold investing. Unfortunately, with individual stocks it works a lot better in 20/20 hindsight than in the real world, where companies' fortunes constantly undergo major changes. The "nifty 50" darlings of the 1960s included Control Data and Polaroid; can you be sure which of today's favorites will not become once-greats? Already Wal-Mart, a favorite of the 1980s, is being questioned as to its long-term growth potential. Companies that U.S.-centered investors consider to be leaders may not be such at all. In many industries, the largest companies are based in other nations; two-thirds of stock market valuation is listed overseas.

You will find selling very difficult. Brokerage firms offer virtually no help, since they have loyalties to companies for which they act as investment bankers (to raise more capital). Brokerage firms have a "buy" bias, always a rosy outlook on the future until a company's prospects are clearly in deep trouble. Numerous stocks are rated "buy" until immediately after announcing disasters from accounting frauds to product-line write-offs to serious growth slowdowns. Investors using discount brokers must of course make selling versus holding an entirely do-it-yourself question; that uncomfortable, forced discipline may be a blessing in disguise.

Selling is also difficult because it requires you to internalize a 180-degree reversal from your prior thinking, in which you've invested lots of money and months or years of emotional energy. To sell, you must conclude that a company that was good and reasonably priced yesterday is sick or overpriced or both, today. Buying opens a new chapter, is done in optimism and hope of great potential, and so represents open-endedness. Selling represents finality, a willingness to accept the current score as final. Selling requires willingly coming to closure. Again, the difficulty people have with this necessary part of investing is a major reason mutual funds have become so popular: one can pay a professional manager to agonize over the facts and the decision.

## Things That Do Work in Stocks

Some types of investing have been demonstrated over many decades and by numerous academic studies and documented investment records to work better than others. Foreign stock markets have higher growth rates than that of the U.S., experience in 1995–1996 notwithstanding. Those economies are growing faster than our mature one. Smaller-capitalization stocks, which involve greater risk of major failures, on average provide higher returns over long periods than do big-capitalization stocks. The latter represent more mature companies and also can be overvalued by institutional investors enamored of past glories. For example, IBM stock was no higher in mid-1994 than it had been in 1984, and dividends had been cut. Stocks that pay dividends, on average, perform better over the long term than do nonpayers. It is easy to lose sight of that historical fact during a frothy speculative phase when companies' shares are bid higher on their rapid sales momentum alone. Companies trading at below-average ratios of price to earnings, price to cash flow, or price to sales consistently provide better returns over long periods (and full market up and down cycles) than do their highly valued counterparts. Companies that add value are better investments than those in basic extractive or commodity roles. Raw materials become mature industries and suffer from price competition, cutting profit margins.

## Six Ways to Improve Your Results with Stocks

**Don't confuse the company and the stock.**   Many investors have difficulty making the subtle distinction between a stock and the company it represents. It is important that you be able to do so. Unless you are a trader using only technical analysis, you probably buy a stock because you believe in its product or service and expect ongoing and growing revenue and profits because of how well the company does what it does. Except in technologically driven industries, the inherent strength of a company is unlikely to change very much from year to year. But its stock price fluctuates sharply much of the time. Sometimes a stock is undervalued and at other times it can be overpriced.

The inherent "goodness" or solid nature of the company very often blinds investors to the current stock price's inappropriate level. This most likely occurs when the stock has risen. If a critic were to propose that the stock seems too high, an owner would predictably respond with a quality judgment, "But it's truly a great company." That may well be true, but for a smart investor the key question is whether the company is worth the present market price. The issue is valuation, not quality alone. Otherwise, logically, there would be no ridiculously high price at which a "good company" should be sold. We readily make value judgments about quality consumer products, but strangely have trouble transferring this skill into the investing arena.

You must separate the inherent virtue of the company from the stock. The stock of a single great company will at different times be underpriced, properly priced, or riding too high. We invoke a sense of value when buying stocks: "This is a terrific bargain," we say when a good company's stock is drubbed in a general market panic. Yet we have great difficulty, because of the known strengths of the company, in ever saying "This is now no bargain at all." A very good test to use in deciding whether to hold or sell is to ask whether you find the stock enough of a bargain to buy at its current price. If not, you should not hold it! (Holding, you see, is buying for another day without paying a commission.)

Excluding stocks under $5 and excluding closed-end funds (which are priced on assets rather than earnings), stocks on the NYSE enjoyed an average earnings gain of about 12 percent in 1996. But on average their stock prices had ranges of about 60 percent from high to low. Thus, much of the time each stock was either undervalued or overpriced. When a stock has made a short-term price move whose percentage clearly exceeds its company's underlying annual growth rate, it is overheated and should be sold or avoided until it cools down. Even though a stock represents a fine company, that does not automatically mean the company is worth today's trading price.

**Exercise discipline in your buying behavior.** A stock's price, from moment to moment, is not a value gauge but rather a barometer measuring the hopes, fears, and other emotions people have about that stock and about the company it represents. As discussed in Strategy 9, disciplined investors learn not to follow and participate in mass hysteria. This means not buying on the announcement of good or exciting news. Good earnings, a new product or contract, and especially a purchase recommendation by a major brokerage house's analyst will drive quick price increases on heavy trading volume.

When the impact of such drivers is dissipated (usually in a week or less), the stock falls back for lack of buying support. At that point, if the news really did make the company more valuable than earlier thought, you can buy smarter and lower! The price graph of Onyx Pharmaceuticals shown in Figure 13.3 shows the temporary effect of favorable publicity. At the point where the rapid rise to about $17 occurred, the company was being featured on a major financial TV show for having a potentially very promising approach to curing cancer. What could be more exciting? Once that stimulus was removed, the stock's price retreated. Buying into such run-ups is a sure formula for disaster, except for very short-term traders who intend to sell in a couple of days.

**FIGURE 13.3**   Onyx Pharmaceuticals

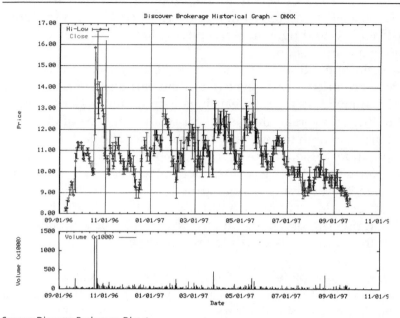

Source: Discover Brokerage Direct

Chasing the strong price momentum of a stock (or a whole industry group, at times) is the longer-term equivalent of buying on good news. Here, however, the stimulus is not fundamentals but rather the allure of the rising stock price itself. Institutions pursuing this approach (and many mutual funds were doing it in 1996–1997!) are in effect saying, "Something good must be happening here (or the stock would not be acting so well), so I need to be on board for the ride." Unsophisticated individual investors make that mistake early in their careers and end up paying for it. Extremely few are the companies that are so fundamentally important (Microsoft and perhaps Intel are examples) that it's truly possible their stocks may never come back to early, low prices.

**Be very sensitive to stocks where institutions hold huge positions and trade actively.**   In gentler eras, a high percentage of institutional ownership was a good indicator for a stock.

"The big boys are smart, and they like it," was the theory. Today, institutional investors have so much money they need to own lots of many stocks just to avoid having idle cash. Ownership of stocks with high levels of institutional ownership, momentum chasing, and a dangerously short-term measurement mentality are a deadly combination for individual stock investors. When mutual fund portfolio managers are measured quarterly for bonus purposes, they become a destabilizing market force by chasing momentum (so as not to underperform) and by dumping ruthlessly at the least sign of temporary disappointment.

We individual investors must know the institutional ownership level of our stocks, so we can guard against downside risk by placing tight trailing stop orders—or by avoiding holding the institutional darling stocks at all! Many readily available sources disclose institutional ownership. The *Standard & Poor's Monthly Stock Guide* lists institutionally held and total outstanding shares (you will need to divide to get a percent figure). The S&P's individual stock reports (the so-called "tear sheets") list the percentage, as do pages in *Value Line*. Several on-line and diskette-based stock databases carry reasonably updated figures on such ownership. And in general you can assume that the biggest-name companies are highly held by institutions.

Institutional herd-mentality selling has become highly visible in the past few years. We see it every week as some company fails by one or two cents per share to meet the consensus of analysts' quarterly earnings expectations. Or when the estimated Producer Price Index rate of inflation is a mere tenth of a percent above the prior guesstimate of so-called experts. The tendency of big holders to sell at the slightest negative provocation is self-reinforcing: Each manager tries to avoid being outperformed, and so must sell when others do in order to not hold a stock that is falling.

Even when no bad news is reported, stocks with high levels of institutional ownership can fall victim to being trampled by the herd. When the market has recently made a strong rally, the stocks that enjoyed the biggest gains become early targets for nailing down profits once the momentum stalls, no matter what the reason. For example, a bad sales or earnings report by a major computer or software technology company can trigger selling in that group, putting the breaks on a general market rally. If major health care stocks had been leaders in that rally, they will be sold down sharply as traders take profits and step aside so as not to underperform. All of this has little to do with fundamental long-term value or true investing. It is short-term speculating in which every player tries to outguess and outmaneuver all the others. Does this help to explain why about 70 percent of mutual funds fail to match their market indices in most years?

Buying by huge players is also a destabilizing factor, and represents a source of short-term price strength you as an individual must be aware of. You can at least be careful not to join the temporary crowd mania, or you can actually also use the strength to be a smart seller. Toro, the company that supplies garden and snow-removal equipment, provides a clear example. The pattern shown in Figure 13.4, called to my atten-

**FIGURE 13.4**   Toro: Winter Wonderland

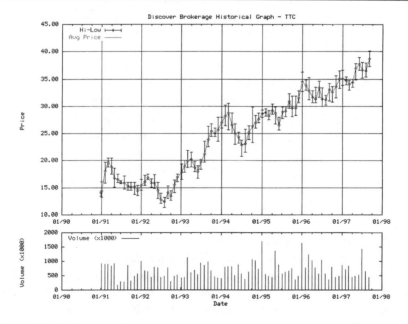

Source: Discover Brokerage Direct

tion originally in a *Wall Street Journal* article, shows the strong influence of news-driven buying. Three temporary price advances well above trend occurred at exactly the times in three out of four recent winters when huge snowstorms hit the New York area. Like commodity traders reacting to a rain storm, institutions rushed to buy Toro's shares even though the vast majority of its business is in lawn gear. Blizzards are more dramatic than watching grass grow!

**Understand charts and technical analysis.** You may not be a technician by intellectual orientation or in practice; however, many market players are watching the charts. The more who do so, the greater the impact that technical analysis has! So you cannot afford to be ignorant of what others know. The sharp interim price gyrations driven by institutional holders, as described earlier, can be seen on a price chart. Often they become parts of formations such as channels and resistance or support levels. You should be aware of those price patterns so your logically reasoned buy and sell decisions can be executed at more advantageous prices than would be the case if you were acting in the dark. Some useful resources in this area are featured in Strategy 30.

**Watch out for the trap of a comfort zone!** In addition to all the economic, business, competitive, company-specific, legal, regulatory, and stock-price risks involved in buying and selling individual stocks, every investor faces another, usually forgotten enemy. That enemy, that bearer of added risk, is inside our own heads. One of the ways our emotions cause us to lose money in investing is by inhibiting our actions until we are comfortable. Whether it is the overall market or a single stock, we seldom can summon the courage to buy quality near the bottom, when all around us are panicking. But months and perhaps 25 percent higher in price later, finally we have developed enough courage to buy—all too often so late in the move we are set up for a loss. Equity mutual funds investors clearly illustrate this tendency, selling or postponing their buying when the market falls and then resuming their heaviest net purchase a couple of months later at higher prices.

Another comfort-zone trap occurs long after a stock has been bought. It occurs in part *because* the stock has been held for an extended period. The company (and therefore its stock price) has treated you well. Your ego has been stroked. Rising stock price measures not only your greater wealth but also your brilliance in choosing this wonderful stock and your courage to stick with it during that brief market downturn a couple of years back (or maybe two or three such phases!). This stock has subtly become a member of the family, a beloved pet, a beautiful piece of art to be admired. When a stock attains such stature, it virtually cannot be sold. The tax liability built up from a long price run adds to the difficulty in parting company. And yet, the world is moving faster and that requires you to be nimble. It is very difficult to part with big winners. And yet many once-great companies (and industries) are past their primes and no longer merit your loyalty, a loyalty that grew in a comfort zone. Be very careful, again, by separating the stock from its company in your mind, to be aware when a comfort zone is forming, and allow yourself to break out when either the market is high or the company itself starts to show signs of losing its former luster.

**Expect bear markets.**    Heresy, you say? The long upward trend in prices from 1982 to late 1997, with only two very short interruptions, is an historical aberration. Do not expect stocks to rise forever, or without significant corrections, or to historically high-risk multiples of earnings. The great bull market that began in 1982 was driven by a massive shift in the political landscape (toward greater freedom and lower taxes, both in the U.S. and around the globe); by a century-rare unwinding of inflation and accompanying drop of 70 percent in interest rates; and by the demographics of an aging baby-boom generation reaching its high-savings years and fearing that Social Security will fail. Can such forces be duplicated again soon, to drive another 15 years of uninterrupted market celebration? Odds would seem to favor less ebullient conditions, and perhaps a return to somewhat less infrequent recessions. The political landscape could reverse; certainly long-term interest rates cannot decline by another ten percentage points again, starting now from under 7 percent. Historically, bear markets average about five years apart and involve drops of at least 15 percent. Do not blind yourself to such possibilities, especially when investing has become fun for an extended period.

# Understand Bonds

**R**ightly or wrongly, many people concentrate their retirement holdings in bonds, either directly or through bond mutual funds. Being familiar with bank certificates of deposit (CDs) and U.S. Savings Bonds, too many investors lazily assume bonds are basically the same as these simple assets. That is a dangerous misconception. Government, municipal, and corporate bonds carry opportunities and risks you must understand well in order to succeed with them. Such awareness is crucial, since many people tilt their portfolios increasingly toward bond holdings later in life.

Bonds involve both good and bad elements. On the plus side, they provide a reasonably dependable stream of known income, important to retired investors. And their likelihood of paying off principal is high, so owning bonds lends a degree of stability to overall portfolio value when stocks gyrate. Bonds' negatives include low (or even negative!) after-tax, after-inflation returns and investors' tendency to view bond positions passively. Also, unless held in tax-deferred vehicles such as an IRA or 401(k), nonmunicipal bonds require current payment of taxes on their interest. Key differences among bonds and other familiar income-oriented instruments are summarized in Figure 14.1.

---

**FIGURE 14.1**    Differences among Selected Income-Oriented Instruments

|  | Bonds | U.S. Savings Bonds | CDs | Bank Accounts |
|---|---|---|---|---|
| Promise to Pay Back | Yes | Yes | Yes | Yes |
| Promise Guaranteed or Insured | Yes if government | Yes | Yes if FDIC* | Yes if FDIC* |
| Periodic Cash Interest | Yes | No | Yes | Yes |
| Fixed Maturity | Yes | Yes | Yes | No |
| Date | Yes | Penalty | Penalty | Yes |
| Liquid before Maturity | Yes | No | No | No |
| Market Traded | Yes | No | No | No |
| Value Will Fluctuate | Not if municipal bonds | Not by some states | Yes | Yes |
| Interest Taxable |  |  |  |  |

\* Up to legally set dollar limit per holder.

---

## Overview of Bonds

The next several pages will explain key concepts so you can understand how the bond market works and therefore how and when to use, or avoid, bond holdings both across a business cycle and throughout your lifetime.

### Nature

A bond is evidence of a borrower's promise to pay the lender. Except with U.S. Savings Bonds, bonds are transferable from one owner to another during the course of their existence. Bonds typically pay interest every six months. Trading markets for bonds are most active where the borrower is prominent and where the size of the particular issue of bonds is large; U.S. government bonds are extremely liquid.

### Issuers

Bonds are issued by domestic and foreign corporations, by foreign governments, by the U.S. government and its agencies, and by municipal authorities (states, counties, localities, and special authorities such as toll road, airport, or utility commissions).

### Taxation

Interest earned on all except municipal bonds is taxable at the federal level (and some municipal debts, referred to as private activity bonds, pay taxable interest). States and localities cannot tax the interest earned on federal bonds. Local and federal taxes apply to interest on corporate and foreign bonds. A realized capital gain or loss on any type of bond (including municipals!) is a taxable event for both state and federal income-tax purposes.

### Guarantees

A promise is only as good as the entity making it. U.S. Treasury securities are considered to be of ultimate quality (in any circumstances short of revolution), since Washington readily prints currency and checks that would always make "good" its promises. Federal agency bonds (Farm Credit Administration, Government National Mortgage Association, etc.) do not have the full faith and credit of the U.S. government and therefore usually trade at slightly higher yields than U.S. Treasury securities. It is generally assumed, but not explicitly stated, that Washington would make good such bonds if circumstances demanded. Foreign governments' bonds are as secure as the issuing nations, but unless such bonds are denominated in dollars, U.S. buyers bear the risk of changes in currency values when considering whether their original principal will be 100 percent returned.

Municipal bonds backed by the "full faith and credit" (meaning taxing power) of the issuer (called general-obligation bonds or GOs) have more assurance of payment than do special-purpose bonds (e.g., bridge, toll road, or airport revenue obligations) not specifically guaranteed by higher authorities. Sometimes states back localities' bonds, improving security and cutting interest costs. Most municipal bonds are very thinly traded. Therefore, owning municipals through mutual funds rather than directly is a good idea.

Some corporate subsidiary bonds may be guaranteed as to timely payment of principal and interest by a parent company. This offers added but incomplete security, since the parent is not immune to failure.

The greatest problem with bonds is that they pay back nominal dollars equal to the original loan amount; historically a given amount of currency tends to buy less over time, so a bondholder gets back less purchasing power than he or she loaned out. (The U.S. Treasury began issuing small amounts of special inflation-indexed bonds in January 1997, seeking to address this problem.)

### Maturities

The maturity date is the date on which the face amount is promised to be paid back. Some bonds (called bills or notes) have maturities as short as a few weeks or months. Corporate and government bonds are usually issued for between 15 and 30 years; shorter maturities are issued if interest rates are more favorable or if a borrower needs to manage its future schedule of cash needs. Very few bonds have longer maturities. Walt Disney issued 100-year bonds in July 1993; Canadian Pacific has an issue of perpetual 4 percent debentures (never maturing) that trade on the New York Exchange bond list; and the British Government issues some perpetual bonds, called Consuls. The remaining time to a bond's maturity is a major determinant in how widely its market price will fluctuate.

### Coupon or Stated Interest Rate

Part of the debtor's promise is to pay interest at a fixed stated percentage of the face amount of the bond. Virtually all bonds pay their interest in six-month installments. For example, an 8 percent bond would pay $40 each six months (totaling $80 per year) for each $1,000 of face value. The dollar amount of interest due remains fixed no matter what prices a bond trades at between its issue date and its maturity. Three exceptions to the semiannual interest practice are U.S. Treasury bills, state and local tax-anticipation notes, and zero-coupon bonds. These securities pay no cash interest; rather, they are originally sold at a discounted price below face value with the accretion taxed as interest. Zero-coupon bonds, issued by governments or corporations, may be of long maturity; the other two types of no-cash-interest bonds mature in one year or less. (Zero-coupon bonds are structurally similar to U.S. Savings Bonds, except that zeros do not provide for redemption on a stated price scale before maturity.) A bond's coupon rate is another major determinant of potential market price volatility between issuance date and maturity.

### Quality and Ratings

Quality refers to the soundness of the borrower and the terms of a specific bond issue (some bonds are designated as subordinated claims to other bonds of the same borrower; some bonds are backed by specific collateral assets while others are not). Quality is generally expressed in terms of alphabetical "ratings" assigned by widely recognized organizations. The most prominent of these are Standard & Poor's, Moody's, Fitch, and Duff & Phelps. The highest rating is AAA or Aaa. Ratings can and do change, sometimes considerably, but these changes are usually a lagged response to news developments. Quality ratings have a significant effect on bond prices, since many institutional investors may buy or hold instruments only above a specific rating. Higher-quality bonds involve less risk to the lender, so they trade at prices that provide a lower yield than bonds of lower quality but with the same coupon rate and maturity date.

### Sinking Fund Provisions

Most corporate bonds of long maturity require the borrower to retire a certain percentage of the issue annually before final maturity. The borrower can do this by repurchases in the open market or by calling in specific holders' bonds for redemption at a predetermined price (usually a bit above face value). Individual bonds are selected for call by drawing randomly generated numbers.

### General Call Provisions

Some bonds may be redeemed at the borrower's option on or after certain dates prior to scheduled eventual maturity. A bond no longer pays any interest after its sinking-fund or general call or payment date, so holders gain nothing by refusing to deliver their bonds. Calls for redemption may be partial or total. In the former case, specific lots are drawn randomly as described above. Call prices (usually above face value on a scale gradually declining over time) are disclosed on the back side of the actual bond; this information is more conveniently available in major statistical services such as S&P and Moody's bond guides. Issuers call their bonds prior to maturity if interest rates have declined enough to let them refinance at a lower interest cost after considering all legal, printing, and commission costs involved. Occasionally an issuer calls in some or all of its bonds after selling major assets (a subsidiary or division, for example), thus generating excess available cash.

### Holder's Option or "Put" Bonds

These have become available since the late 1980s in response to takeover activity. They allow holders to demand full early repayment in the event of specified corporate events (typically a hostile takeover of control). They are often issued to guard in advance against hostile takeovers, since the would-be acquirer would need enough cash to pay off the bonds, thus raising the total necessary to effect the transaction. A put option protects holders from a possible downgrade in quality, which would occur in the case of a leveraged transaction. This can be an important protection for creditors, who do not, like stockholders, get to vote about the takeover.

## Protection in Bankruptcy

Priorities of corporate bondholders' claims are always below those of tax authorities and wage earners. They usually are below those of trade suppliers. Bond claims come before those of preferred and common stock holders. Depending on the chances for long-term survival and rehabilitation of a distressed company, bondholders may come out whole (with overdue interest paid and principal claims eventually met), or less so. If liquidation of the company's assets is forced, generally bondholders get less than full face value (and shareholders would then get nothing). Often a settlement package is offered in which bondholders are given newly issued common stock in exchange for wiping out some or all of their bonds' face value. Bondholders do have a vote on such bankruptcy settlement proposals, but these votes are often dominated by large institutional holders, so individuals have no effective voice. As stated earlier, the bondholder's guarantee is only as strong as the issuer itself.

## Convertibility

Some issues of corporate bonds may be converted or exchanged at the option of the holder into a number of shares of common stock in the issuing company. This is done by turning the bonds in to the issuer (thus ending the stream of semiannual interest payments). If the issuing company's stock price rises significantly, the conversion feature will force the bonds to trade at a premium price over face value because they can be readily converted at any time and the newly received stock sold at market price. Convertible bonds usually pay a lower interest rate because they contain this possibly valuable "kicker" feature. Convertibles are also usually subordinated to other debt and therefore do not have very high quality ratings. An issuing company can effectively "force" holders to convert if its common stock has risen substantially. By calling its bonds for cash repayment in 30 or 60 days, the company effectively forces holders to accept stock (worth more) rather than cash. Many companies in growing industries use convertibles in this way repeatedly.

## Accrued Interest

Stock prices trade "ex-dividend" by roughly the amount of the upcoming payment on a trading day two days before the record date; in these cases, one party gets all of each dividend payment. Bond prices are handled differently. In between semiannual interest payment dates, bonds trade at prices quoted excluding interest; each trading day, more interest is added on top of the quoted price, and the buyer pays the seller the accumulated amount on top of the trade price. For example, a 9 percent bond of $1,000 in face value pays $45 interest each six months. If that bond is sold midway between the interest record dates, the buyer would pay the seller the agreed trading price plus $22.50 of accrued interest. The buyer would later collect the full $45 coupon when it is due. Each holder pays taxes only on the net interest received. If a 9 percent bond is traded one day before its semiannual interest-record date, the buyer will pay the seller $44.75 on top of the agreed trade price. That is the accrued interest to date. The buyer will be entitled to the whole $45 semiannual coupon payment a day later, and so will have earned $0.25 net for one day.

## Bond Prices

Bond prices fluctuate every day. Price changes are driven by the combination of quality, coupon rate, time remaining to maturity, and the prevailing level of interest rates. Except when a sudden, dramatic corporate event occurs, interest rates are the dominant factor affecting bond prices. Otherwise, perceived quality changes only slowly over time; time to maturity shortens minutely each day; coupon rate is fixed. Bond prices are figured from what traders call a "basis book" of numerical tables indicating price levels that generate effective overall yields to maturity (popular "financial calculators" are preprogrammed to provide the same answers quickly).

## Price Quotations

Bond prices are quoted in percentages of their face value. Thus, a $1,000 bond quoted at "97" would be traded at $970, or 97 percent of face.

### Yields

Bonds trade not based on cash yield alone, but instead as a function of the yield to maturity that investors require at any given time based on the four factors listed earlier. Yield to maturity is a moderately complex mathematical formula taking into account the cash interest return (annual coupon divided by current price) and the implied return created by the difference between current price and face value or first call price.

Bond prices move in the opposite direction of interest rates. Any given bond promises to pay a fixed number of dollars in interest each year. Since that interest stream is fixed for the bond's life, market price (the only thing that can change!) must move up or down in order to make the bond provide a currently appropriate net rate of return.

If a bank offered 1 percent per year, or a mere $10 interest, on a $1,000 one-year CD, you would not buy such a deal, since it would not be worth a full $1,000 to you. You would be willing to pay only some amount less than $1,000 that would net you today's "going" one-year rate, such as perhaps 5 percent. If a bank today offered to pay 15 percent interest on 5-year CDs (as many did in 1980 when rates were sky-high), you'd jump at the chance. You'd actually be willing to pay more than face value for such a deal, because you are willing to earn a net rate somewhat lower than 15 percent. But conventional CDs are not negotiable, so you could not actually make such a deal to buy above face value. You can sell bonds to any willing third-party buyer, at any price mutually agreed!

Here are a few quick examples of how the aftermarket sets trading prices for existing bonds: If XYZ Corp.'s 8 percent coupon bonds have one year until maturity and if today's going rate of interest for bonds of their quality is 8 percent, the bonds will trade at face value for a net yield of 8 percent to maturity ($80 divided by $1,000 market price). But suppose prevailing rates for one-year bonds of such quality were just 7 percent, as in a lower-inflation or slack economy. Investors would willingly pay more than face value to get $80 of interest. They'd pay almost 101 percent of face value, because they would be compensated for that extra $10 or 1 percent in price paid above the $1,000 redemption value by getting an "above-market" income

**FIGURE 14.2**    Price of 8% Bonds at Various Yields to Maturity Over Time

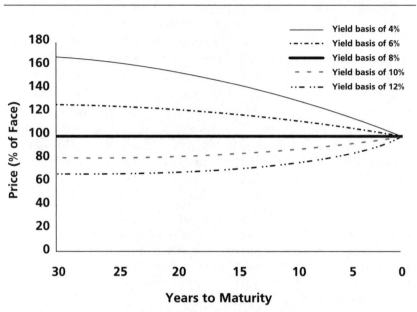

stream of $80, instead of 7 percent, or $70, during the bond's remaining term. In effect, these investors would be getting some extra income by paying some extra price to even it out. If prevailing one-year rates were at 9 percent, this 8 percent bond would trade below par, or at around 99 percent of its face value rather than 101 percent, of course! The prices of 8 percent bonds under various prevailing interest rate conditions and remaining to maturity are illustrated in Figure 14.2.

Now suppose that prevailing rates (9 percent) are above the coupon rate (8 percent) and the bond still has many years remaining until maturity. Investors would discount the price of the bond considerably more than 1 percent. Why? Because they will insist that the discount in price makes up the 1 percent yield shortage (8 percent coupon versus 9 percent rate demanded) for each remaining year until maturity. A two-year 8 percent-coupon bond would trade a bit above 98 percent, or $980, on $1,000 face value) to provide a 9 percent yield to maturity. In a 9 percent yield environment, a 25-year-remaining 8 percent bond would

---

**FIGURE 14.3**   Leveraged Effect of Interest Rates on Bond Prices

---

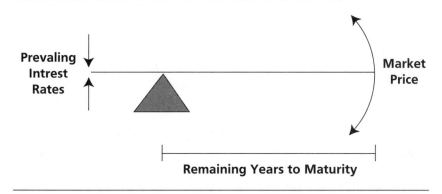

trade much deeper below par, to make up 25 years of differences. Its price would be approximately $900. The mathematics work such that the longer the time remaining to maturity, the wider the bond's price change. Also, the lower the coupon, the greater the discount if interest rates rise. Zero-coupon bonds therefore involve the greatest potential for price fluctuation. When interest rates fall considerably, prices of callable, high-coupon bonds will not rise as far as the basis-book formula would predict. This is because buyers will not risk paying a high price based on an expected full life to maturity, only to then suddenly see their bonds called away at a lower price. When rates are down, bonds trade on a basis referred to as "priced to call (date and price)," which assumes the earliest possible call will occur.

The easiest way to remember what happens to bond prices is shown in Figure 14.3's picture of a lever and fulcrum. For any given amount of up-down change in interest rates (at left) the bond's price (at right) will move in the opposite direction by more or less depending on the length of time (horizontal) remaining to its maturity.

## Bonds Are Not One-Decision Investments!

As indicated in Strategies 7 and 8, you should not consider any individual investment, once bought, as intended to be held forever. This is every bit as true with bonds as with stocks!

People are inclined to view bonds as single-decision instruments, probably because each bond's very name includes a maturity date (e.g., XYZ Widgetcorp Senior 8 percent Debentures, due July 1, 2019). Likewise, one is accustomed to holding CDs to maturity—a product of inertia and, not incidentally, that "substantial penalty for early withdrawal." And holding U.S. Savings Bonds to maturity was also a childhood habit.

Bonds are traded every day, just as stocks are. Prices are determined by supply and demand in the short run, implying that price-limited orders should be used when buying and selling. The appropriate price level for each bond is set by its coupon rate, quality, time remaining to maturity date, call provisions if a factor under prevailing interest rates, and the present and expected level of interest rates. Bonds of two corporations with all such factors in common will be substantially similar in price because sophisticated holders consider such instruments to be essentially interchangeable. Dow Chemical is "the same thing as" BankAmerica Corp. if both are single-A rated. The larger the lot involved, the more liquid the market, because institutions are the major aftermarket traders. It is difficult to find a willing buyer for an odd lot such as $7,000 face value without making a price concession. Usually 25 bonds or more ($25,000 face value) represents a round lot to bond traders; $100,000 lots are even easier to trade.

It is inconceivable that prevailing interest rates will remain unchanged during the 25- or 30-year life of a typical corporate or government bond. With the world economy and individual companies changing so rapidly, it is now a reasonable bet that the quality rating of any given corporate bond may change, for better or worse, at least once during its life. Chrysler Corporation paper moved from investment quality to junk and back again in the period from 1970 to 1990. Exxon remains triple-A rated, but IBM has been stripped of that honor. Municipal bond ratings must not be assumed to be carved in stone. New York City bonds have been upgraded partially since its budget crisis of 1975. Orange County, California, bonds were called investment grade until its 1994 pension-fund derivatives fiasco led to bankruptcy. In a fast-changing health care environment, a county hospital could be shuttered and its bonds could fall dramatically. Bond prices tend to fluctuate less wildly than do stock prices, because stocks are more influenced by emotions; stockholders get what is left after bondholders get their promised interest and principal back. But bond prices definitely do fluctuate!

During your remaining investing lifetime, interest rates will not be stable. They will be influenced by election results, cyclical economic expansions and contractions, the dollar's value against other major currencies, and commodity inflation rates. When you perceive significant shifts coming in the economy, you can and should adjust your bond holdings accordingly. This does not mean you need to miraculously be able to divine exact tops or bottoms in interest rate cycles. By catching the major parts of secular or even just cyclical swings in interest rates, you will be able to capture total returns well in excess of coupon rates during bond bull markets, and will be able to avoid earning lower (or even negative!) returns during bond bear-market phases. If you limit your bond holdings to high-quality issues only, it can be fairly stated that avoiding losses is easier in bonds than in stocks. This is because "all" long-term bonds move together while many individual stocks can lag for corporate news reasons during a bull market in stocks. Buying and holding bonds passively until they mature is the strategy of a helpless victim, a person content to take whatever life dishes out on average. You can and should do better than that! Economic conditions and the direction of Federal Reserve policy are not guarded secrets; use the information you see and feel to your investment advantage.

Before 1965, bond and stock markets usually moved in opposite directions. Recession meant falling stocks and rising bonds as interest rates would drop. Expansion meant higher profits and higher interest rates, so stocks would rise and bonds would decline. Since the Vietnam War era, markets have become highly inflation conscious, so bonds and stocks have often moved up or down together. High inflation means high interest rates, implying lower price-earnings ratios, since stocks compete with bonds on a total-return basis. Low inflation or disinflation has come to be good for both stocks and bonds simultaneously unless caused by a deep recession. In 1995, Congress laid out a plan to balance the federal budget by the year 2002. If that discipline is indeed followed and thereafter maintained, it may be that bond and stock prices will again decouple as in the pre-1965 model.

Whatever the actual details may be, a no-change scenario in major economic variables is the least likely outcome for the balance of your lifetime. Therefore a buy-and-just-hold-for-maturity stance on bonds is not justified. Typically, you'll lean toward a gradually increasing proportion of fixed-income holdings in your asset mix as you age. This fact alone makes it increasingly important that you pay active attention to bonds over time. When the outlook for inflation and interest rates is highly uncertain, you should shift your mix from long-term to short-term bonds, or gravitate to medium-term maturities as a half-way solution. You may do well to "ladder" your maturities, keeping some assets deployed in bonds of several different maturities at all times so you can never be completely wrong no matter what interest rates do. As each holding matures, you use its proceeds to buy other bonds whose terms and returns then appear most attractive.

## Bond Pitfalls and Opportunities

As discussed earlier, buying and holding bonds to maturity can result in far from optimal results as you passively ride out major shifts in rates and prices. Following are factors that have major influences on interest rates, which of course translate into the opposite direction of bond prices:

- *Inflation*—Rising inflation means falling bond prices. Falling inflation means rising bond prices. Lenders do not loan money at rates they fear will not compensate them for loss of purchasing power. Interest rates are always set above expected inflation rates (although in hindsight such expectations may prove right or wrong).
- *Business cycle*—Expansion ups demand for credit, raising rates and dropping bond prices; recession cuts credit demand, dropping rates and so rallying bond prices.
- *Depression*—The recessionary effect noted earlier works only for highest-quality issuers; risk of default depresses lower-quality bonds' prices until the depression, or expectation of one, passes.

- *FRB policy*—The Fed eventually gets what it wants, because it has the power to change rates in various ways. It usually works on short-term rates, where its power is most direct. The effect on long-bond rates is often the opposite after a short time. If the Fed raises short rates it slows expansion, eventually lowering long-bond rates. This was seen in 1994 and into 1995.

## The Importance of Quality

Chasing high yield by buying "junk bonds" can be a mistake, especially if they are bought or held beyond the strongest part of an economic cycle. Defaults greatly increase during recessions. As discussed much more fully in Strategy 16, high yield comes with high risk attached. High yield is very tempting because it appears to provide a guarantee of an attractive return. That promise is sometimes a mirage, however, because cash return is not always total return. In the final analysis, only total return (cash yield plus or minus price change) is what matters. You need to consider carefully whether an extra 2 percent of current yield is worth buying at the risk of possibly losing 50 percent of capital if a default occurs.

The higher the quality of bonds you own, the more easily you can play the part of the contrarian investor with assurance. For example, if you own U.S. government bonds only, you can effectively ignore possible default. Then, when prices are down you do not worry whether they're down because of possible failure. Your attention is entirely focused on when inflation abatement or Federal Reserve Board policy will point to a drop in rates. Then, fully knowing you will not catch the exact bottom, you can confidently "buy low" and enjoy superior returns with low risk.

Some people are highly attuned to legal tax avoidance. They prefer to own municipal bonds rather than taxable bonds. Sometimes they make that choice regardless of the objective facts (the relative yields after taxes), and such a blind preference can be a financial mistake. Which type of bonds make a better choice depends on the relative creditworthiness of local versus federal versus corporate bonds, which varies over time. The higher your marginal tax bracket, the more sense high-quality municipals make. In certain circumstances, such as those involving taxation of Social Security benefits, municipals can make more sense no matter what your bracket. These aspects are covered in more detail in Strategy 26.

## The Bond Fund Alternative

Many investors choose to invest in bonds indirectly, via bond mutual funds. If you opt for bond funds over individual bonds, you still must understand the fundamentals covered in prior pages so you can make intelligent choices about which funds to own and when to switch or to sell them out entirely. Buying and holding bond funds forever makes no more sense than doing the same with individual bonds. The next several pages cover the not-trivial differences between bonds themselves and the funds that own them.

# Understand Differences of Bond Funds

**O**ver time, income-oriented investments will become a bigger part of your overall asset mix—if indeed they are not so already. When well used, bond funds can be very useful devices for building your retirement assets and for providing some balance against sharp fluctuations in equities. You can arrange things so that your bond funds' current income avoids current taxes because it is received in your 401(k) plan or IRA or Keogh accounts. Classically cited advantages of funds are diversification, professional management, immediate liquidity at a fair price, divisibility of investment into exact owner-preferred amounts, power to buy or cash out specific dollar amounts when desired, and ability to reinvest earnings immediately and automatically without commission costs. For many investors, that is a powerful package, especially while their overall bond holdings are modest in value.

Notwithstanding their attractions, bond funds can be misunderstood and misused, possibly causing damage to your wealth—exactly where you thought you were playing it safe, as millions of investors sadly discovered in the bond bear market of 1994. This strategy discusses those troublesome areas and offers guidance on the profitable ways to use bond funds. One huge difference is that a long-term bond fund will not act the same as a long-term bond does. Why? The fund never "reaches maturity" unless it is a term trust. And of course another big problem is that a fund may not invest in exactly the same way as you wish it would. By selecting carefully, you can control that one.

## Major Misconceptions

### Constant Value

All too many bond-fund investors, particularly those who are recent bank-CD refugees, incorrectly believe it's impossible to lose money in a bond fund. By its nature, a mutual fund is a managed collection of underlying individual securities. So, since bond prices fluctuate, the net asset value (NAV) of a mutual fund holding bonds will likewise rise and fall.

The upside of that news is that you can enjoy capital appreciation from bond funds, since they can rise in value. This is useful only for nonpassive investors—people willing to shift their holdings around occasionally rather than hold them for life. Economic contractions usually bring about declines in interest rates. When interest rates fall, bond prices rise. A single bond might not do well in a recession, but a portfolio should advance on average—a key benefit of a bond fund.

One of the subtle misperceptions about bonds (and therefore bond funds) is that your interest stream is your actual return, or somehow your minimum reward. To the contrary: From year to year, the price-fluctuation component of your fund's total return often will be larger than the cash-income component.

Since a long-term bond's price fluctuates in the opposite direction of interest rates, the per-share value of a fund containing such bonds changes considerably. If prevailing rates moved by 1 percent from 8 percent up to 9 percent in a 12-month period, your total return on a bond fund full of long-term bonds would be slightly negative for that period. You'd get your 8 percent cash return but would suffer a paper loss of about 10 percent in market value of your shares. Of course, the good news for the active investor is that when rates fall, your total return will be considerably greater than the coupon rate. When rates fall back from 9 percent to 8 percent, a fund full of 8 percent bonds would rise in NAV by about 11 percent, on top of the interest currently paid out. Figure 15.1 shows the price fluctuations of one of the longer-existing bond funds. In many years they exceeded the fund's income distributions.

Such moves are not hardly rare. Just recently, the 30-year U.S. Treasury benchmark "long bond" moved from a 5.75 percent yield basis in late 1993 to a surprisingly high 8.25 percent just 13 months later, only to reverse to as low as 6.50 percent again by mid-1996. Bond fund investors who correctly foresaw most of those swings were handsomely rewarded. Those who sat passively with their bond fund holdings all through that period suffered a modest net capital reduction and the queasy sensations of a roller-coaster passenger.

In short, bond fund prices move! Perhaps investors' 25-year familiarity with constant-NAV money market funds has contributed to a belief otherwise. Some investors were sold bond funds with the pitch that "it will get you a higher yield than your money market fund," but without the appropriate clear warning that capital will fluctuate in a longer-term bond fund.

### Bank-Sold Funds' Safety

Impressive marble columns, rich walnut desks, and gleaming vault doors down at your bank convey a solid feeling. These appearances, plus the widely known fact of federal insurance behind bank deposits, probably contribute mightily to a terrible misconception: that funds sold in a bank lobby are somehow guaranteed or safer than other funds. Don't think that for even a minute!

To their credit, the banking industry and the National Association of Securities Dealers (NASD) have made mighty efforts to point out that bank-sold and bank-managed funds are in no way insured or guaranteed as to safety or performance. They've even begun displaying a little logo with the letters "FDIC" inside a circle, covered by a red slash mark. Prospectuses must bear a legend warning that no insurance of principal or return is involved. Funds are now required to be

**FIGURE 15.1** Bond Fund of America, Weekly Net Asset Values, 1990–1997

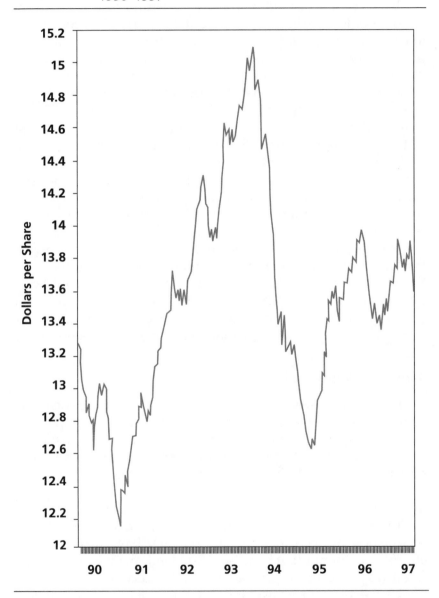

sold in an area of the bank physically separate from the deposit-taking teller booths, to help reinforce the distinction from bank deposits. Numerous psychological experiments have demonstrated that people tend to hear what they want to hear, and they still seem to associate banks with total safety, which they mistakenly transfer to bank-sold funds. The sharp bond bear market of 1994 reduced but did not eliminate the number of innocents. Many of the funds you can buy in a bank lobby are literally the same funds you could purchase from a stock broker. All bond (and equity) funds are managed by human beings and their portfolio securities holdings rise and fall in value daily, doing well or badly over the long term depending on manager skill.

### Income Streams Guaranteed

Only a U.S. government bond can be assumed absolutely safe as to timely and full payment of principal and interest, and even that would apply only absent a revolution or takeover in war. But for all practical purposes in terms of your investment program meaning anything enduring, the statement is true.

A bond fund is not at all the same as an individual bond, however. Even if it holds only U.S. government bonds, your bond fund could reduce its income distribution. That will happen due to any of three causes:

1. Some high-yielding bonds held will mature or be called, forcing reinvestment of cash at lower rates.
2. When interest rates fall and new investors contribute new dollars, the manager can then invest only in lower-yielding bonds.
3. If interest rates are lower at times when distributions are paid and reinvested, these have the same effect on average yield as new money. The average yield on the total portfolio will thus be a bit lower, forcing a slight reduction in monthly income distributions per fund share. Your fund pools all its monies and shares the resulting returns equally (per share held) among all holders regardless of who joined the family first.

Government-bond funds are least prone to dividend cuts (but not immune!) because the great majority of U.S. government bonds are not callable, but the two other factors still operate.

Funds investing in corporate bonds and especially in mortgage-backed securities are highly exposed to cuts in their distribution levels. When interest rates decline greatly, many companies call in their old high-coupon bonds and refinance at lower cost with new bonds. Likewise, municipal bonds typically offer only seven to ten years' protection against being called. If your fund held those high-coupon bonds it will get its principal back early but will no longer receive the stream of high semiannual coupon payments. It will be forced to reinvest the proceeds at new, lower interest rates then prevailing. Thus, it will lack the interest income to support paying you the same distribution per share as earlier.

When rates decline, a bond fund can either cut your monthly distribution a bit or continue to pay it. But to do the latter it must dip into capital, in effect paying you some of your own principal back. Mortgage-backed securities are quite sensitive to changes in rates, since homeowners refinance their mortgages or buy new homes and pay off the old mortgage upon sale. Funds holding such securities basically have no call protection available to them. They initially offer higher yields than government bond funds, but those cash streams are less likely to be sustained.

To recap, no fund's distribution can be guaranteed. The bonds it holds may be extremely default-safe, but the periodic income distribution could be reduced. Any salesperson who even hints to the contrary is either massively underinformed about how bond funds work, or is committing fraudulent misrepresentation. Run the other way if you receive such a sales pitch!

### Complete Safety of Government Bond Funds

If you define total safety as a combination of an absolutely guaranteed income stream plus impossibility of decline in principal value, then even a government-bond fund fails both those tests. Cuts in the income stream were explained earlier. The capital you invest in a government-bond fund is exposed to reduction from four causes:

1. Bond prices fluctuate opposite to changes (rises) in interest rates, so your fund's share price will change in rough proportion.
2. The fund might pay distributions exceeding its net income in order to keep shareholders pacified. If it does so, the excess comes out of your capital. For example, if a fund with a per-share NAV of $10 earns (after expenses) $0.75 per share but pays you and other shareholders $0.80, it draws down its net asset value by that five-cent difference. Now less capital remains available to earn income in the future, so the fund has begun a downward spiral by overpaying its income stream. Owners will see on their Form 1099s a money amount in the box called "nontaxable distributions." But before buying, look at the historical table in the fund's prospectus or annual report. If words like "overdistributed net income" or "distributions in excess of amount earned" or "return of capital" appear, this means capital is being paid out.
3. Government-bond funds may be allowed by their investment policies to utilize options, futures, or other derivative securities that could create either gains or losses in net asset value even though the fund must stick to government bonds. Zero-coupon bonds or stripped Treasuries are examples. These fluctuate very sharply in response to small changes in interest rates, and so drive changes in your fund's value per share. Thus, while an individual U.S. government bond may be guaranteed against default on its interest payments and will eventually pay 100 percent of face value, a fund as a whole cannot be guaranteed never to suffer a loss.
4. Finally, many fund holders might decide to redeem their shares in a depressed period, thereby forcing the portfolio manager to sell off some depressed bonds to raise enough cash to pay off the departing holders. Bonds sold low will not benefit the fund's holders by later recovering; they're gone forever. Such a process can operate to create real losses in a government bond fund even though all underlying bonds it owns are "safe" if held to maturity.

### Equating Bond Funds with Bonds Themselves

Each individual bond has a specific maturity date. Other than term trusts, bond funds have no such thing as a "maturity"; funds have unlimited life unless shareholders vote to liquidate. A long-term bond fund whose prospectus says it will always hold a portfolio of 25- to 30-year maturity bonds will do exactly that. In 20 years, it will hold a different collection of then-25- to 30-year bonds and its NAV will fluctuate as those long-term bonds do. By contrast, what is now a 30-year individual bond will become a five-year obligation after 25 years pass. That bond will eventually move to 100 percent of face value at or just before its final payback date, regardless of interest rates' level at that time.

So owning a bond fund will almost certainly not get you the same results measured at a critical date (such as retirement) as would owning a target-maturity term trust or individual maturity-chosen bonds. That can be a plus or a minus: If you own a long-bond fund and interest rates are way down when you choose to retire, you can cash in at a premium and get a higher total return than if you'd chosen individual bonds or a term trust targeted to come to face value at the same date. Conversely, if you're unlucky enough to need to cash in bond fund shares at a certain date while interest rates are way up, your principal value will be impaired.

Bottom line, don't confuse a long-term bond fund with a long-term bond, for they will surely treat you differently.

## Specific Sinkholes

Now you know that even in dealing with highest-quality bonds, funds do not provide "guarantees." But even in funds dealing with high-rated bonds, there lurk several danger spots.

### Derivatives: Unsafe Stuff Hiding in Supposedly Safe Funds

Just as institutional program trading was a bogeyman for stock investors in the 1980s, so in the early to mid-1990s derivatives began to bedevil bond-fund investors. Derivatives burned fund investors for their greed and ignorance. It is well established that investors naturally gravitate to anything that appears to promise high yield, or a high return without risk. And, no matter how hard regulators work to prevent it, investors hear contrived or incomplete pitches from professional sales experts and rely on that verbal information rather than fully reading a fund's prospectus. (Much litigation and arbitration activity centers on the second point.)

If you hold but a very few insights after completing this book, one should be that there's no "free ride" in the investment world. You must shoulder risk to obtain anything above a meager return. In an area of hoped-for safety such as bond fund investing, you must be ever mindful of the parallel between risk and potential return. High total returns can be achieved in bond funds only when the interest-rate cycle proves favorable and you actually sell near its bottom (price peak) and capture your capital gains; or when significant risk has been taken. Any bond fund offering a cash return exceeding the rate available on long-term bonds (less about 0.75 percent for expenses) is doing something beyond simply buying and holding bonds. In recent years, that "something else" has in most cases been using derivatives. The wider that differential between a bond fund's "promised" yield and underlying long-term bond yields, the more exotic and risky are the techniques being used.

The tender trap usually begins with a safe-sounding name. While safe-sounding securities certainly make up the large bulk of a fund's portfolio, it's the balance of the equation that seeks to add yield and in that process exposes your money to added risk. The hook takes the form of potentially higher return. Your sales professional will almost never be able to explain and quantify the risks; in many cases the investment techniques were invented via computerized modeling and have not been available to be proven in the real world of past market cycles.

What is a derivative, anyway? Reduced to its simplest essence, a derivative is any separately manufactured financial instrument whose price is determined on the basis of values or fluctuations in other defined instruments. By this definition, convertible bonds and stock-purchase warrants are not derivatives because they were issued in that form by a corporation as part of its financing.

But an exchange-traded option is an early generation derivative, since it was not created by GE or GM, but instead by the

Chicago Board Options Exchange (CBOE). The trading price of that option is driven by its underlying value, which in turn is based on GE's or GM's stock price. The wide array of exotic derivatives available in the institutional marketplace of 1997 makes 1970s-vintage CBOE-type listed options look as basic as a child's milk-wagon pull toy. You need to know what derivatives your fund might use, and then select funds that match your tolerance. Strategy 2 stressed the importance of understanding whatever you own. Fortunately, mutual fund prospectuses are becoming easier to use under the driving force of SEC Chairman Arthur Leavitt. Plain and concise English is his primary agenda. Recently adopted and proposed prospectus rules require cover-page and clear inside statements about degrees of risk, some in bold-face type. Some 1997-pending rules require question-and-answer dialogue. Until now, much risk disclosure language could be hidden in dense boilerplate called a Statement of Additional Information (SAI), which few investors know exists and even fewer know how to obtain.

Finding disclosure about derivatives is a bit tricky, since the word itself is seldom used, with only the names of specific instruments or contracts spelled out. Look at the back cover of the prospectus, which has a table of contents. Find captions such as "risk factors" or, more commonly "investment techniques and practices." There you'll see what sorts of exotica may be mixed in with your high-grade bonds. Among the more commonly used devices are interest-only strips, principal-only strips, caps, floors, collars, options, futures, options on futures (!), and inverse floaters. These are derivatives. They have various purposes, and can be used to limit risk. However, money managers are measured primarily on performance rather than on risk avoidance. Therefore, lots of funds use derivatives in speculative ways, in an attempt to enhance their income streams or per-share principal values.

Unfortunately, it's entirely possible for a prospectus disclosure to be simultaneously misleading and legally accurate. And it is exactly in this swampy, high-risk area of derivatives where such anomalies lurk. One of the most common is a statement such as "the fund may not commit more than 5 percent of its assets to initial margin deposits to secure financial futures contracts or to premiums associated with uncovered option writing." Anyone who has done futures trading or has written an uncovered ("naked") option knows all too well that capital risk is unlimited when the market moves against you. Therefore, putting only 5 percent of one's assets in initial deposits or option premiums sounds misleadingly benign; when that 5 percent is bet the wrong way, massive damage ensues, in no way limited to 5 percent. Many derivatives invented in the early 1990s were constructed using assumptions that markets would not move more than a certain amount in a given period. Unfortunately, such assumptions were far from guarantees; in some cases, such as the big bond bear market of 1994, they proved false in short order.

An enlightening exercise would be to phone a fund group, prospectus in hand. Say you note that only 5 percent of the assets can be invested in such-and-such, but then directly ask how much money would actually be lost if those investments went as bad as they possibly could. You'll probably be put on hold; the eventual answer, likely after some fancy verbal dancing, will amount to "we can't say exactly." Whatever the specific answers, you will find the call a sobering experience.

My advice? If you wouldn't willingly trade commodities contracts, sell short, buy in a heavily margined account, or write uncovered puts or calls, don't own any bond fund that does those—or considerably more exotic—things. Hundreds of bond funds do stay within the straight and narrow. If you would not allow yourself to dabble with your risk capital in those ways, for sure you should not enter such swirling waters with your serious, safe-money dollars. Had the sudden and sharp bond market decline of 1993–1994 lasted more than just a brief 13 months, its damage might have done more good. Only late in that period did the press became focused on derivatives-disclosure problems. Had bond prices kept dropping much longer, many funds' managements and boards of directors would have terminated use of these techniques, even if only as a defensive marketing strategy to retain and attract assets. Only a few did. Like a chronic alcoholic, much of the fund industry did not quite hit bottom on derivatives, so it failed to take a lasting cure.

### Other Unproven Gadgets

The word *new* has sold a lot of laundry detergent, so it is not surprising to find it in financial products marketeers' tool kits. Newness implies excitement, open possibilities, similar positive concepts. Unfortunately, investors too often let that appeal override what should be their first reaction, namely to wonder how this undeniably unproven approach will stand the test of time and adversity. That caution is especially warranted with "serious" money like bond fund dollars! A very wise research director I once served said there are only two kinds of companies (and their managements): those that have encountered trouble and those that will. Applying that thinking to new investment instruments or techniques means that any adversity will by definition be unprecedented and therefore will contain great risk of total calamity. Newness as a point allegedly favoring an investment idea is convenient for a salesperson in two ways. First, no prospect can raise any hard examples of how well (or poorly!) this new concept has actually worked in the past. And second, when something later goes wrong, the seller can often get away with, "Well, who would have imagined *that?*"

Yield enhancement was a favorite marketing technique with bond funds in the middle and late 1980s. Then, investors were regretting not having locked in century-high yields a few years earlier; everyone wanted a way to recapture yesteryear's yields. Imagine the excited gleam in a broker's eye upon learning that while U.S. government bond yields had dropped below 10 percent, it would be possible to offer clients a 12 percent or higher yield on a bond fund containing only such high-quality bonds! It was all "possible" through the magic of yield enhancement. Translation: The portfolio manager was selling options against the bonds in the fund, and the premiums received were to be paid out to fund shareholders as additional income.

That would have worked just fine if rates had stayed in a narrow range and not kept falling. Well, they did continue to drop. As a result, the funds found their entire portfolios called away when the options came to settlement month. The portfolio manager not only lost out on all but a small amount of price appreciation, but also faced the need to reinvest the resulting cash from sale of former portfolio bonds in other bonds then yielding 9 percent or less rather than 10 percent. Some funds actually played and lost this same game three or four times before giving up on it. Investors' yields declined with each round of forced 100 percent portfolio turnover, and they missed capital appreciation in a long and strong bond bull market. But, yes, the idea was indeed new!

The details changed, but a few years later the theme was the same: High-yield (read: junk) bond funds became a rage around 1989, the latest way to get an above-market yield. The pitch: Default rates had been low (Of course! There'd been no recession for an extended string of years!), and diversification (via a fund) took care of the risk of choosing a single junk bond unluckily. The nasty recession of 1990–1991 brought junk funds to their knees. In the early 1990s, emerging nations' debt became the next "new" way to get higher yield supposedly with minimized risk. This, too, became a disaster, when all such debt melted after the Mexican peso flotation. Strategy 16 will take you though the high-yield hurdles in more detail.

Particulars of course will continue to change, making it impossible to predict exactly what shape the bond fund potholes of 2005 or 2015 will take. But, be assured, their common theme will remain newness. Think of it as unproven-ness. Not a very attractive attribute for a place to put a chunk of your serious retirement money, is it? (John Kenneth Galbraith's concise but marvelous 1990 volume, *A Short History of Financial Euphoria*, cites new financial gadgetry and belief a magic elixir has been found as basic elements of fads that precede debacles. [Nashville TN: Whittle Direct Books, 1990.]) If you're being sold a fund with an allegedly attractive new-sounding feature, ask your financial sales expert to find instead a long-existing fund that has used a similar, or preferably identical, approach. There and only thus can you see actual annual returns proving how this purportedly wondrous new approach holds up under adversity.

Ten years' data provides the valuable perspective of one or even two complete business cycles. That added cycle can be crucial, since each expansion or recession may have had different causes and a distinct collection of primary victims and adverse effects. The more different environments in which you can test an idea, the better off you will be. Insist on seeing an annual report, not just the prospectus. These are shorter, less formally written, and discuss actual in-practice rough edges more fairly than does a prospectus, full of carefully crafted forward-looking hope phrases.

Bottom line, when investing serious money whose returns will determine your standard of living permanently, why play with new, when old has worked in the past and is provable? With all the keen investment minds being so highly paid, if an idea is great, why was it not discovered and perfected long ago? Little and probably nothing miraculous can be discovered to enhance bond fund returns without adding risk. Newness helps a salesperson sell, but may harm your financial health. Which is more important to you?

# Don't Trip Over High-Yield Hurdles

*H*igh yield means high risk. If risk actually were low, many more investors would be willing buyers at a lower-yield level and the issuer of those securities would not be forced to pay such a high rate to attract capital. The market is not lacking information and professional investors are not collectively stupid. You may not perceive what the exact risks are or how serious the threats may be, but clearly others do or else the yield would be lower! Price is set as a means of discounting any income stream by a required return, or yield. High demanded return means high perceived risk.

Unless you spend a major amount of time researching economic trends and investments, I strongly advise against holding individual junk bonds, those rated below double-B. Their default risk, historically, has been somewhat below 10 percent. But you can lose virtually 100 percent of your capital if you are unlucky enough to choose the wrong one. Mutual funds that assemble portfolios of high-yield bonds are much better bets. However, holding such funds over a long term is not appropriate. Periods of lowest default risk begin about two years into an economic expansion and last until business has just begun to roll over into its next recession. If an expansion is lengthy, this guideline will allow you several years of above-normal returns with progressively decreasing default risk. If the expansion phase includes or causes renewed strong price inflation, bond prices will come under pressure in the latter part of your holding period; at least your fund's high yield will protect you against loss of purchasing power better than those of higher-quality funds. Once in recession and until somewhat after the next expansion starts, funds of high-quality bonds are a much better bet.

## High-Yield Hurdles

Yield sells. There's no simpler way to express a major reality (and trap) of Wall Street—investors are sold relatively easily on any investment idea that provides a high yield. The higher that yield, the easier the sale. Prospectuses discuss the risks in legalese boilerplate, but few prospective investors actually read a prospectus in depth. Existing stocks and bonds virtually shout "buy me" from the financial pages, flaunting their double-digit cash returns. You must see and avoid tripping over the following four high-yield hurdles.

**Hurdle 1: Believing the unbelievable.** Older Wall Street hands are repeatedly amazed by how short investors' memories are. People most heed whatever kind of mistake has most recently bitten them. That bias, plus the passage of time and probably a subconscious desire to block out painful past experiences, explains why reaching for high yield repeatedly exerts its damaging grasp on our heads.

To be alert for the siren call of unbelievably high yield, you need to define what is beyond credible. There is no simple, constant number acting as a definitive stop sign. High yield is relative to average yield at any given time. As this is written, in summer 1997, cash returns exceeding 8.5 percent and certainly those over 9.5 percent serve as strong caution signals, while long-term U.S. Treasury bonds are yielding about 6.6 percent. But in the middle to late 1980s, AAA bonds themselves yielded

10 percent or a bit above. Then, rates above 13 percent to 14 percent were cautionary. A reasonable rule of thumb is this: Always know what the current yield on 30-year Treasury bonds is, since that defines acceptable returns for low-risk investments; add 300 basis points, or 3.0 percent, the same thing, and consider that resulting rate as a significant danger signal for bonds. At a 400-basis-point spread or more, be extremely wary.

With common stocks, different rules apply. In *Barron's* or a similarly authoritative reference source, look up the current yield on the S&P 500 Industrials (which is less volatile and therefore more dependable than that on the Dow Jones Industrial Average of just 30 stocks). An individual stock yield of 2.5 times the S&P 500 yield, and certainly three times that benchmark, should serve as a danger signal. This is a relative measurement rather than a misleadingly simple "one yield fits all times" guideline. Beyond this, compare yields within an industry group. Major oil companies' stocks provide above-average yields, which you should compare to calibrate the yield for any one within that industry. Similarly, utility stocks and REITs are numerous and therefore provide statistically reliable comparisons. (For more information on utilities and REITs, see Strategies 18 and 19.) Within those fairly homogeneous groups, more than about 200 basis points above average should act as a strong caution signal. An easy first source for defining the prevailing range of yields and so the implied threshold of high risk is *The Value Line Investment Survey*. Its individual stock reports, conveniently clustered by industry, display yield prominently at the top of the page.

Allow a little more upside freedom of yield differential for publicly traded limited partnerships (LPs), because these suffer life in a systematically inefficient market. Nearly all institutional investors and many individual investors shun them due to their real or imagined tax complexities. An energy pipeline structured as an LP might yield about 9 percent while an equally healthy one structured as a corporation would yield 5 percent to 6 percent.

Unusually high cash yields are usually not credible indicators of long-term, sustainable income streams. In bonds, they signal a real danger of default. For stocks, unusually high yields more often than not say that knowledgeable investors believe a dividend reduction or outright omission is ahead. Those investors have sold and forced price down in anticipation. Unfortunately, large numbers of gullible investors, and those whose thinking is governed by inertia or denial, will find themselves "surprised" by a bond default or a dividend cut and will react by selling only after such news; price will then fall even further. Sophisticated investors shy away from high-yield situations until after the bad news is already out, thus avoiding damage to their capital and any "surprising" reduction in their income streams.

While some individual situations may work out, too many will prove disastrous. The more out of line a specific security's yield is with averages or with yields on benchmark high-quality investments, the greater the danger of loss. It is very difficult to resist the lure of a high yield. That extra several percent may suppress your tendency to disbelieve there is real danger. Your willingness to believe will, however, in no way reduce the amount of actual risk. It just exposes you to dangers while you wear your blinders.

**Hurdle 2: Temporarily guaranteed distributions.** A very common way yield-hungry investors set themselves up for a fall is by investing in situations that provide temporarily high yields, usually based on some sort of guarantee. These are common in yield-oriented initial public offerings, often when a newly created entity is spun off by a related sponsor. An example might be a restaurant or hospital operating company raising capital by transferring its real estate to a REIT or an LP, leasing the property back, and guaranteeing the dividend stream on the new entity's stock for a period of maybe five years.

In such temporary-guarantee situations, investors focus on the present income stream and pretend it will last indefinitely. They also rely on the apparent security of a guarantee by a third party, often one whose name is fairly well known. They focus on the attractions and ignore their limits. They ought to read the prospectus language about the support period by mentally appending these words: "and after that all bets are off, since it will need to sink or swim on its own merits." Sobering language like that would deter most investors, if it actually got read. But offerors and underwriters are covered by language that specifically names a date or says "five years." Their ready legal defense amounts to, "We warned you by saying five, and not six or more years; didn't you read what the prospectus clearly said?"

Be extremely wary whenever a dividend guarantee period exists. The financial credibility of the guarantor must be considered, since a weak guarantor makes any promise nearly worthless. Second, you should understand that the offering, including its limited guarantee period, is specifically structured to provide high front-end cash returns but then deliver no more than what return is guaranteed. Afterward, the underlying business will be the sole source of further distributions.

The offeror and its underwriters know that an unusually high yield such as they are temporarily guaranteeing will attract a lot of investors and provide the needed capital to make that distribution guarantee doable—for a while, but not forever. Often such a public offering will raise more capital than the business actually needs, precisely so that those extra dollars raised can be used to pay excessively high distributions in the guarantee period. Buyers will be getting back their own money rather than an economically viable return on their money! Compare your 1099-DIV from a corporation, or Schedule K-1 from a partnership, with your cash return—return of capital occurs where cash received exceeds reportable taxable income.

Following is an actual instance of a guarantee-period public offering. (Note: This was one of the most squeaky-clean situations in recent memory. Disclosure of the impending end of guaranteed distributions was made in every quarterly and annual report. Toward the latter stages, that disclosure was immediately followed by a notation of what cash available for distribution would have been if the guarantee had not been honored.) The company is American Restaurant Partners LP, whose Class A units (symbol: RMC) trade on the American Stock Exchange. It is a large and profitable Pizza Hut franchisee. The partnership's IPO was made in August 1987 at $10 per Class A unit. These securities carried an annual $1.40 basic annual distribution rate "until such time as cumulative distributions equal $10, the purchase price of the units," which worked out to the second calendar quarter of 1994.

The annual history of high, low, and December 31 prices and then-current cash yields for the Class A units is shown in Figure

16.1. Total annual returns (actual cash received plus or minus price change per share) are also indicated. Note that these were almost never even close to the "expected" return indicated by the cash yield. Rather, they were driven primarily by declining interest rates and, eventually, by the sharp 1994 drop in distribution rate.

**FIGURE 16.1.**  Historical Data on American Restaurant Partners LP

| | Dollars per Unit | | | | | | | |
|---|---|---|---|---|---|---|---|---|
| Year | High | Low | Dec 31 | Distri-bution | % Yield* | 20-Year UST Yld | Yield Spread | Total Return % |
| 1987 | 10.63 | 7.63 | 9.50 | 1.40† | 14.74 | 9.23 | 5.51 | −3.3‡ |
| 1988 | 10.88 | 8.88 | 9.00 | 1.40 | 15.55 | 9.10 | 6.45 | 9.5 |
| 1989 | 10.50 | 8.13 | 10.25 | 1.40 | 13.66 | 8.00 | 5.66 | 28.9 |
| 1990 | 11.63 | 9.25 | 9.63 | 1.50 | 15.58 | 8.27 | 7.31 | 8.5 |
| 1991 | 10.38 | 7.88 | 9.13 | 1.50† | 16.44 | 7.56 | 8.88 | 12.2 |
| 1992 | 12.09 | 7.69 | 10.63 | 1.50 | 14.11 | 7.29 | 6.82 | 32.9 |
| 1993 | 15.09 | 9.00 | 11.38 | 1.60† | 14.07 | 6.26 | 7.81 | 22.1 |
| 1994 | 11.13 | 7.25 | 5.88 | 0.64† | 10.89 | 7.97 | 2.92 | −38.9 |
| 1995 | 7.00 | 5.50 | 6.00 | 0.64 | 11.67 | 5.85 | 5.82 | 13.0 |
| 1996 | 7.25 | 5.38 | 5.88 | 0.64 | 10.89 | 6.30 | 5.59 | 8.6 |
| Spring 1997: | | | 5.31 | 0.44 | 8.28 | 6.73 | 2.50 | −7.7§ |

\* Based on annual rate excluding extras
† Year-end annual rate excluding extras
‡ Partial year, including one interim dividend
§ Return for first quarter of 1997

This history shows that, until the rate was cut in 1994, the units gradually exhibited a widening premium cash return over long-term Treasury bonds. This was because sophisticated investors were calculating and discounting what would happen in 1994 and beyond. The distribution rate would be reduced (as it happened, to $0.64 annually and even lower in 1997) and in 1994 less sophisticated investors would exhibit shock at the cut and sell out, driving the units' market price lower to a level then providing a more sustainable, real-market return. Those who had read and believed the frequent disclosures were planning on a drop in price, compensated for by an excessively (but temporarily) high cash distribution.

Those who ignored the temporary nature of the guarantee bought their units in a mistaken or naïve belief that a 14 percent or higher yield could be sustained. Most striking in that table is the year-end 1993 information—with just two more quarterly distributions payable at a $1.40 annual rate, buyers were still willing to pay over $11 per share, apparently oblivious to or fearless of a likely plunge in price once the new distribution rate would become established after mid-1994. But that price decline surely took place! The bottom-line lesson is that there is no free lunch in the investment world, even when a strong brand franchise such as Pizza Hut underlies one's investment. And, for the record, after almost ten years, one had undiscounted dividends plus ending market value (before capturing tax-loss benefits) of $18.09, for an average internal return well under 7 percent without dividend reinvestment—a far cry from the 14 percent so apparent at the IPO.

**Hurdle 3: False comfort from the yield.** "Well, at least I know I'll get that high yield every year" are 12 fatefully naïve famous last words too often regretted later. Getting *at least* that high dividend or interest income, on a net basis, requires all of the following conditions:

- The bonds do not default or, in the case of a common stock, the dividend is voluntarily continued by the directors.
- Investors do not begin to perceive any rising danger that would cause them to lower the price.
- Yields in general don't rise, dropping the security's price.
- In the case of a non-U.S. security, that nation's currency has not fallen in value against the dollar, forcing currency translation values to move adversely.

The first two points are specific to particular aspects of the individual investment vehicle itself, whether debt or equity, and the associated risks have been covered earlier. The last two involve external but nevertheless real elements that can cut a security's market price irrespective of the fundamental health of the issuer.

The strongest telephone or electric utility company's stock can confidently be predicted to fall in price when interest rates rise more than a tiny amount. The stock or bonds of the strongest foreign company or government will be worth less in U.S. dollar terms if that other nation's currency falls in value (gradually or suddenly) against the dollar. By sheer mathematics, it then takes fewer dollars to buy the same number of other currency units, so that security will be worth less in dollars.

While you may invest mainly for income, especially in later years, never forget that the total return on your investment is what counts. Current income received plus or minus change in market value is your true return. So it is inaccurate to say you will "at least receive the current income." In saying that, you're focusing on one part (the quoted cash dollar return), which is neither the total picture nor a guaranteed minimum part of overall return. It is neither, being merely the most visible (and you hope predictable) piece of the puzzle.

**Hurdle 4: Buying high-yield investments at just the wrong time.** Investors greedily demonstrate yield reach-back syndrome, which has been evident since the early 1980s. Reach-back is driven by a yearning for higher yields once available on safe instruments. Remember 16 percent CDs and 14 percent–plus Treasury bonds back in 1980–1981? Every step of the way down from those century-high peaks, yield-hungry investors have sought ways to grab yesteryear's market rates. The only way has been to move to lower quality. The progression has included, in sequence, moves to mortgage-backed securities and funds, then to quality corporate bonds, to junk bonds, then leveraged municipal-bond funds, and most recently to international bonds.

The most desperate reach to lower quality occurs at the most dangerous time in each cycle. Interest rates, if allowed to move without undue intervention from Federal Reserve Bank policy changes, would make valleys somewhat after each actual cyclical low in the economy. That period in which long-term rates decline—prompting investors to reach back for yesterday's yields by sacrificing quality—is when the economy is weakening or still in process of bottoming out after a recession. That's exactly when credit risk among lower-quality debt issuers is rising and highest: through and just after the end of a recession.

Investors react cyclically to their bond market experiences just as they do in stocks: with some delay in response to what has already become obvious. After a disaster (such as defaults during a recession) they become cautious and flee to quality, even though that means accepting lower cash yield. Gradually, as economic conditions start to improve, bond buyers become a bit more comfortable, extending their willingness to own some less-than-top-quality credits. In the fullness of a boom, they gain confidence and look even deeper into the quality pile. Once the economy has just peaked and rates break and begin declining, buyers seemingly forget any pain from the last credit debacle and willingly reach back to get higher cash yield, which is available only from low-quality bonds. That reach-back occurs after economic activity has already peaked, meaning exactly when default risk is starting to rise. Therein is the final hurdle that can trip yield-hungry investors—low current yields and several years' comfortable prosperity prompt income investors to embrace junk bonds (and junk-bond funds) exactly at the wrong time in a cycle, namely just when default risk is rising. The further rates fall (as recession deepens), the greater the urge to reach for higher yield.

# Be Smart in How You Use Mutual Funds

$S$ince the mid-1970s, millions of investors have largely abandoned direct purchase and holding of individual stocks and bonds in favor of professional management and presumed lower risk, by investing through mutual funds. Even that change has hardly resulted in simplification. There are now more mutual funds than stocks listed on the NYSE and AMEX combined. Some less-than-ideal patterns have developed in investors' behavior in mutual funds. In this strategy, you'll learn about the major pitfalls of fund investing and suggested remedies. These pages offer no advice on what particular funds to buy or sell; our focus is on types and styles of fund investing that serve either well or badly.

## History of the Fund Phenomenon

From 1980 through 1990, U.S. investors' assets in mutual funds grew tenfold, to $1 trillion. Then, by early 1997, they more than tripled again to $3.4 trillion—equal to over $13,000 for every living person in the nation. Funds have clearly become the investment medium of choice. Their shares, after all, can be redeemed daily for exactly their true current worth, on any given day, while individual stocks and bonds trade erratically at times in reflection of emotional reactions to news events. Funds provide three other attractive features: built-in diversification, professional management, and the power to buy or sell an exact dollar amount when desired—impossible with stocks or $1,000-denomination bonds.

Other factors that I believe draw investors to funds include the ability to sell (some classes of shares) free of commissions—both a financial and a psychological consideration for some—and the fact that fund investing shields one from frequent solicitations by brokers urging decisions to sell and buy. Funds generally suggest long-term commitments, providing a sense of conservative posture and allowing a holder to feel relaxed about choices already made. Relatively few people enjoy dealing with financial matters; mutual funds deliver a mental feeling of relief, by letting you say, "There, I've taken care of that."

## Major Mistakes People Make with Mutual Funds

### Buying Shares with the Wrong Sales Loads

We will not reopen that tired, decades-old debate about no-load versus load (i.e., sales-charged) funds. The bottom line is performance net of costs, with due allowance made for any need for assistance in selection. Those who enjoyed a magnificent average total return of 28.5 percent from the Fidelity Magellan Fund in the years 1980–1989—or even an average 18 percent in the years 1985–1994—would enthusiastically assure any doubters that paying a 3 percent front-end sales charge was well worth the long-term reward. But load funds do not systematically outperform no-loads. Investors now have access to vastly more information on funds through newspapers' tallies, magazines' numerous feature stories and tabulations, computer-searchable databases, and even the Internet. This information democracy has rendered financial sales professionals less necessary, or even unnecessary for many. Still, other investors need and prefer knowledgeable assistance and are willing to pay sales charges for it. Is it "better" to buy a major appliance "blind" in a discount outlet or to pay more in a full-service retail store and receive expert assistance by having questions resolved in advance?

If you get help and advice in buying fund shares, you should expect that in some form you will pay for that service. The person involved in selling you your shares is compensated on an incentive (read: "commission") basis; you, as buyer of the product, will inevitably pay for all services rendered, including that of selling to you. The following discussion pertains to funds other than those entitled to use the phrase "pure no-load," which has a specific meaning under SEC rules.

There are five major types of sales charges on mutual funds; you should decide which model best matches your time horizon. Some funds impose only one, while others charge in more than one way.

1. Front-end loads
2. Redemption charges
3. Spread loads
4. Annual 12b-1 fees
5. Contingent deferred sales charges

**Front-end loads.** Front-end loads come out of your invested capital the day you buy a fund. Legally they can run as high as about 8 percent, but in recent years competitive pressures have cut them mainly to about 4.0 percent to 4.75 percent. If you invest $10,000 in a front-end-load fund with a sales charge of 4 percent, your shares will be worth $9,600 at the end of the day when you buy them. You will have $9,600 and not $10,000 working for you. (You actually pay an effective charge of about 4.16 percent on the net amount you invest in the fund.) If you want help from a financial sales professional in choosing a fund, paying a discrete amount in the beginning, and preferably nothing else later (!), makes sense if you will hold for the long term.

**Redemption charges.** These come out of your proceeds every time you sell some (or all) of your fund shares. Suppose that over a period of seven years or so your original investment doubles from $10,000 to $20,000 (a realistic long-term average 10 percent return for equities). If you had bought a back-end fund with a 4 percent charge, you will see an $800 redemption charge on its $20,000 sale, leaving you net proceeds of $19,200. This leaves you with the same ending wealth as if you'd bought a 4 percent front-end-load fund. Your net $9,600 investment there, after commission, would reach $19,200 if it exactly doubled.

**Spread loads.**   These seek to reduce buyer resistance to paying high loads all at once, either when buying or when selling. A typical spread load might involve 1 percent per year on the purchase date anniversary, for perhaps seven years. This does not present any chance to avoid the full load by selling after just one or two years—the fine print discloses that the full anticipated amount of load will be captured via a lump-sum charge on sale if it has not already been taken through annual 1 percent assessments. One key question for which you need to get a written answer: Will the annual percentage charge (in the above example, 1 percent per year) be applied to the original value of the account or to its future actual value? If your fund provides a positive return, a percentage applied to actual value will represent a higher dollar burden on your originally invested sum than the stated rate (7 percent in total, in this example). Generally, spread loads are somewhat of a gimmick enabling an easier sale; I would avoid them, since in the early years they set up a psychological barrier to perhaps-appropriate sale decisions.

**Annual 12b-1 service fees.**   A fund management company can levy these charges, limited to 1.25 percent per annum, against the assets of the fund for marketing expenses. (The name refers to section 12b-1 of the Investment Company Act of 1940, which permits them.) The basis for such charges is an assertion that existing holders' interests are served through economies of scale if a fund grows larger due to added marketing paid for by the charges. The 12b-1 fees also can be used to pay sales personnel for providing ongoing service to existing shareholders. That help may relieve a fund company of expense by allowing it to employ a smaller client-service staff. Part of the service provided would include being available to offer comfort and encouragement not to sell during temporary downturns in the market. A

12b-1 fee is figured as accruing expense of the fund daily, as it invisibly slices a tiny fraction of a cent off the net asset value.

Two major drawbacks of 12b-1 fees are that they apply to current values of your shares, therefore representing more than the stated percentage annually on your original investment if your value has risen; and that *they can continue as long as you own the fund.* If you own a fund charging an unlimited annual 12b-1 fee of 1.25 percent, after 20 years you will have paid 25 percent, which will have been applied to the presumably appreciating value of your account, not just to your first investment. My advice is that there are so many other funds available (literally several thousand) that I would avoid those imposing 12b-1 fees, especially if anticipating long-term holding. Many funds are sold with no front-end load that "turns off" the prospective buyer, but then impose the greater long-term burden of 12b-1 fees. As a memorable auto oil filter commercial said, "You can pay me now or pay me (more) later."

**Contingent deferred sales charges.**    Known as CDSCs for short, these redemption costs decline over time to zero depending how long shares have been held. A typical CDSC might step down over six years by 1 percent a year, finally arriving at zero. If you sold in less than 12 months, you would surrender 6 percent of your proceeds; in the 23rd month, then 5 percent; and so on, to no charge after a full 72 months. Such charges usually apply separately to each additional fund-share investment you make, which starts its own clock running. This structure appeals if you expect to be a long-term holder and truly believe no emergency will upset that plan. However, remember that there is no free lunch on Wall Street: CDSCs are often imposed in classes of shares where annual 12b-1 fees also apply. Therefore, even long-term holding will not entirely escape charges for the fund's marketing costs.

Many funds now offer a range of share classes. Each class has the same investment portfolio but is assessed a differing stream of charges depending on the sales fee basis chosen. Often "A" shares are front-end loaded, and other plans carry different letters. You should fully understand all your options before buying. Fortunately, regulation now requires representatives to disclose and explain all the options before making a sale of one.

This helps protect buyers from a minority of salespeople who tend to sell a class of shares paying more sooner rather than what serves a client's needs best.

A mutual fund's prospectus must include, in its very earliest few pages, a clear table showing estimated "costs you would pay" assuming a $1,000 investment ($10,000 starting in mid-1997), over various holding periods. These costs include the annual expenses of the fund (as differentiated from the commissions described earlier) and are based on the required assumption of a 5 percent average annual return on investment. Where charges are levied based on value of holdings rather than original cost, the table understates your true future expenses when your gross return is over 5 percent.

Here's the bottom line: If you will be a long-term holder, you should prefer a single, front-end charge rather than another type or combination, since those others typically cost more in the long run. This, of course, assumes you did not start out by choosing a no-load fund in the first place.

### Chasing Recent Leaders

If you glean little else from this book, I hope you have learned not to follow the crowd. To make sure, please reread Strategy 9. Appropriately armed with useful contrarian understanding and more control over your own emotions, you'll be better able to resist the temptation to chase after recently leading funds. Constant exposure to magazine and newspaper articles regarding mutual funds, and lately probably also to PC software for selecting funds, poses a definite danger in this regard. Alexander Cockburn said many years ago that the first priority of a journalist is to confirm existing prejudice rather than to contradict it. Putting that differently, what is familiar rather than strangely upsetting is what sells magazines. The financial media repeatedly run articles featuring which funds or styles of investing have performed best over the past 12 (or fewer) months.

January issues are especially notable for this tendency. Read them if you will, but try not to inhale deeply while doing so. In the investment world, what has been hot soon will be not! Long history shows that markets experience rotation of leadership. At a macro level, stocks will outperform bonds for a time and then will fall back as bonds do better. On a micro level, certain industry groups, investment styles, or economic themes that catch the imagination of investors will provide returns temporarily above long-term norms. Examples are value versus growth investing, cyclical versus consumer industries, large-cap versus small-cap stocks, defensive versus high-technology stocks, and so on. Over the long term, a company's stock price will tend to increase at the rate of its earnings growth. This is the pull of fundamental value. Anything else requires a sustained net expansion or contraction of the price-earnings ratio. But in the short term, investor psychology and a tendency to jump on the latest bandwagon causes prices to rise for a while much faster than the underlying fundamental growth rate. Such expansion of price-earnings multiples is unsustainable.

Outstanding interim performance by mutual funds reflects portfolio selections that took advantage of latest rotational leadership within the market, either actively or passively. Sector or single-industry funds are most prone to being leaders (or laggards) over short time frames. In 1992 health care stocks were on top. The next two years were halcyon times for financial industry stocks. Then 1995 featured technology issues, and 1996–1997 the huge-cap S&P 500-type stocks. Such rotation of leadership drives performance by diversified funds too, although not as strikingly. Unless a fund is committed by fundamental policy to market-weighted balance across industries (as an index fund would be), the portfolio manager attempts to "beat the market" and thereby earn salary bonuses by positioning assets in industries outperforming the overall average. This is described as "overweighting" certain sectors or industries and "underweighting" others. Even if a fund is not specialized in one industry, its results will shine when it has emphasized those industries, sectors, or themes that have worked best lately. Weightings can be changed for fundamental reasons, but lately these changes mainly reflect raw price-momentum chasing.

Individual fund managers tend to have personal favorites or comfort zones in investing. One may like health care companies while another is enamored of semiconductors and software. One manager will lean toward stocks mainly on an undervaluation basis while another primarily rides fast-growth companies with 40x multiples, for better or worse. Their respective funds will rise to the top of any ranking scale when those styles or approaches have lately been most successful. Inevitably, what has moved up to an extreme will then pause or suffer a setback while some other part of the market becomes the leader. As a result, those funds that have done best over any recent short period like a year or 18 months are unlikely to be able to sustain their leadership positions. (A stopped clock is right twice a day but predictably will not give good answers at all other times.) How long "a while" is cannot be predicted. Fad cycles do not conveniently come in predetermined lengths.

Because of internal market rotation, buying funds that have recently been hot can lead to frustration and long-term under-performance. This amounts to chasing yesterday's favorites. The danger is greatest when the past advance has been strongest for longest. At that point, "everyone" just "knows" that you absolutely must be invested in the widget industry, and it becomes very lonely to resist jumping into the game just when prices are farthest out of line with long-term reality (value). Remember, what applies in individual stocks directly drives performance of mutual funds as well. Once literally everyone interested has bought into an investment concept, there is no one left with available cash to do further buying and therefore price will lose momentum and start falling as earlier buyers become impatient or nervous. Consensus (meaning unanimity of opinion) in the market marks a turning point in the opposite direction, necessarily and inescapably. Remember that caution when reading lists of recent fund winners!

Another note about mutual fund rankings: Many investors rightfully eschew one-year performance as a guide, but instead look at three-year, five-year, or longer periods. This approach contains a hidden pitfall. While you think you're examining long-term performance, outstanding latest-year results are included in, and therefore dominating, a several-year average. A better way to look at a fund is on a year-by-year basis. This has three advantages: it shows how consistently the fund performed at or above benchmarks; it shows whether one year's huge success is driving the overall "average" return; and it shows how volatile the swings up and down were, which will help you determine your personal emotional staying power with such a fund. Tables in prospectuses and annual reports are required to show separate annual returns for five and ten years if the fund is at least that old.

Bottom line is this: Don't chase recent winners; instead, seek consistent performers. If you have a sufficiently independent streak, choose funds that have good long-term records but that have recently underperformed due to rotation in the market. In the next leadership change, they are likely to come back and overperform. In spring 1995, a large funds-management organization's president publicly stated that he runs his own IRA plan exactly that way. Each year, he rotates assets into the company's worst-performing nonsector fund and out of its recently heroic performer. His results have consistently been well above mean.

### Imagining Nonexistent Diversification

People easily back into this trap by buying funds managed by various companies. Because they've bought multiple brand names, they feel diversified. Risk-lowering diversification occurs only if they've bought funds with different investment objectives. A portfolio consisting entirely of Fidelity Destiny, Twentieth Century Ultra, Berger 101, Janus Twenty, Invesco Dynamics, and Founders Special actually has six funds all doing the same job and no other investment approach represented. Great in a roaring bull market, but a predictable disaster in the next bear cycle! While each such fund might hold 200 stocks on average, those six funds would be unlikely to be diversified over 1,200 stocks. Many names would be owned in four, five, or literally all six funds. Thus, owning those funds would involve perhaps 400 stocks rather than 1,200—and those likely will be of the high-flier flavor. No anchors to windward, no value protection, no international representation, nothing counter-cyclical. One down quarter by one major semiconductor company or an isolated earnings aberration by a consumer megastock, and all six funds would land in the tank together.

The moral of the story is that numbers of funds do not make for diversification; only differences in investment style do. Buying even two funds that invest essentially the same way will overweight your holdings to that approach, necessarily robbing other kinds of assets of their proper allocation. Unless you have a demonstrated history of frequent switching and consistently successful contrarian timing of the market, you should steer away from multiple funds of one type. This pothole is easier to avoid than ever before: Each day's listings in the *Wall Street Journal*—and in some other major papers—includes codes showing every fund's investment objective. Check for matches on your list and make some rebalancing changes!

### One-Decision Investing

As noted elsewhere in this book, many people feel uncomfortable making financial decisions. They fear making a serious money mistake and accurately predict their inability to choose the one best fund or individual stock from among the several thousand available. Mutual funds, marketed as they are with a heavy dose of reminders to be a long-term investor, provide their owners with comfortable feelings based on the classic combination benefits of professional management and diversification. Being a long-term investor adds to one's sense of conservatism and therefore furthers the tendency to buy and hold "forever." That serves the fund's management company well but is unlikely to work ideally for you, except by relieving you of the discomfort of making choices more than once. Several major kinds of changes should prompt you to at least consider moving from one fund to another:

- Economic shifts such as significant changes in interest or inflation rates, major technological revolutions, and similar events can render yesteryear's winning investment strategy a likely future long-term loser.
- Demographic megatrends clearly will have major effects during your investment lifetime. Around the year 2000, birth rates will decline again and an aging population will save more, borrow less, and buy more things typical of seniors' lifestyles. Companies booming in the 1970s or 1990s will not fare as well.
- Tax and regulatory changes also can have profound effects. Whole industries or sectors can be greatly helped or hurt by changes in the latest "wisdom" from Washington.

Changes in deductibility of interest expense, a major shift in capital-gains tax policy, or new depreciation rules are just a few examples.

- Departures of key people in your mutual fund company's management team are increasingly likely. Since the early 1990s, there have been many mergers among management companies. Sometimes a resulting cultural change will drive key people such as senior economists or investment strategists to depart. Your fund, whose past success may have been driven by their insights and skills, will be a victim of such shifts.

- Your portfolio manager may leave or be replaced on a rotating basis due to internal promotion policies. With someone else at the helm, whose style almost certainly will be different, your fund is likely to perform differently. The many changes at Fidelity in 1995–1997 had unsettling effects on investors.

- Mushrooming fund size may impair chances of continued strong performance even if key personnel stay in place. It is less possible to manage a huge (multi-billion-dollar) fund adroitly than when the fund was smaller, say under a billion. This is especially true where the investment objective by its nature is specialized. There will simply be a limited supply of undervalued asset-play stocks, merger candidates, micro-cap growth companies, or true critical technology leaders from which to choose at any time. As a fund grows, its manager is pushed to buy stocks further down his or her priority list; as a result, performance will tend more toward the average. If your fund has grown tremendously in size, these considerations might justify a switch.

- You and your needs will change during your investment lifetime. With age, you will want less risk and be less inclined to seek the big winners than you were decades earlier when you had more time to overcome an early loss. Your income-oriented funds during high salary years may best be tax-sheltered municipals; after retirement, a taxable bond fund probably will make more sense. Perhaps an inheritance or a major business event (sale or serious setback) will change your overall asset mix and/or risk tolerance at some point. Such factors argue for being flexible rather than buying and holding a particular fund for a lifetime.

One development that began to be evident in 1994 offers some possible assistance for those who are incurably unable to sell and move on to other investments. A few management companies began offering lifestyle types of funds that have target maturity or retirement dates (see Figure 17.1). Each such fund itself will change its investment mix over the years ahead, gradually evolving from a capital appreciation vehicle to a conservative income-oriented portfolio as its holders age. You simply buy one whose target is your expected retirement time or your statistically predicted year of death; the fund changes while you keep holding it, reducing your need to switch funds as you mature through life's stages.

**FIGURE 17.1**    Examples of Lifestyle Funds

| Brand Name | Target Years | Adviser |
| --- | --- | --- |
| BT Investors LifeCycle | Short, medium, long | Bankers Trust (800-245-0242) |
| Fidelity Freedom | 2000 by 10s to 2030 | Fidelity (800-544-8888) |
| Kemper Horizon | 5, 10, 20 hence | Zurich Kemper (800-621-1048) |
| Masterworks | 2000 by 10s to 2040 | BZW Barclays Global (800-835-5472) |
| StageCoach Lifepath | Same as Masterworks | Same as Masterworks |
| Time Horizon Portfolios 1-3 | Short, medium, long | Bank of America (800-451-8377) |

Such funds will well serve investors who otherwise would buy and hold forever despite their changing personal needs. They do, however, contain a potentially important hidden eventual drawback. In the final few years when you will be close to retirement, high inflation and interest rates could sharply depress long-term bond prices, impairing the capital value in such a fund then heavily positioned in that asset class. By instead owning a varied collection of individual and more conventional funds over which you have full control, you would be in position to avoid the damage to bonds by moving out of bond funds and into money market, natural resources, or real estate funds for those later years.

Remember that one size does not fit all, nor will any single investment approach work ideally throughout your lifetime. Would you own the same home, the same car, and the same type of wardrobe for an entire lifetime? No single fund (other than lifestyle funds, which have not yet been proven by time) is likely to meet your personal needs forever. Be flexible, learn to trade in the old for the newly more appropriate and stop worrying about perfection. Better to make a move that moderately (if imperfectly) betters your long-term results than to let indecision freeze you in a fund that predictably will not serve you well for the rest of your life.

### Selecting Less-than-Desirable Fund Types

This practice can rob you of good performance. Three types in particular come to mind. One is the high-yield (think the more blunt "junk-bond" designation) fund, which is tempting but, as shown in Strategy 16, is not equally appropriate across a full economic cycle. Two others, also income-oriented, present underperformance traps. These are utility funds (for more information on that industry, see Strategy 18) and so-called equity-income funds.

My objection to utility and equity-income funds is that they are sold on the basis of generating high income, but use common stocks to achieve that end. Your portfolio manager is then under pressure to deliver high income from a common stock portfolio. High income inherently means high risk, and no common stock's income stream is at all guaranteed. I believe the equity-income fund is, to paraphrase a popular song, looking for income in all the wrong places. Investors find these funds a comfortable buy because they seem to offer the best of both worlds: income, necessary or seemingly attractive, plus the cachet of equity, which they've been reminded provides higher total returns than bonds over the long term. But equity-income funds do not invest in the broad range of stocks providing those kinds of high returns. Such funds concentrate in mature industries such as steel, utilities, and major oil companies because they pay high dividend yields.

Much better is to own either an honest "balanced" fund or a set of two separate funds that respectively provide income and capital appreciation from two different groups of investments. A balanced fund always invests between 40 percent and 60 percent in bonds and the complementary percentage in stocks. Each asset class does its own job in the overall mix, and the portfolio manager looks for the best available investments within each sphere. Likewise, in two totally separate funds, you can get professional selection of growth stocks and of bonds from specialists whose total investment focus is their one specific investment objective. Neither fund's manager needs to settle for a best-available combination of hoped-for income and hoped-for growth from common stocks. You as the holder create the desired asset mix while each fund pursues its separate goal internally.

### Confusing Bond Funds with Actual Bonds

This potentially costly mistake was discussed at some length in Strategy 15 but deserves a renewed mention. Bond funds offer the well-known list of funds' advantages. But their key difference centers on maturity. Individual bonds have specific maturity dates, when (assuming no default) principal will be paid off regardless of the then-current level of interest rates. You should ladder or manage your bond maturities to match your declining principal-risk tolerance as your age rises.

Other than term trusts, bond funds never have a maturity! You would not be as well served to buy a new collection of 30-year bonds at age 70 as perhaps at age 40. But continuing to own a long-term bond fund does exactly that to you. That fund will never mature but instead will always hold an updated collection of long-maturity bonds. A long-bond fund, by its nature, exposes you to major movements in net asset value because it will always own long bonds. Those bonds will certainly rise or fall in the opposite direction of interest rates' moves. So owning a bond fund will almost certainly not get you the same results measured at a critical date (such as retirement) as would owning a target-maturity term trust or maturity-chosen individual bonds.

Therefore, if you prefer owning bonds through funds rather than individually, you must switch periodically to progressively shorter-maturity funds as your tolerance for loss of capital declines with advancing age.

# Be Smart about Utility Investing

*S*uccessful investing, whether in general or specifically for retirement, requires diversification. Spreading your resources across several asset classes exposes you to gains that might pass you by if you focus exclusively on one type of investment. Having eggs in several baskets protects you against a sharp decline in one area of the markets that could significantly impair your total capital. You should pay special attention to this second risk if you're prone to action after reading financial items or watching popular financial TV programs.

Most individual investors instinctively gravitate toward seemingly safe investment areas when looking toward retirement, and even more so after they've reached that life stage. A major attraction that adds a sense of safety to any investment is its stream of current income. Therefore, retirement-conscious and other safety-oriented investors feel a natural pull from utility stocks. This strategy identifies and helps you avoid the common errors in utility investing.

## Times Are Changing!

Utility stocks, while having a legitimate place, are by no means a single magical solution. Nor are they best serving your needs if bought and held forever. Do not assume that the world will remain frozen in suspended animation, with conditions never changing from when you bought a particular stock, bond, or mutual fund. Even the seemingly mundane areas of telephone, electric, water, and gas services have undergone massive changes in recent years; many shifts are still in process!

Since the early 1970s, consumers' environmental awareness and government agencies' regulatory activity have risen, sharply changing life for water, electric, and gas companies. Rapid technological innovation and AT&T's forced divestiture of its seven "Baby Bells" have revolutionized the competitive and strategic environment in the once-staid communications business. In just 20 years starting in 1973, electric utilities were rocked to their foundations by three sea changes: first the OPEC oil embargo, then the antinuclear backlash spurred by the Chernobyl disaster and Three Mile Island near miss, and, lately, major new regulatory initiatives that change rules deciding which company produces the power your local utility connects to homes and businesses.

The natural gas pipeline business has felt a regulatory revolution since the mid-1980s: FERC rules have turned the transport network into an open, toll-competitive interstate highway rather than a collection of previously private local roads. One major bankruptcy and hundreds of lawsuits were the most dramatic results; dividend cuts and omissions, formerly rare, became common.

Now, water companies face a future of rising scarcity. Standards for product quality will continue rising and so cost of their product will rise sharply; predictably, consumer backlash against high prices will press regulators to squeeze rates, repeating the electric industry's 1970s cycle of trouble.

So what investors of past generations viewed as quintessentially safe investments (even better than safe: with rising dividends) now require great vigilance. Does this mean you should recoil in fear and horror, never again to consider or hold a utility stock? No, but you must understand and learn how to steer around the potholes in utility investing. (For more information on utilities investments, you may wish to consult my book, *Plugging into Utilities,* McGraw-Hill, 1993.)

Three problems potentially confound your success in utility investing. Two are internal—things within an individual investor's head; only one is fundamental, driven by the facts of the companies in the industry. These three areas of mistakes in utility investing are:

- Personal inertia
- False comfort zone
- Overemphasis on current yield

## Overcoming Personal Investment Inertia

More than in any other industry, utility stock values are driven primarily and directly by dividend income rather than growth prospects. Classical theory, as now quantified in the dividend discount model approach, holds that proper valuation of any equity security is driven by the expectation and discounted valuation of a future stream of dividends. Prices may swing (widely!) around such true value. Transient excitement or disappointment over future earnings prospects, flowing from current news developments, is merely a proxy for changes in estimations of a company's future ability to pay its owners a stream of cash returns on their investment. Earnings matter because they represent potential for, in fact enable payment of, dividends.

Utility investors are more concerned with income than with growth, usually too much for their own good. They've chosen a vehicle primarily for income generation, with some hope for future growth, since it is a common stock rather than a debt. They expect no wonderful new products, key patents, openings of exciting new markets, no technology breakthroughs wiping out competition—all those things that equity investors look for in growth stocks or more speculative situations. Utility investors see their dividend stream and discount it by an appropriate yield defined by ambient conditions in the bond market. They pay little heed to wiggles in quarterly earnings, knowing those are principally determined by weather, economic conditions, changes in rates permitted by regulators, and extremely complex accounting conventions. Utility investors ask, What have you done for me lately? What's the dividend? And, What is the outlook for inflation and therefore for interest rates?

At least that's what rational utility investors should ask. Too often, however, they do nothing after buying a utility's shares. This is a psychological problem, basically driven by inertia, that lazy trap of buying and holding forever. A historically slow pace of change in utilities' fortunes lulls their investors into comfort and complacency.

Investors in utilities also know that prices for their stocks, much like quotations for bonds, are driven primarily by changing levels and expected trends of interest rates. When interest rates rise, bond prices fall; bond prices rise when interest rates fall. So, people are willing to pay more dollars for a given income stream when interest rates are low, and less for the same stream when rates are high. Alternative opportunities (including utility shares) in a highly liquid marketplace impose discipline on prices.

Utility stock prices are governed by market-yield logic: They move in the opposite direction as interest rates. (They also react to actual and likely changes in the rate of dividends being paid, whereas bonds pay a fixed income stream barring default.)

As clear as the two parts of a utility stock's price formula are, investors seemingly fall into paralysis once they buy these shares. Probably the central reason for this inertia is bad experiences in forecasting future interest rates. Where economists labor hard for just partial success, we mere mortals throw up our hands in defeat. We give up. We seem to assume changes in rates may well be random, implying any of our choices or actions are as likely to be wrong as correct. So we refuse to play a perceived 50-50 game that is also burdened by commissions costs.

A subtle but even larger cost, however, is potential injury to our fragile egos. We greatly prefer being proved right over being shown wrong. Since fear is a stronger motivator than greed, pain avoidance outweighs pleasure pursuit. This is very true for utilities investors, who by nature are somewhat risk-averse. We'd instinctively rather take no action we clearly could regret than take some action that only "might" benefit us. It's strangely clear that this mental calculus rules at the time of the very difficult decision about whether to sell our investments, while the pleasure-seeking and venturesome sides of our nature make buying decisions much less stressful. We don't like the odds surrounding selling, so we hide our heads like ostriches. We refuse to sell because it might be a mistake. The fact that our utility stock pays a meaningful stream of dividends contributes to our tendency to prefer holding over selling. "Well, at least I'll get that nice yield," we think to ourselves. With a no-dividend stock, we more clearly perceive the speculative nature of holding and are more easily persuaded to sell when we see clouds on the horizon in the form of a likely rise in interest rates. But a nice dividend yield holds us in place.

How can you overcome this trap, which otherwise will see you holding your utility stocks up and down, and up and down again, through major economic and interest rate cycles? The key is to remember the math: Movements in interest rates, which directly drive movements in utility stock prices, are much larger in percentage terms than is either the current cash yield or the rate of dividend growth!

Over the very long term, dividend income provides somewhat over half the total return from utility shares. But in the interim, interest rates fluctuate much more than the current dividend yield. From October 1993 to November 1994, the 30-year Treasury bond moved from a 5.75 percent yield basis to 8.25 percent. That meant a 43 percent increase in the denominator of the fraction in which income is divided by required yield. Bond prices, to use the Street's politest description, tanked. The Dow Jones Utility Average dropped by over 31 percent, a decline never seen in any year in the previous 100.

Sure, the 1994 bear market in bonds and utilities was unusually severe, the equivalent of a 100-year flood. But even moderate changes in interest rates, those not uncommon in any given year, generally exceed cash yields on bonds or utility stocks. A rise from 7 percent to 8 percent in prevailing interest rates is a change of 14.3 percent, which translates into a 14.3 percent drop in the price of a utility stock (ignoring the effects of any rise in dividends). A 14 percent price drop is more than twice the current cash yield, leaving the investor both one year older and well behind in real dollar wealth for his or her inaction.

Holding on is foolhardy in the face of clear evidence of where the interest rates winds are blowing. We didn't know exactly how great the total rise would be, but it was very clear that the Fed was intent on smothering possible inflation and would raise rates as needed to do so. Once rates were clearly rising, we knew we'd missed the exact top in utility prices. But failing to stand aside because we didn't know exactly how bad the bear market would be (something you must make yourself understand clearly you will *never* get right!) was not a good reason for holding on. It was like refusing to jump from the roof to a rescue boat because you did not know precisely how high the floodwaters would rise.

Perfectionism is a problem utilities investors must overcome. Perfectionism seeks to protect our fragile egos. It leads us to take no action at all when we are less than 100 percent certain of the future. Refusing to take any investment action that even *might* be a mistake will provide you with a frozen, dysfunctional portfolio.

But it gets even worse. Paralysis driven by perfectionism sets you up for an even bigger mistake later. You will not sell before the top for fear of missing more gains, and will hold on just past the top for having missed it, and will still hold as the decline drags slowly on and values seem more juicy. But chances are dangerously high you will overcome your perfectionist paralysis at just the wrong time. At the very bottom, fear will finally take over, and you will sell out in panic. Consuming fear, but of what? That the utility you own will actually drop all the way to zero while the company, realistically, will indeed live on? No, at the bottom what finally moves you to a precisely wrong action, selling out, is that you can't stand any more pain to your ego over how wrong the stock's decline proves you've been! You cannot allow it to get any worse. You want out, even if in your heart you basically know the stock is cheap.

To be successful in overcoming inertia with utility stocks, do three things:

1. Remember that moves in interest rates will have far more effect on your investment return than the several percent of current yield you are getting. Then act on that knowledge (i.e., sell) when you see signs of a rise in rates.
2. Accept your own imperfection and get on with investment life. Sell when it seems like the thing to do, looking

forward (to capital preservation and the chance to buy back in happily lower later on). Don't look back to the exact top missed, something you can do nothing about.

3. Remember that selling decisions are inherently always more difficult than buying. When you bought, you let the prospect of a gain overcome your fear of loss. Now, at time to sell, make yourself do that again. Deny the strong pull to do nothing because you might be making a mistake. If you'd done that at buying time, you'd still be stuck in a bank money market account.

## Getting Out of Your False Comfort Zone

Much too often, people confuse a stock with its underlying company. This is very likely in utility investing, for a subtle reason. So be on high alert to avoid this pitfall.

Psychologically, we tend to project from a general understanding to a specific situation, even when that is not necessarily logical. All humans need groceries, we demand health care, and we wear clothing. These are provided by grocery stores, by drug companies and hospitals, and by clothing manufacturers. A false comfort zone ensnares us when we carelessly assume that any company in those industries whose stock we have bought is going to be fine because it provides an essential product or service. The more basic or essential the economic activity involved, the more easily we fall into this mental trap. "How can a supermarket chain go belly up?" we ask. Well, it can, or it could slip into prolonged or permanent marginal operation, barely making ends meet, providing investors no profits but continuing to offer jobs and to help serve its neighborhood's grocery needs. Any company in a basically necessary business can go far downhill for any of multiple reasons. Regardless of whether the business actually dies, its investors can lose 100 percent or painfully close to that. Involvement in an essential part of the economic chain does not ensure success. Assuming it does will ensnare you in the false-comfort-zone trap.

Utility stock investors are highly prone to this pothole. Utility stocks, by their nature, virtually scream at us: "How could they turn the lights (or the telephone, or gas, or water) off? Of course they can't. And, unlike the supermarket, they don't even have any competition!" (Well, at least until recently they didn't.) The flaw in reasoning then follows immediately: "Therefore my utility stock is safe."

Oh, really? What if there is a nuclear plant accident? Or if the water turns out to be contaminated and a million people sue in a class action? Or if cellular phones actually do emit dangerous waves? Or if a gas line explodes and a court rules the company was negligent in maintenance? Or if an elected or appointed public utility board bows to consumers' demands for unrealistically low rates? Some company will still provide each one of the four essential utility services for everyone. It probably will continue to be the one in which you bought stock. But it might not do so at a revenue level allowing enough profit to maintain its physical plant assets and pay you those dividends you started out expecting. Your company might survive, but marginal survival is not why you bought stock. Borderline profitability means you'd be better off in bonds, where at least the income stream probably will continue, and where they owe you the arrears if they suspend. A reduced or omitted common dividend will never be made good.

Ah, yes: dividends. A history of nearly 100 years of uninterrupted quarterly dividends certainly would tend to give you some reassurance about your utility stock, wouldn't it? Ask the folks who owned Consolidated Edison in April 1974 when its directors ended just such a string of regular dividend checks because of exploding rises in oil prices due to the OPEC embargo. Their income was cut off and their stock price dropped to worse than half in short order. The plain truth about any company's dividends is that they are not guaranteed. They do not happen automatically. They are voted on by the directors every three months. When push comes to shove and cash is short, no long tradition of consecutive dividends means anything. Banks don't cash dividend checks on reputation or tradition.

It is not my intention here to pick on Con Ed. They simply were the first utility in the modern era to omit their dividend. In the ensuing two-plus decades, a few dozen other boards have found it necessary to follow suit. Over a hundred utility companies have at least reduced dividends. I'll repeat: Dividends, unlike interest, are not guaranteed. Investors all too readily fall into a false comfort zone by saying they can't turn off the essen-

tial utility service, and they've always treated me well by paying (even sometimes raising) my dividends in the past.

Following are four tips that can help you overcome this trap
of false comfort with utilities' stocks:

1. Separate in your mind the essential nature of the company's utility service-provision role from any hope of
   guaranteed safety in its stock. The essential industry is
   not the company, is not the guarantee of any profit, is not
   the assurance of a dividend check, is no assurance the
   stock price will not fall (especially when interest rates
   rise, as discussed earlier).
2. Accept that the past is absolutely no guarantee of the
   future. Utility companies are only starting to face the
   brave new world of competition. They remain regulated
   by the dead hand of government, and move slowly if for
   no other reasons than their own size and corporate cultures. Therefore, think of every quarterly board meeting
   as one in which the dividend is a debatable item. If the
   company is still rolling along nicely, dividends will be
   maintained or possibly raised slightly about once a year.
   But if there are signs of trouble, don't consider a dividend sacrosanct. It is neither that nor automatic.
   Dividends are not promised, as interest is.
3. Don't let a utility company's staid, solid image lull you
   into forgetting that change is ever faster. This means
   your company must keep improving just to keep from
   falling backward. Competition and technology are
   greater problems for your once "safe" utility stock than
   years ago. Be vigilant for disturbing trends: Lean toward
   selling, since it is better to be safe than sorry.
4. Follow dividend signals coming from the boardroom
   without any rationalizing. Dividend policy, and especially any change in it, is the closest legal thing to inside
   information you can have. Directors know what is happening, even if they do not give details by press release!
   *Never buy or hold a utility stock whose dividend is not being
   raised.* How long would you stay with an employer
   whose highest executives decree they cannot afford to
   give you a raise? You'd conclude the ship was leaking

and scurry to jump ashore. When the percentage growth rate of dividends is reduced (say from 4 percent to 2 percent a year, for example), sell the stock and go elsewhere. That is a first sign of trouble. Don't ask for the details; directors meant exactly what they did.

## Resist the Lure of High-Yield Utilities

Here, as with bonds, more is not better. So when a stockbroker calls and suggests you should buy a utility stock that yields more than the average, or more than several others you can easily find in your newspaper, run the other way! High yield is a trap (review Strategy 16). Securities markets are relatively efficient. Brokerage research departments, big bank and insurance companies' investment staffs, well over 100 utility mutual funds, and several rating agencies spend a lot of time studying utility companies' securities. These stocks' prices move fairly smoothly, driven mainly by demanded yields.

Yields are the market's way of assigning a risk premium to each utility stock (or each corporate bond). A utility company whose outlook is rosy will probably be raising its dividend consistently by several percent annually. A company that is fairly healthy but growing slower will raise its dividend more gradually, maybe about 1 percent or 2 percent a year. Companies in trouble will have stopped raising their dividends. The market efficiently assigns low yields to the safest companies and requires high yields of the most risky. Astute investors charge risk premiums when buying stocks whose dividends will not increase and might even be cut or omitted. It works just like an insurance company that charges higher life insurance premiums for hang-glider enthusiasts who smoke and overeat. Actually, because so many individual investors mistakenly search out high yields, prices for higher-risk utility stocks are higher (and their yields lower) than they really should be to account fully for the chances of adverse dividend news. So the market is not perfectly efficient.

No individual investor is likely to be more informed than the collective mind of the market that is assigning prices (based on yield premiums) to utility stocks. When you buy high yield, you're taking on high risk, whether you understand it or admit it or not. Resist all temptation to buy high yield. Just as your overall portfolio, even in retirement, should not be 100 percent invested for income, here too you should aim for solid total return rather than current cash return alone. A rising dividend rate will drive a rising stock price as long as interest rates are not working against you. To the extent you do not fully anticipate a rise in interest rates, a rising dividend in a utility stock will buffer your losses. A utility failing to raise its dividend provides no such help. And it should raise your worry level. Sooner or later, most high yielders will bite you!

Overcoming the temptation and accompanying danger of high-yield utility stocks takes no elaborate or sophisticated formula. All it takes is discipline. Invest in utilities for total return, insisting on a rising and not decelerating dividend rate. When offered or tempted by high yield, follow the elegant advice of former First Lady Nancy Reagan: Just say no.

## Two Other Areas of Concern

Two other problems bedevil utility investors. While they're not as badly hazardous as those discussed above, they do merit mention.

### Dividend Reinvestment Plans

Virtually all utility companies offer dividend reinvestment plans (DRIPs). These are convenient ways of reinvesting and thereby of compounding your income from these stocks. Participation tends to foster a habit of loyalty to the company, and that is a subtle trap. You may be holding your original block of shares in certificate form while accumulating other "book entry" shares via the DRIP. Therefore, when it comes time to sell a utility, you must issue two sale instructions—to the broker and the DRIP. Have a letter to the DRIP typed and ready simply to date and mail. Don't let the DRIP itself act like a loyalty anchor. Actually, it would be a good idea to go down to a nominal position, such as one or five shares, so you could later reenter the stock via the DRIP at zero or minimal commission. But do this only if your sale is driven purely by the interest rate cycle. If the company violates the dividend rule laid out above, it is indicating corporate illness and you should sell 100 percent of your position. DRIPs are wonderful devices unless they subtly trick you into staying with a troubled company!

### Utility Mutual Funds

Utility mutual funds had nearly $21 billion of U.S. investors' dollars in early 1997, even after some loss of value and some heavy redemptions in the 1993–1996 period. I personally am not favorably disposed toward utility funds, and I'm sorry if that offends my friends in the funds business or brokerage community. Mutual funds are manufactured financial products. The bigger the fund, the more management fee the adviser earns. There is nothing wrong with that, any more than when selling more fries raises profits at Wendy's. But what sells utility mutual funds most readily is not good for investors' safety or asset growth. High yield sells utility and bond mutual fund shares, making them more tempting. Extra salt on fries makes them taste better, too.

The points made about high-dividend yields from individual utility stocks apply equally to utility mutual funds. Read the prospectus carefully before you invest money. My personal advice as a former utility stock analyst is to reject those utility funds that say their investment objective is high current income. Consider only those that specifically emphasize total return including growth of capital driven by rising dividends. (As a matter of disclosure, I must remind you that I am employed by Lipper Analytical Services, Inc., the leading firm that tracks and ranks funds' performance and expenses. As a matter of policy, the firm makes no recommendations as to purchases and sales of individual funds.) There are very few such utility funds.

The vast majority of utility funds represent a clearly suboptimal compromise: They look for high yield in all the wrong places (stocks, where income is not guaranteed); and they must seek yield because that's what sells utility fund shares. I believe an investor is better served, assuming the choice to use mutual funds, by owning a good growth stock fund and, separately, a quality bond fund. Reasons for that point were given late in Strategy 17. A utility fund manager is hostage to trying to serve two masters: the shareholder and the marketing department.

And a utility fund, like any other fund, can suffer from its own success. The more money it attracts, the further down the list of relatively attractive holdings it needs to venture to keep all the cash invested without violating diversification and overconcentration guidelines. You as an individual utility investor can do better by owning just a very few of the most choice situations, determined by their dividend growth rates. And you will save the roughly 1 percent annual expense ratio too.

# Be Smart about REIT Investing

*L*ike public utilities, real estate investment trusts (referred to for short as REITs) are among investors' traditional favorites for income. Not all REITs are the same, of course: some involve greater risks than others. This chapter points out risky situations to avoid and desirable elements to seek when investing in REITs. And as with utilities, while REITs may be attractive they do not alone constitute a complete investment portfolio.

### REITs in Brief

Real estate investment trusts enjoy a special place in the U.S. tax system. Due to Internal Revenue Code Sections 856–858, REITs, like mutual funds, are considered conduits for income and therefore escape the double-taxation burden borne by investors in other types of corporations. If a trust complies with all applicable regulations, it qualifies for REIT tax treatment and therefore pays no federal income tax. Principal requirements are that a REIT cannot participate in the operation of any business or trade, must have at least 75 percent of its assets in and income derived from real estate (through lending, leasing, or a combination), and must distribute at least 95 percent of its otherwise definable taxable income to shareowners each year. Also, if any person or entity, or combination of related persons or entities, beneficially owns more than 9.9 percent of any given REIT's shares, that REIT loses conduit status.

There are two basic kinds of REITs: those that own real estate and others that lend on real estate. Some REITs contain a mix of investments, but most are virtually or 100 percent devoted to one style. Real estate investment trusts can invest in a variety of property types: residential apartment complexes, office buildings, shopping malls, health care facilities, and storage units are most common. Major risks faced by REITs are geographic concentration, specific tax and economic exposures, and tenant quality. Some REITs, particularly in the go-go days of the 1970s, engaged in one or both of these financially risky practices: using too much leverage or "borrowing short to invest long." Would-be REIT investors must look at all such risks.

## As Usual, High Yield Should Be Your Red Flag

Once again, being contrarian and counterintuitive will serve you well when investing in real estate investment trusts. Strong total return rather than high cash yield should guide your choices.

Three sorts of high yield should signal prudent investors to look elsewhere. These are high yields relative to the competition, simply unbelievable yields, and guaranteed distributions.

### High Yields Relative to the Competition

As mentioned in Strategies 16 and 18, investment markets are relatively efficient. Much professional analytical and press energy is devoted to examining and understanding publicly traded companies' finances and business prospects. Thus, prices of securities in these companies reflect the combined judgment of knowledgeable participants in the marketplace. Just as insurance companies demand higher premiums for taking on higher risks, informed REIT investors charge a risk premium for investing in less-secure situations than for comfortable ventures. So, when you see two REITs providing significantly differing cash yields, expect to find that the higher yielder carries more risk. You must choose whether to accept that added risk, not grab blindly for it.

One way to assess what other investors perceive has been happening is to check relative returns over time. You can easily track such information from readily available sources such as the *Value Line Investment Survey.* Its section on REITs provides names of comparable entities; you can track their relative yields over time. Select about ten (deliberately including a variety of asset types) and construct an average of yields for several years. Your results might look like the table shown in Figure 19.1.

**FIGURE 19.1**   Average Yields for REIT R and REIT I

| | **Cash Yield in Percent** | | | | |
|---|---|---|---|---|---|
| **Yield** | **Current** | **1 Year Ago** | **2 Years Ago** | **3 Years Ago** | **4 Years Ago** |
| Average | 6.5 | 7.5 | 8.0 | 8.0 | 7.5 |
| REIT R | 8.4 | 8.5 | 8.5 | 8.2 | 7.7 |
| REIT I | 6.8 | 8.0 | 9.0 | 9.2 | 9.0 |

REIT R formerly traded at a yield just slightly above average some three or four years ago. But lately, even as overall yields have fluctuated up and then down in line with general interest rates, investors have perceived increasing relative risk in REIT R and therefore will pay less for a dollar of its income stream (i.e., they will demand a higher yield) in relation to those of the rest of your average. Investors believe REIT R has become more risky and so now demand a higher yield relative to other available alternatives. Note that even though its yield has declined slightly from a year ago to the current time (8.5 percent to 8.4 percent), REIT R has moved to a significantly higher yield relative to the average, whose cash yield has recently fallen (with overall interest rates) from 7.5 percent to 6.5 percent in our example. That is a signal of probable trouble for REIT R: perhaps a dividend cut is likely. (By contrast, REIT I has been improving in the minds of investors. Formerly it traded at 1.5 percent above the average (9 percent against 7.5 percent) but that gap has narrowed over time.)

Changes in relative yield should not be ignored. They provide a significant signal that investors have seen a shift in relative risk. Before investing in a REIT with an above-average yield, you should do a lot of reading to discover why that yield difference exists, particularly if it's been growing. If you cannot find any apparent reason, assume that you have missed what others know; do not assume the market is wrong. Once you have identified the point of perceived quality difference, you can then evaluate intelligently whether you think the marginally higher yield is worth the added risk to your capital in case things actually do go sour. How much might dividends be cut if a major tenant or borrower defaults; how big a drop in share price would that probably cause? Is the risk of that percentage loss worth the extra cash yield you now receive? In sum, high and especially rising relative yield should be a strong caution signal prompting serious study before you invest. It should not be an absolute bar to buying, but should make you highly circumspect.

### Unbelievably High Yields

If yields are too good to be true, they probably will soon prove untrue. In examining REITs, you can use the same sort of logic you would in considering bonds or utility stocks—if a company's current cash yield is grossly higher than those for most other stocks in the industry, it is because informed opinion in the marketplace expects a dividend cut or omission, probably soon. While this rule-of-thumb figure differs at times, consider it definitely a bright red flag if yield on one member of a REIT peer group is anywhere around 50 percent higher than that for the average. In a high-yield period, this would mean perhaps 15 percent against 10 percent; in a low-inflation, low-yield climate, maybe 9 percent against 6 percent. One tipoff to possible trouble, as discussed regarding utility stocks, is the failure of trustees to raise the distribution rate in the latest year. Such information is easily found in the *Value Line Investment Survey*, the S&P *Monthly Stock Guide*, or in S&P's *Individual Stock Reports* (often called "tear sheets").

### Guaranteed Distribution

One situation (although not the only one!) leading to an unbelievably high yield can be the existence of a guaranteed distribution rate. High yield certainly sells more individual investors than does lower yield. Because high yield is a magnet for investor dollars, many income-related public offerings are structured with a temptingly high initial annual distribution guaranteed for some specific period, often three to five years. That high initial yield entices investors to buy, making the public offering work. Sometimes the distribution rate is backed for a period by a related company. (If there is a distribution guarantee, a good test is whether the guarantor company owns a significant part of the REIT; if not, suspect trouble ahead.) Typically the quoted annual payment stream is not supported by current earnings, and in some cases not even by cash flow or "funds from operations" as REIT accounting calls it. Investors are being paid back part of their money annually in that guarantee period. Thereafter, all bets are off—except the odds-on bet that distributions will be slashed or wiped out, driving the stock's price to plummet.

As advised in Strategy 16, never buy a common stock with a temporarily guaranteed distribution, either in the IPO or in the aftermarket. Instead, wait until the guarantee period has passed; then, see what amount directors declare when they have full discretion. That rate is more likely a sustainable payout on which you can price the security more reliably. Where you see a very high yield on a few-years-old REIT, do not buy the stock until you have obtained and thoroughly read the company's initial offering prospectus, its latest annual report, and Form 10-K! Look for discussion of the distribution rate and whether there was (or still is) a period of guaranteed minimum payments. A telltale clue here is failure to raise dividends gradually from year to year. A flat dividend is a big warning that you must look deep beneath the surface.

## Equity versus Debt REITs

Investors seeking attractive financial rewards are better served in the long term by owning equities (stocks) than debt securities. But such logic does not necessarily carry over into the much more illiquid area of real estate, particularly when inflation rates are low. Here, being a lender rather than landlord may work best. If and when real estate appreciates strongly in value (as it did during the high-inflation period of 1966–1981) one can do exceptionally well as an owner. But in economic circumstances such as those of the late 1990s and into the 21st century, inflation will not be as likely to paper over and bail out shaky investments.

Suppose one or more tenants of a shopping center fail to renew their leases. The owner (possibly an equity REIT in which you hold shares) faces a major reduction of monthly cash inflow and must scramble (marketing and remodeling costs will jump) to secure replacement tenants. A lender holding a mortgage note on the shopping center property (perhaps a bank, but maybe as easily a debt REIT in which you own shares) is in a considerably stronger position. It is protected because the owner (that landlord now scrambling to fill those empty spaces) will lose the entire shopping center by defaulting on the mortgage. The borrower must do whatever possible to avoid foreclosure, while tenants have a much easier path out of trouble by just closing up and walking away. They've pledged no valuable property as security. That is why I prefer the greater security of a REIT portfolio that is either entirely or heavily concentrated in mortgage loans over one that is primarily a landlord. A possible exception would occur where a REIT has one single major tenant that guarantees the local leases. As examples, two REITs in that situation are Universal Health REIT (Universal Health Services, the hospital operator, is the guarantor and a shareholder) and U.S. Restaurants (whose largest tenant is the Burger King system). In such situations, if the guarantor is considerably larger than the leases it is backing and considerably larger than the REIT, a useful level of comfort is provided.

## Other Sources of Risk in REITs

Other principal sources of risks in REITs are lack of diversity in terms of geography or business type, tenant quality, and financial leverage.

### Lack of Diversity

Like a securities portfolio, a REIT property list involves lower risk if diversified than if concentrated. California, the real estate rocket of the 1970s and 1980s, saw its success fizzle out in the early 1990s as unemployment rose, property prices fell, and foreclosures mounted. In a shocking historical reversal, many families left there "for better opportunities elsewhere." A REIT concentrated in a single state or region could be quite vulnerable in such circumstances. That was illustrated in the energy belt's local depression that lasted for much of the 1980s.

Here, incidentally, were two more illustrations of useful comfort-zone test (what feels awfully comfortable may be awfully late!). Just about the time when everyone was convinced that oil would go to $70 a barrel or more, and when everyone in the country "knew" that California real estate goes nowhere but up, those bubbles burst. No economic trend lasts forever. The more familiar the story through recent repetition, the more you need to question it before investing late in a cycle. Because real estate cycles are generally long and exceed single recession/expansion phases, this comfort-zone trap is especially crucial to avoid when investing in REITs. The fact that REITs are usually financially leveraged makes careful examination even more important.

Another good type of diversification is by property type. A REIT owning a mix of apartment buildings, shopping malls, medical centers, parking lots, and office buildings is at lower risk than one specializing in one type of realty. Suppose tax treatment of residential properties changes, resulting in a building boom that gluts the market and reduces rental rates. Suppose another OPEC embargo or a major rise in energy taxes discourages driving to vacation hotels. Major tax changes or regulatory shifts can harshly affect an entire industry or class of realty assets, making a concentrated REIT a secondary but certain victim. In such cases, REIT portfolios concentrated in the affected property type would be severely endangered.

Here again, I find one positive exception, although it probably will not last forever. The U.S. population is aging, and life spans are being extended by medical science. This implies a rising number of nursing-home beds will be needed. Much has already been done to control costs of medical care, and certificate-of-need rules in place for about 20 years act as a brake on reckless overbuilding of hospitals. For these reasons, at least for the next generation or so, health care REITs that are diversified in terms of geography, tenants, and facility type seem attractive. Acute and old-age care will be in demand. If one assumes our capitalist system will remain in force, property rights will be protected and economically fair rents will be paid on such essential facilities as hospitals, outpatient surgery centers, and nursing homes, which will pay their mortgages. Even in the fading potential circumstance of nationally controlled health care, someone must pay the rent. Had the 1993 Clinton health care plan been enacted, incomes of drug companies and of doctors would have been in more danger than rents on health care buildings. Indeed, one could argue that "health care for all" would have meant higher occupancy rates and therefore even stronger coverage of REITs' rent and mortgage revenues.

### Tenant Quality

Tenant quality bears examination. A trailer park arguably carries more risk than a high-end apartment complex. A major shopping mall whose anchor tenant is Sears or Wal-Mart (a national corporation with a credit rating at risk standing behind the lease even if one local store should close) is a better bet than a strip mall whose only tenants are local small business owners. At the other end of the spectrum, too much of even a seemingly good thing could pose a risk. One high-quality tenant for many facilities (a hospital chain, for example) can pose a danger, particularly in a highly regulated or heavily leveraged industry. Suppose the hospital chain expands too fast on debt financing, or suffers a care-quality or bogus-billings scandal, or relies too much on Medicaid clients. A one-tenant or one-debtor REIT could sink with its related party.

### Financial Leverage

No matter what type of property a REIT may own, whether diversified or not, overly aggressive financing is a very real risk. So much in the investment world, surprisingly, is counterintuitive. For example, the seeds of future losses are usually sown in situations where risk seems low: in businesses that have been highly successful, and late in economic expansion cycles when prosperity is greatest. In these environments, corporate leaders become confident and so do their lenders. Memories of past difficulties are overshadowed by visions of greater profits to be gained from further good times.

REITs can undertake two major types of financial risk: overleveraging, and borrowing short to invest long. Both are easily detected in quarterly or annual financial statements.

**Overleveraging.**    Here, investors should examine historical ratios and look for recent deviation, and look at peers' ratios. Overleveraging is a REIT manager deciding to add more debt to gain a higher net percentage return on the base of assets owned by shareholders. This trap is usually fallen into late in an economic cycle; few investors have the courage to take on added leverage at the bottom of a recession. The press release or annual report will speak of "taking advantage of new and expanded opportunities" via added borrowings; the debt/equity ratio on the newest balance sheet will be higher than in any recent year. The REIT will be setting itself up for a fall when the next downturn occurs. No trustees will be able to see ahead and forecast exactly what that next calamity will be, or of course they would not presently support taking on extra risk from added debt. Just because the coast looks clear now (that comfort-zone idea again!) doesn't mean added debt will prove a safe undertaking. If your REIT is among the later ones in its group to take this step, odds are even higher that the cycle is already aging and that a fall will come soon.

**Borrow short/invest long.**    Real estate is a long-lived and illiquid asset. If it is to be financed (as it usually is), it must be carried with a long-term loan. Temptations to borrow short term are very alluring. Short-term interest rates are usually lower than longer-term rates. That difference makes the spread between gross income (rent to be received) and carrying cost (interest, or total annual payments) wider than if one borrows at a higher, long-term rate. Short rates are usually most depressed around the low point of an economic cycle. Borrowing short then usually entails the risk that when permanent replacement financing is eventually to be done, rates will have moved higher in an expanding or more inflationary economy. In a worst-case scenario, no financing might be available at all (a tight-money period) or will be available, but only at such high rates that the property now loses money for its owner.

The most insidiously dangerous form of short-term financing is that involving variable rates, such as those tied to prime or LIBOR. Here interest rates are initially very low but there may be no cap on eventual interest cost. Here is one more area where common sense derived as an intelligent consumer has easy application in investing. We all know people who refinanced their homes (or purchased new ones) in 1993 at wonderfully low rates through adjustable-rate loans; they probably used their extra borrowing power from those low monthly payments to borrow more than they otherwise would have. When the rate-reset dates arrived, they suffered payment shock as their monthly mortgage bills jumped by $300 or $500. You may have considered such a loan. If you took one, you were gambling on rates staying low or going lower (or on your income rising sharply to cover the risk). Rejecting such a loan option despite its low starting rate, you made a safer, longer-horizon choice against borrow short/invest long.

Impose on a REIT an expectation that it will be similarly sensible, forgoing the bait of a near-term addition to profits to avoid major problems from narrowed long-term margins or a credit crunch later. Borrow-short/invest-long danger is easily visible on a REIT's balance sheet. Find the schedule of maturities of loans payable in the footnotes; look for total short-term debt (including lines of credit) significantly above past years' ratios. Unless your REIT has already purchased a loan commitment for long-term financing, effectively locking in its future cost, you should be concerned. That fact would also be in the footnotes.

## Signs of Good Health in REITs

There are several similarities between utility and REIT investing. Investors have long been cautious about investing in utility stocks whose dividend payout ratios (dividends as a percentage of earnings) are high. That caution applies as well in the REIT field, but here what is "high" is considerably different. Payout ratios at or exceeding 100 percent of reported earnings are common and in many cases are not dangerous. Why? Reported earnings are figured after a noncash accounting entry for depreciation has already been subtracted. Therefore cash available for distribution to holders (or "funds from operations," FFO) is actually more than reported earnings per share. You should avoid REITs that pay out 100 percent or more of FFO, since that means they are neglecting maintenance.

It is not realistic to prescribe a specific ratio of dividends to either earnings or cash flow that is safe for all REITs, since circumstances vary considerably. Instead, fall back on a simple but highly reliable test: dividend growth. As discussed earlier regarding utilities, dividends are a choice made consciously and after due deliberation by informed trustees. If they are raising dividends gradually each year, that is a good sign. Absence of growth, or a slowdown in growth, is legal inside information and you should never ignore it. Management may say dividend growth has temporarily been shelved in favor of other business priorities. The bottom line, however, is that the press of such other needs is now more serious than in past years when trustees had enough confidence to raise dividends. To translate, risk has risen. Common sense will tell you to sell and go elsewhere without delay. Your single best sign of continued good REIT health is a rising distribution rate.

# STRATEGY *20*

# Embrace Some Esoterica: Partnerships and Convertibles

$O$nly active short-term traders should even consider such exotic items and commodities, options, futures, and various new-age derivatives. Books devoted entirely to those subjects are available; we will not cover them here. Two somewhat complex investment media that should be understood by serious individual investors are limited partnerships and convertibles securities.

## Limited Partnerships

Most investors instinctively glaze over when partnerships are mentioned. Virtually all institutional investors avoid them due to the tax complexities involved in reporting to their investors. Such systematic nonparticipation by a significant constituency should alert you to the potential that herein lies an undervalued asset class. While being shunned or ignored does not automatically make all limited partnerships (LPs for short) bargains, the field is worth understanding and study.

A partnership is a nonincorporated entity involving more than a single owner engaged in business. The Internal Revenue Code provides special taxation rules for partnerships. While a corporation is taxed at the corporate level and any dividends are then taxed again when received by shareholders, a partnership does not pay income taxes at the entity level; it passes its income or losses directly to its partner-owners, who then include those items in their tax returns. In the 1970s and 1980s, a burgeoning industry of lawyers and underwriters started packaging almost every conceivable kind of business activity as partnerships and selling them to investors. Until some changes in the tax code occurred (mostly in 1986), LPs were created mainly as tax shelters—certain businesses (especially oil and mineral exploration, cattle feeding, and movie production) generated major paper losses while the partners' actual financial exposure was limited contractually. Under more restrictive current tax legislation, traded LPs starting in 1998 will be limited to real estate and energy.

Many investors remember the occasional scandals involving partnerships in past decades and reflexively refuse to become involved. Even those who are better informed about today's legitimate LP investment opportunities know that partnership participation makes for a more complex and sometimes-delayed tax return. Because large numbers of investors turn off regarding LPs, some are priced in the aftermarkets at relatively inefficient or bargain prices. This makes them interesting for those willing to do some homework and to file moderately more complex tax returns. (Virtually all publicly traded LPs supply not only the required K-1 forms but also diagrams or charts indicating the schedule and line on which each specific item of income, deduction, and credit should appear; following these directions is a detailed but not particularly difficult task.)

Where are the interesting LP investment opportunities? Mainly in energy and pipelines. Look for real for-profit economic activity rather than purported tax sheltering. Pipelines generate fairly predictable revenue and profit streams and their heavy asset requirements provide depreciation deductions that enhance cash flow. Absence of tax at the entity level provides for potentially attractive yields. Some investors in the retirement phase can arrange their finances as to keep themselves in the 15 percent federal income tax bracket; here an income-generating LP investment effectively is taxed at less than half the normal corporate rate, adding to net return. The absence of institutional buyers/holders in LPs artificially lowers their trading prices, again enhancing yield for those willing to undertake the tax reporting required.

### Caveats

There are five possible pitfalls to owning LPs:

1. You definitely should consult a tax specialist about possible implications for you. The more complex your other financial affairs (write-offs, etc.), and especially the higher your income level, the greater the chance that an innocent LP investment may cause more tax problems than it is worth. Complex partnerships, such as those involved in coal bed methane extraction, are most prone to creating such situations.
2. Again, after consulting with tax experts, be careful about owning an LP inside an IRA or similar tax-deferred account. Your income from an LP is measured not by the cash distributions you receive but by the net profit it generates for tax reporting purposes. This amount is unknown until after the LP's fiscal year ends. Your IRA can run afoul of the unrelated business taxable income (UBTI) rules, which are designed to limit direct participation in a business. To pay the UBTI tax, an IRA would effectively be making a premature disbursement, and you know the penalties and complexities that implies.
3. Future changes in tax laws could have negative consequences on market valuations of partnerships you buy under prior rules. It has happened in the past. Realistically, the energy industry has fairly strong clout in Washington and is unlikely to be devastated unless an extremely antibusiness Congress and President coexist.
4. Make sure you are not buying an item with a temporarily guaranteed cash income stream about to float free to its truly sustainable level. Some LPs were originally marketed with such features. Ask for the original prospectus.

5.  I would advise against investing in some of the presently popular subsidized housing deals that do not trade in the aftermarket. I offer this advice in the interest of always knowing what you own and what it is presently worth. Many produce very attractive returns, but these violate one of my major rules for safety by not being quoted daily in the media. What you cannot see you cannot be as sure of!

## Convertible Securities

Convertible securities are considerably less complex than partnerships and involve none of the same tax complexities. Not a huge amount of publicly traded convertible securities exists, and therefore these are not widely followed by Wall Street analysts (who tend to focus on items that are traded in huge amounts by institutional investors). So, here again, convertibles potentially represent a moderately inefficiently valued niche in the investing landscape that can be profitably exploited.

A convertible security is a corporate bond or preferred stock that the owner (investor) can choose either to hold in its original form or, once and forever, to convert into common shares. Corporations issue convertibles because they effectively provide the chance to issue equity today at the hoped-for higher prices of tomorrow. Also, interest and dividend rates demanded on convertibles tend to be lower than on straight senior obligations, making the issuer's cost of capital lower.

Here is how a convertible security typically is structured. A convertible debenture (bond) is issued in multiples of $1,000, like any nonconvertible would be. Suppose the company's common stock is trading at around $20 per share, and the company is growing and eventually will need to issue more stock to expand its asset base. The company might sell convertible debt allowing holders the right, at their sole option, to exchange or "convert" the bonds into shares of common stock. In our example, the conversion ratio might be set at 40 shares per $1,000 bond. The immediate value of a bond if converted would be only $800 (40 shares trading at $20 each), but if the stock performs well over several years, the bond probably would become more valuable for its conversion feature than for its income stream alone.

Suppose that the stock does appreciate, say by 50 percent to $30 per share. Each $1,000 bond can be converted into 40 shares, and so would trade at not less than $1,200 (quoted as a bond, at 120 or 120 percent of face). Since the bonds also continue to pay interest as long as an investor holds them as bonds, they would actually trade at a small premium above their "conversion value" of $1,200—unless the dividends receivable on 40 shares of common were higher than the interest on the bond itself.

The investor in a convertible security has two possible ways of making money: the bonds earn interest and they also offer an upside "kicker" because they can be converted at the holder's option into common stock, and that common stock might rise in value. So the lender (bondholder) has the usual rights of a bond but has a possibility of becoming more wealthy if the company's stock does well. Is this a free ride, a bonanza investors should never pass up? Not really. The owner of a convertible security gets only part of the appreciation in the common stock, if any; the bond or preferred stock also pays a lower income stream than it would if no kicker were built in. In the example above, a 50 percent rise in common share price resulted in only a 20 percent appreciation for the bonds, although from that price upward the relative appreciation would be virtually the same in percentage terms. Also, because convertibles are usually subordinated in the order of creditor rights, they are not very strong acting if the company's fortunes turn sour. Their relatively low coupon or dividend rates offer only partial downside price protection in a bad bond or stock market.

What price is right for a convertible? Generally, if there actually is conversion value above the face value, experts say not to pay a premium of more than three years' net difference in income. You figure the interest from holding the bond, subtract the dividends (if any) you'd get if you converted into stock, and pay no more than three times that amount in addition to the actual current conversion value. If this sounds a bit complex, consult the *Value Line Convertibles and Warrants Survey*, which tracks all the details on convertible bonds and preferred shares.

One added point: While it is true that conversion is done only at the choice of the owner, a company issuing convertible securities can sometimes "force conversion." Thus, while the owner has ultimate power to decide, in certain circumstances only one decision would make sense, namely to convert. Suppose the stock in the earlier example traded at $40 per share. Each bond would be worth $1,600 if converted. If the issuing company calls the bonds for redemption at $1,000 each, all rational holders would convert rather than allow the company to pay them just $1,000. Thus, the company forces the bonds to become stock; former bondholders must then decide whether to remain stockholders or to sell out and reinvest their assets elsewhere.

Convertibles in many cases are fairly small issues and therefore do not always trade in highly liquid markets. Therefore many investors prefer participating via mutual funds. Another very interesting opportunity is to invest in convertibles through any of the roughly ten closed-end funds specializing in this area. Such funds typically trade at discounts to their actual net asset values, offering greater yield and possibly more upside potential. Closed-end convertible securities funds are listed in *Barron's* and the *Wall Street Journal* every Monday as part of the special table of closed-end funds showing net asset value, market price, and premium or discount. In a market that feels high but still "wants to go up," convertibles provide an interesting combination of moderate upside and somewhat limited downside price potentials; closed-ends trading at a discount add more value to that formula.

# STRATEGY *21*

# Create the Right Asset Mix Now

*F*ar too many investors have an asset mix that was unplanned, one having evolved as an accidental byproduct of individual past investment purchases that have since gained or lost value at widely varying rates. This strategy shows the importance of planned asset allocation, suggests examining all assets of various types as part of a single integrated whole, and discusses the high importance of diversification across asset classes. Strategy 22 will extend the concepts raised here by suggesting a gradually shifting asset-mix path for the balance of your lifetime.

## Consider the Overall Picture

When most people think of investment assets, they focus on the most common types: bank accounts, stocks, bonds, mutual funds, and perhaps their retirement plan. It is important to look at all your assets and consider them together as an overall mix or blend. Are you holding a fair-sized block of stock (or do you have options) in the company you work for? Do you have a trust fund that either throws off fixed income currently or perhaps will provide a lump-sum payout at some future date? Do you own income-producing real estate or hold a mortgage note paying you interest or principal? Do you have entitlement to a pension income stream that may be fixed or slightly indexed after starting at some future date? These and other kinds of assets ought to be factored in as parts of your "investments" picture. Your stocks, bonds, and mutual funds are not the entire list of components.

Figure 21.1 compares assets other than your conventional stock/bond/funds portfolio.

---

**FIGURE 21.1**   "Unconventional" Assets

---

| Type | Equivalent To | Implications and Other Considerations |
|---|---|---|
| Stock/Options in Your Employer | Specialty equity fund: one industry | Reduce or avoid other stocks/funds in same field. |
| Trust Fund Income | Bonds paying interest, no principal payback | Lighten bond fund position in favor of equities. |
| Pension Entitlement, Social Security; Fixed Annuities | Bonds paying interest, never any principal | Lighten fixed income investments in favor of more equities. |
| Mortgage Receivable | Bonds (if has a balloon); otherwise limited-life trust | Deemphasize bonds and other real estate. |
| Income-Producing Realty | Undiversified REIT or REIT fund; a mature dividend-paying stock | Avoid heavy REIT exposure; lighten bonds and blue chips to favor aggressive equities. |
| Raw Land | Inflation-hedge assets | Reduce/avoid gold and resources stocks/funds. |
| Lump Sum in Future (Trust/Estate) | Bonds maturing or called | Use proceeds to rebalance total asset mix at time received. |
| 401(k) or Similar Investment Plan (Includes IRA and Keogh) | Stocks/bonds/funds in which invested (note any company stock!) | Tax shelter for bond income; no tax losses for stock losses. |
| Variable Annuities | Stocks/bonds/funds as invested | See 401(k), above. |

---

Suppose, for example, that you work for a biotechnology company in which you own stock or have some stock options or appreciation rights, and that your spouse works for a government agency and will eventually be entitled to a fixed pension. Your situation is highly dependent on the success of your company, so you would be best to avoid owning other biotech stocks or a health care sector fund. Your choice of growth funds might lean a bit more toward the conservative than average and would avoid funds that are overly weighted in biotechnology stocks. Your spouse's pension in effect gives you a synthetic triple-A bond that will always pay income but will never mature and cannot be sold for its principal. Your bond holdings should therefore be tilted away from governments and toward world income and domestic high-yield funds; your stock/bond mix should count the capitalized value of the pension income stream as a bond and then lean more heavily towards stocks and stock funds than another family would.

It would be a good idea, perhaps this very weekend before you can forget, to make a list of all your assets (including future income-stream entitlements such as pensions) just as if you were doing the planning that precedes drawing up a will. Value each asset and classify it according to its debt versus equity character. You may be surprised to discover your overall balance is fairly heavily weighted toward fixed income (particularly when Social Security is included). As a result, you may need to shift securities holdings in your personal account and/or in retirement plans away from bonds and toward equities.

## Why You Must Practice Diversification

Clearly, it is risky to place all your dollars into any single asset class. Risk, used here, means both uncertainty as to result as well as possibility of loss. While preretirement asset building through growth rather than income-now investing is clearly the path to potential maximum wealth, it also involves higher risk during any short time period. Diversifying across major asset classes, or types of mutual funds if that's your chosen route, therefore makes sense. Not all asset classes see prices rising or falling at the same time or at the same rate. For example, gold or related stocks would rise with faster inflation while bond prices would fall. While Strategies 4 and 5 made a case against a maximum-safety/income-now approach, the other end of the spectrum is also too extreme, even for young investors. The three big dangers of a maximum-aggressive growth path are that:

1. *You might panic and quit at just the wrong time.* This could happen during some sudden painful "crash" or late in one of the grinding bear markets that come along every so many years.
2. *A major bear market or even a quick crash might occur at just the wrong time.* The "wrong time" could be shortly before or exactly when you plan to retire and convert your portfolio from a growth vehicle into a generator of spendable income. If this should happen, your principal would be impaired badly, adversely affecting your financial quality of life in retirement by cutting your income stream.
3. *When you begin investing, particularly if a large single sum is involved, you might enter in an already excessively high market.* The temptation to "go for the gusto" is of course highest after a long bull market in stocks has lowered fear of losses.

Reducing uncertainty of overall return is important for more than financial reasons. Investor psychology, unless managed with strong and deliberate discipline, can confound the best-laid plans. Greed and especially fear can take hold, and these powerful emotional drivers have their greatest chances of causing trouble at exactly those times when the price for any mistake is largest. Greed becomes strongest primarily at and near tops, when staying aggressive for too long carries maximum potential for loss. Fear grips you, predictably, at bottoms. Just when the greatest risk to your capital's future growth lies in not holding and not buying stocks, is when you are most tempted to dump everything and retreat to lick your wounds in the comfort zone of CDs and money market accounts.

So, diversifying your holdings across asset classes produces two important benefits: It moderates fluctuation in your overall wealth, making it less likely you'll panic near a bottom; and it limits the amount of assets exposed to your possibly making the mistake of bailing out at just the wrong time. Diversification means your chances of making a big mistake (typically at a bottom, but also at a top) with all you have will be greatly reduced.

## How Much Diversification Is Required?

Just "x percent in stocks and y percent in bonds" (while better than 100 percent in either one) is too simple a rule to do the risk-narrowing job well. The prior discussion has used the concepts of "stocks versus bonds" or "equity versus debt" as shorthand references to proper asset mix; in reality, more than two broad asset classes are involved. Not only is there often a divergence between bond and stock trends, there also are differences over time among small-company shares, big-company stocks, and international equities (let alone the stock markets of individual countries). That's why diversifying across multiple asset classes is important: It produces true risk reduction, the process of narrowing the uncertainty as to your overall outcome.

A minimum mix should include the following:

- Domestic growth stocks (or growth and income, depending on your age)
- Domestic bond funds
- International equities
- Resources, precious metals, or both
- "Cash" or a money market fund, to park reserves so you can take advantage of occasional substantial declines in other asset class prices—and as a buffer against life's emergencies

Some would further require separating the domestic equity portion into both small-company stocks and large-cap stocks. Others would argue that a single, very broadly diversified equity mutual fund can include the necessary weighting of resources exposure, making that added specialty area unnecessary as a separate item. Some advisers counsel a mix of value and growth approaches as well.

## Should You Do It with Stocks or with Funds?

Academics debate how many individual stocks, even if carefully chosen so as to have low correlation with each other, make up a sufficiently diversified list. Between eight and twenty seems to be the dominant range of conclusions. Any given mutual fund is by its nature already diversified, in some cases holding up to several hundred stocks (or bonds). Early in life, when your investment portfolio may be limited in size, both a need to diversify and the imperative of limiting transactions costs argue for using funds rather than individual stocks. Later on, as your investible asset pool grows and your expertise (and perhaps available study time) increases, buying and selling individual stocks as well will make more sense. Unless you devote extensive time and become somewhat expert, some areas of investing appear best left to professional managers and cry out for the diversification that mutual funds provide. These include investing overseas (how can you know all you should?); high-yield or "junk" bonds (do you dare take the risk of choosing just one or two?); and perhaps high technology and small companies (how can you do all the initial and ongoing research needed to handle this area really well?).

While it might take over a dozen well-mixed individual stocks to truly diversify, a smaller number of funds can do the job. For example, you should choose one each of these types or "investment objectives": domestic stocks (maybe two, separated into small and large companies), international stocks, bonds, money markets, and possibly resources. While it is important to cover all these major asset classes, it is of much less importance and sometimes little true value to own more than one or two funds pursuing a common objective. Especially in the cases of large funds owning hundreds of stocks, two or more same-objective funds will simply own for you many of the same stocks twice. So diversify across fund types before adding more funds that have the same investment objective.

Fortunately, it is relatively easy and convenient to diversify appropriately all within a single major mutual fund family, since many of them offer full menus of every imaginable type of fund. Many fewer fund groups offer specialty sector funds, and you may have strong interest or confidence in a certain sector or industry and wish to own such a fund. The rapid development of funds supermarkets (Schwab, Fidelity, Jack White, Scudder, and others) has now made it easy to choose, and move money among, funds offered by several management companies in a single-account format.

The bottom line is that you will need a minimum of between four and six funds in order to diversify properly. One that investors often skip, due to some combination of caution and lack of familiarity, is an international stock fund. Two-thirds of all stock value is in companies listed outside the United States, and most of the rest of the world will grow faster in the future; both of these facts are major arguments for overseas diversification. Global funds allow their portfolio managers to invest anywhere in the world including U.S. stocks. Owning such a fund takes away your control over asset mix, however. That is because your fund's manager might decide to make a significant reallocation of domestic versus overseas stocks, effectively changing your personal balance. My opinion is that you can control your diversification more deliberately by owning separate domestic and international (but not global) stock funds.

This strategy has made the case for diversification and names the minimum mix of asset classes one should own. We have not yet specified particular percentages of assets that you should assign to any asset type; the reason is that this will vary depending on your age and risk-taking propensity. The next strategy elaborates on that aspect in some detail.

# STRATEGY 22

# Adjust Your Mix Going Forward

*I*nvesting is a lifelong activity, not a single set of stress-inducing choices made once and forever. An investment program cannot prudently be put on automatic pilot. As you move through different stages in life, not only will you be adding assets to your portfolio while income exceeds spending but also your investment mix should shift gradually toward lower risk.

Your need to invest for higher returns gradually diminishes as you mature toward a retirement target date. This is fortunate, since your emotional and financial tolerance for those wider swings that accompany higher average returns also will decline as you age. Having noted that fortunate coincidence, just how much should you allocate to each kind of asset at various stages in life? Many financial planners recommend the "rule of 100" as an answer to this allocation problem. That rule says:

> Hold in common stocks a percentage of your assets equal to 100 less your age in years.

Following this rule, a person aged 30 would hold 70 percent in stocks and 30 percent in bonds and money market instruments. At age 65, his blend would be 35 percent stocks and 65 percent in income-producing items. Even at age 80, the rule would still call for 20 percent in equities. The reason for this suggested formula, which points toward a more aggressive stance than most people envision, was covered in Strategies 4 and 5: Inflation requires that you achieve a high overall rate of return to protect your assets' buying power. Inflation cannot be counted upon to end conveniently when you'd like, namely when you retire. Inflation will require that your spendable income must increase, or else you must live off principal or do so even faster than planned.

## The Rule of 105

I believe your greatest financial risk may prove to be a chance that you outlive your assets, which means outlasting a source of comfortable income. The two major threats making this a very significant possibility are inflation, already discussed in detail, and improvements in medical science. What if heart disease and cancer are conquered? We'll live much longer on average than now projected; the Social Security deficit will explode; and our need for financial self-reliance will become pivotal. Make no mistake about it: In the 21st century, there will not be enough younger people still generating Social Security and other tax revenues to support the expanded cohort of retired citizens who will want no less than current and preferably increased benefits. Specifics of the eventually adopted solution are impossible to predict, but here is its broad shape: Those best situated will be people who've made provision for their own needs rather than hoping against reality that they can count on a mainly free ride.

This unnerving prospect, that rising longevity could bankrupt your retirement finances, prompts me to recommend that you adopt my proposed "rule of 105":

Hold in common stocks a percentage of your assets equal to 105 less your age in years.

Taking this approach will produce significantly more total assets because the mix will at all times have been heavier (versus by the rule of 100) in those categories (domestic and international stocks) that produce higher total returns over time. As shown in the tables provided in Strategies 1 and 4 a little extra average return means a lot more in total spending power over a lifetime. A move to the rule of 105 is most important for women, because they live longer, making the one-size-fits-all rule of 100 less adequate for their needs than for men's. For an example of how the rule of 105 plays out over a lifetime, see Figure 22.1.

**FIGURE 22.1**    Rule of 105, Lifetime Target Bond/Equity Mix

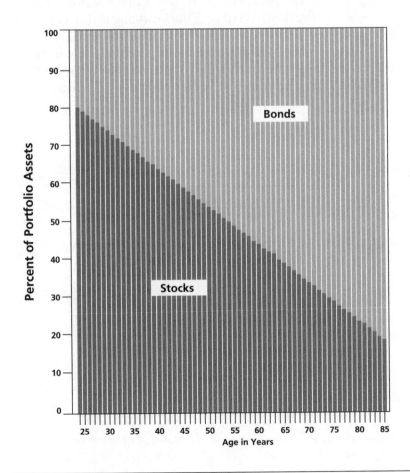

## Asset Allocation for a Lifetime

Just saying *stocks* and *bonds* is inadequate, as noted briefly in Strategy 21. Greater detail as to asset allocation is necessary, since those two broad headings encompass many variations. Figure 22.1 features a proposed model for shifting your asset mix over time.

Using either the rule of 105 or the allocation table in Figure 22.2 should not be a slavish exercise. You would unnecessarily spend commission dollars to rebalance your total assets once annually, as driven by your age, or to precise percentages. But these models should serve as guidelines. My best-results suggested approach would be to track your asset allocation annually and to prune back in the volatile areas when they reach several percentage points above the desired curve. This kind of shifting can have you taking actions every few years (perhaps each three to five), and will reduce risk by pulling some dollars off the table in high-volatility asset classes when they have most recently risen nicely for a few years (an example would be reducing U.S. stocks after

**FIGURE 22.2**   Suggested Percentage Asset Allocation over a Lifetime

| Asset Class | Life Stage | | | | | |
|---|---|---|---|---|---|---|
| | Young Age (20–35) | High Earning Age (35–50) | Glide-Path Age (50–65) | EarlyAge (65) | Middle Age (75) | LateAge (80+) |
| MM | 10% | 10% | 10% | 20% | 20% | 30% |
| HQB | 10 | 10 | 20 | 20 | 40 | 50 |
| G&I | 20 | 20 | 20 | 20 | 30 | 20 |
| GS | 30 | 20 | 10 | 10 | 0 | 0 |
| INT | 30 | 30 | 20 | 10 | 0 | 0 |
| LQB | 0 | 10 | 20 | 20 | 10 | 0 |

Key:  MM: Money market funds
      HQB: High-quality bonds: U.S. government, municipal, investment-grade corporates
      G&I: Growth-and-income stocks and such funds
       GS: Growth stocks, including small-caps, or such funds
      INT: International (non-U.S.) equities, or such funds
      LQB: Lower-quality bonds: medium-quality corporates, high-yield bonds; perhaps
           some foreign bonds

1996 and shifting into lagging overseas shares or funds). Occasional switching will allow bull markets to run in your favor and will keep you from having to make switches every single year, although you definitely should examine the situation annually. Doing that examination in November (perhaps over the long Thanksgiving weekend) or early December will allow you to make moves with current-year tax effects in mind. In paring back stocks, for example, you could sell a loser this December or postpone taking a gain until next January. Such timing could be especially valuable if the new year will see you retire and fall into a lower tax bracket.

### An Example

Let's look at what would happen to a reasonably well-balanced portfolio over a five-year window as its separate asset classes perform at different return rates, and then see how that portfolio's owner might then shift assets in response. In Figure 22.3, the investor is 40 years old at the beginning, and has a $100,000 asset pool allocated into five classes, considering personal accounts, an IRA, and a 401(k) plan combined.

By the time she turns 45, her portfolio, enjoying the benefits of a U.S. stock market growing faster than its historical rate of 11 percent, and feeling little effect from low inflation, has increased at just over an 11 percent average rate and now stands at $168,800. For the sake of simplicity, assume no asset additions due to the burden of current tuition payments. The portfolio now needs rebalancing both because of differing recent growth rates and to reduce the equity component from 65 percent to 60 percent due to the passage of five years.

Note that the suggested sales are shown in round-dollar rather than precise terms. The new (60 percent) mix of equities is slightly more heavily weighted to international and to resources than was the 65 percent total five years earlier; those sectors gained less in the recent past. Since there's just a whiff of higher inflation, bonds were slighted a bit in favor of money market funds. In general, what has recently done quite well is pared back and the laggard classes added to, thus reestablishing her desired balance. This approach has the desired effect of contrarian selection, in which it is assumed future improvement will occur in depressed sectors and recently strong areas will soon pause.

**FIGURE 22.3**  Example of an Investor's Asset Mix at Ages 40 and 45

|  | US Eq | Int Eq | Nat Res | LT Bds | MMFs |
|---|---|---|---|---|---|
| **At Age 40** |  |  |  |  |  |
| Funds* | $40 | $20 | $5 | $25 | $10 |
| Five-Year Growth Rate/Year† | 15 | 13 | 3 | 6 | 4 |
| **At Age 45** |  |  |  |  |  |
| Value | 80.5 | 36.8 | 5.8 | 33.5 | 12.2 |
| Percent Allocated | 47.7 | 21.8 | 3.4 | 19.8 | 7.2 |
| Desired Percent | 37 | 18 | 5 | 30 | 10 |
| Desired Value Now* | 62.5 | 30.4 | 8.4 | 50.6 | 16.9 |
| Approximate Sales | 18 | 6 |  |  |  |
| Approximate Additions |  |  | 3 | 16 | 5 |
| New Values | 62.5 | 30.8 | 8.8 | 49.5 | 17.2 |

* All values in figure are in $1,000 increments.
† Effective average growth rates are shown, net of interim fluctuations. No asset class is likely to appreciate at any constant rate. High volatility of annual returns lowers net results below the mathematically expected average return—a loss effect that increases with volatility. For example, a 10 percent gain and 10 percent loss (in either order) produce not breakeven but a 1 percent loss; a 20 percent gain and 20 percent loss result in a 4 percent net setback.

Key: US Eq = U.S. equities (includes large and small caps)
Int Eq = International (non-U.S.) equities
Nat Res = Natural resources (gold, energy; such funds)
LT Bds = Long-term bonds (government, lesser high yield)
MMFs = Money market funds

## Never Abandon Diversification

Unless you have a very cool disposition and have fervently adopted contrarian principles, the markets will occasionally make you greedy, fearful, or frustrated. For example, if international stocks go virtually nowhere for three years running, you'll be tempted to abandon that "boring" arena and chase domestic stocks that have been doing very well (greed). Or if stocks or bonds fall considerably for many months or a year, you will feel a tug in the gut urging a retreat to money market funds. Resist those impulses! In Figure 22.4, you can see the best, worst, and average returns for 1986–1995 in the major asset classes. Figure 22.5 presents the range of annual percent returns for 1986–1995 in the major asset classes.

This was a period of generally declining interest rates and included only one worldwide recessionary phase rather than the two more commonly observed in ten years on average. U.S. stocks outran their historical norms by over 4 percent per year. Returns for 1996 were excluded from this figure because they would bias the results further above historical norms.

No one is consistently able to predict the relative movements in multiple asset classes, so trying to do so will cause frustration. You probably can achieve slightly above-average results by adding to asset classes that have lagged for two years running and taking money off the table after two years of outsized gains. You will surely lose by following the recently hot trends. The gradual and occasional rebalancing described earlier automatically provides periodic discipline and contrarian selection at the margin.

## Increased Attention Required Near Retirement Age

Capturing fortuitous gains and avoiding the risk of giving them back increase as you near retirement. The two reasons for this need are that you will have fewer years to hope for any recouping of losses and that your working years provide the last chance to add new assets to the pot—another means of replacing losses or shortfalls. In addition, you will face one or more possibly major decisions regarding your retirement or profit-sharing plan assets when you retire. Timing might not be ideal, and could well be out of your control.

If stocks are down when you turn 65, it will take great courage to let your equity assets rise and recover rather than freeze or reduce your equity percentage to gain greater income and feel less at risk. For this reason, it would be best if you start reallocating every other year at about age 56 and then each year from 61 onward. That way, you will capture any outsized gains in domestic or international stocks and put some into less volatile asset classes right away. You will have more pain over

**FIGURE 22.4**  Ten-Year History of Variations in Returns, 1986–1995

|  | **Best** | **Average** | **Worst** |
|---|---|---|---|
| U.S. Stocks | 38 | 14.9 | −3 |
| International Stocks | 70 | 14.0 | −23 |
| International Bonds | 35 | 13.7 | −3 |
| U.S. Bonds | 27 | 11.3 | −6 |
| 90-Day T-Bills* | 8 | 5.7 | 3 |
| Diversified Mix† | 29 | 12.4 | 1 |

\* Approximate proxy for money market funds
† Equal starting amounts in all five asset classes annually

giving back or losing a given percentage than the pleasure you'd add by winning an equal amount. Your mode will be taking pleasant gains if they show up but generally tapering your risk as first priority.

Tax considerations will become more important as your first year of retirement approaches. Say you are 64 and plan retirement a year later. If stocks zoom, you would do better to sell a growth mutual fund in your IRA account or 401(k) plan (where tax on the gain will be deferred until years in which you make withdrawals) than to sell a solid long-term growth stock that probably will not lose much until you retire and then take the gain while in a lower bracket. You would want to take any taxable securities' losses before retiring rather than the year after, to increase the value (bracket) of the write-off in tax-dollar terms.

**FIGURE 22.5**  Ranks of Asset Class Performance

| | 85 | 86 | 87 | 88 | 89 | 90 | 91 | 92 | 93 | 94 | 95 | 96 | Avg |
|---|---|---|---|---|---|---|---|---|---|---|---|---|---|
| U.S. Government Bond Funds | 4 | 5 | 6 | 5 | 4 | 1 | 3 | 3 | 5 | 5 | 3 | 6 | 4.16 |
| Gold Funds | 6 | 2 | 1 | 6 | 1 | 6 | 6 | 6 | 1 | 6 | 6 | 5 | 4.33 |
| Growth Funds | 2 | 3 | 4 | 2 | 2 | 3 | 2 | 2 | 4 | 3 | 1 | 1 | 2.41 |
| High-Yield Bond Funds | 3 | 4 | 5 | 3 | 6 | 4 | 1 | 1 | 3 | 4 | 2 | 3 | 3.25 |
| International Equity Funds | 1 | 1 | 2 | 1 | 3 | 5 | 4 | 5 | 2 | 2 | 4 | 2 | 2.66 |
| Money Market Funds | 5 | 6 | 3 | 4 | 5 | 2 | 5 | 4 | 6 | 1 | 5 | 4 | 4.16 |

# Consider These Simplification Options

*M*any people, especially those who are not fully comfortable with mathematics or who don't actually enjoy financial activities, would vote for maximum simplicity if given a chance. That desire to have someone else, presumably an expert, "do it" is a major reason mutual funds passed $4 trillion in assets around mid-1997. This strategy presents three fast-growing fund phenomena aimed at further simplification of investing for those so inclined.

## Index Funds

An index fund seeks to replicate the performance of a recognized security price index. Some academics, including Burton Malkiel, believe that stock price movements are mainly random by nature and so attempts to "beat the market" by individual or even by professional portfolio managers are doomed to failure. The fact that about 70 percent of mutual fund portfolios fail on average over the long run to exceed their market benchmarks is cited as supporting evidence for this theory, which is known as the random-walk or efficient-markets theory. Index funds appeal to those who believe the theory or who see the performance evidence and willingly give up trying to outperform broad market averages.

As of spring 1997, some $475 billion, or over 15 percent of total fund assets, was invested in funds tracking the S&P 500. These portfolios buy and hold all, or nearly all, of the 500 index component stocks in proportion to their capitalization weightings in that index. Stocks held by index funds are sold only if shareholder redemptions force some liquidation, or if an index component is replaced, which happens a handful of times a year, usually driven mainly by mergers.

Index funds present some appealing characteristics to various investors. For trustees of union or company pension or profit-sharing plans or for those who select funds to be available in an employer's 401(k) plan, index funds are safe choices. Safe not in the sense of preventing losses, but in the sense of being unassailable as wrong. An index fund can't beat the market, but more importantly will not prove an unluckily chosen laggard. Because these funds are managed mechanically, mainly under guidance of computer tracking programs, expensive star portfolio-manager talent and industry analyst salaries are eliminated. Therefore, index fund advisory fees are very low. Custodial, marketing, legal, and other costs are also modest, so overall expense ratios are far below those of actively managed growth and income funds. This cost savings directly aids performance and greatly appeals to small and large investors alike. Another subtle appeal of the index fund is that one need not worry about a star portfolio manager defecting, retiring, or losing his or her touch: Management is impersonal, passive, mechanical.

A top appeal of index funds is their so-called tax efficiency. They've historically allowed asset buildup over time with only extremely minor taxes being paid along the way. Mutual funds must pay shareholders at least 98 percent of net realized long-term capital gains as distributions every year (or, if they retain the gains, pay federal income tax at a corporate rate above that of holders). But since index funds do scant selling of portfolio stocks (their annual turnover ratios typically are in the low single digits), they realize only small gains and so create little tax liability each year until a fundholder chooses to sell.

You might find it attractive from a tax-control standpoint, and in terms of total return, to invest some of your personal taxable portfolio money in index funds. When it gets large enough to justify holding individual stocks, your IRA or Keogh plan can do so tax-efficiently because any gains on those stocks' sale would be tax-deferred (but realized losses would produce no current-year write-offs). Likewise, dividend- and interest-producing stocks, bonds, and funds are more tax-advantageously held in an IRA, Keogh, or 401(k) plan. So from a tax viewpoint, index funds might be better used in a taxable account than within a tax-sheltered account.

While S&P 500 index funds are vastly the most popular, many others exist. Some track small-cap stock indices such as the Russell 2000, or other market measures. Still others track various regional or world securities baskets maintained in the Morgan Stanley international indices. Since March 1996 it has been possible to buy separate index-emulating funds, each of which invests in one of 17 countries. These WEBS, or World Equity Benchmark Series, created by Morgan Stanley, trade on the American Stock Exchange. If you're attracted by prospects in Hong Kong, Mexico, or Germany but fear bad luck in picking wrong individual stocks, these overseas index types of vehicles deserve consideration.

One note of caution on index funds: Through mid-1997, their effects had yet to be observed in a bear market. Since an S&P 500-based index fund must own exactly those stocks in proper proportion, it doesn't hold cash reserves to accommodate redemptions. In a prolonged market downturn, if investors burden such funds with unrelenting redemptions, this would force sales of the 500 underlying stocks, which would thus become depressed bargains. A torrent of investor money flowing into index funds in 1996–1997 pushed major market indicators up faster than the broader list of stocks and contributed to an appearance of ongoing market strength. The opposite could occur in a protracted downturn. Remember program trading's effects in 1987? They took a lot of blame for the severity of the October 19 meltdown.

## Funds of Funds

A 1996 change in Securities and Exchange Commission regulations enabled an upsurge in forming and selling so-called funds of funds. True to their names, these mutual funds buy and sell shares in other funds rather than investing in individual stocks or bonds. Funds of funds are controversial: They involve some duplication of costs as each fund layer carries its own expense structure. Regulations of the SEC bar a fund adviser from collecting fees on the duplicated assets when its fund of funds buys shares in another of its in-house funds. But double expenses do apply, and when a fund of funds buys shares of an unaffiliated fund (a Schwab Fund holding some of Baron Asset Fund, for example), both management companies do collect advisory fees on essentially a single asset, namely your investment dollar.

Why would funds of funds exist, given that expense drawback? For the convenience of individual investors who despair of the decision-making and paperwork complexity of diversifying their own portfolios of funds. They want asset allocation or a chance to ride the hot streaks of currently popular portfolio managers, but feel they lack the time or expertise to accomplish it well on their own. Millions of investors have given up on choosing (and then needing to decide whether to sell or continue holding) individual stocks, opting instead for mutual funds' diversification and professional full-time management. In the same way, U.S. investors by mid-1997 were confronted with over 9,500 separate funds available in over 15,000 classes of shares (with differing load and redemption fee structures); that blizzard of choices can feel overwhelming. A fund of funds is a marketeer's answer to this need: Simplify and get all you want in our one fund, they propose.

Broadly diversified asset-allocating funds of funds make most sense from this I-need-help viewpoint. Within prospectus-defined limitations, the portfolio manager invests in a short list of other funds. Perhaps one or two each for large-cap and small-cap growth stocks; value stocks; government bonds; emerging country equities; junk bonds; and foreign high-yield bonds. Typically, no more than some named percentages will be invested in foreign-oriented funds, in bond funds, or particularly in junk bond funds.

Those readers expert in mutual funds might ask, why not just buy a conventional flexible-portfolio or asset-allocation fund and escape that second layer of expenses? The answer lies in two advantages a fund-of-funds portfolio manager has. First, such funds almost always focus on buying no-loads, so they incur no commissions costs when trading. Second and probably more important, a fund of funds can move into or out of an entire asset class in a single stroke, not needing to buy or sell numerous separate stock or bond positions. In effect, a fund of funds gets an easy ride, forcing portfolio managers of those funds it picks to execute many individual buy and sell trades in sometimes treacherous markets.

Here are two examples of how this works. In early 1997, stocks in India, Thailand, and Korea were reeling from scandals and political turmoil. A fund-of-funds portfolio manager could in a single phone call sell her entire XYZ Pacific Region fund position of perhaps several million dollars, forcing that other portfolio manager to liquidate individual stocks in Seoul and Bombay. Or, if small-cap biotechnology stocks suddenly become the rage, a fund-of-funds portfolio manager can make a single fund purchase in Hotstock BioFund and thereby pass on the costs and work of buying individual stocks that are already soaring to the person who manages that fund. If that fund-of-funds manager makes a good and timely call, her shareholders benefit from instantaneous asset repositioning.

Other more narrowly focused funds of funds aim at a single investment objective such as growth or income. These own multiple funds pursuing the same goal. In theory, the fund-of-funds' manager might identify and ride with particular fund managers currently having hot hands. Also, this approach to growth could capture expertise from several managers who practice different investment styles. A single fund of growth funds would own at least one each of small-cap, mid-cap, large-cap, value-oriented, and perhaps world growth funds, blending the returns of all and not missing any style. An income-focused fund of funds would own at least one each of a junk-bond fund; a world bond fund; a U.S. government or mortgage securities fund; a short or intermediate corporate fund; a money market fund; and perhaps at times an emerging-markets debt fund. Again, the hope would be to find the smartest or hottest managers specializing in all different types of bond investing.

In 1996 alone, the number of funds of funds jumped from 26 to 64, and additional names were in the regulatory and marketing pipelines as this was written during 1997. Only time will tell whether investors, often influenced by media articles, will vote for the convenience advantages or the cost disadvantages of funds of funds. But now you understand their pluses and minuses. That the Charles Schwab organization has created three funds of funds (with gradations of aggressiveness) indicates its confidence that many investors find convenience and simplicity attractive. Schwab OneSource, the leading mutual funds supermarket, was launched by the same market research and marketing decision-makers. And hindsight tells us what a smart call that was. For a list of the funds of funds that existed in April 1997, see Figure 23.1.

## Life-Cycle Funds

Another area of recent fast growth and development in mutual funds is the so-called life-cycle or lifestyle fund. This new entry is also designed for one-decision simplicity. As a self-directed, proactive investor who has read more than 20 of this book's strategies (and probably some others) on how to do things in detail for yourself, you may question the need for single-decision funds. Let's take a look before you make your final call.

Life-cycle funds are created to ease decision pain for investors who know their asset mix should change over time, as discussed in the preceding strategy. But when does one do that: annually, every five years, when one market sector seems high, or by mechanical formula? Such problems rob decision-averse people of sleep and boost antacid sales. Enter the bright marketeers with an innovation. Each life-cycle fund is targeted at people of a particular age or who plan to retire in the same year. Many such funds include those year numbers in their names. An ABC 2022 fund, for example, would be for those whose sights are set on retirement in that year.

How do such funds work? The portfolio manager very gradually shifts the mix of investments from more to less aggressive over time. Thirty or 40 years before its target date, a life-cycle fund will hold a large majority of assets in stocks, likely includ-

**FIGURE 23.1** Funds of Funds as of April 1997

| | |
|---|---|
| API TRUST:CAPITAL INCOME | NATIONS LG:IN&GR; INV |
| API TRUST:GROWTH FUND | QUALIVEST:ALLOC AGGR |
| DVSFD INV ST:AGG STR | QUALIVEST:ALLOC BAL |
| DVSFD INV ST:CON STR | QUALIVEST:ALLOC CONSV |
| DVSFD INV ST:MOD STR | QUALIVEST:ALLOC GROWTH |
| FIDELITY FREEDOM 2000 | SCHWAB CAP:ONESRC BAL |
| FIDELITY FREEDOM 2010 | SCHWAB CAP:ONESRC GR |
| FIDELITY FREEDOM 2020 | SCHWAB CAP:ONESRCE INTL |
| FIDELITY FREEDOM 2030 | SEI ASST:DSFD CSV INCM |
| FIDELITY FREEDOM INCOME | SEI ASST:DSFD CSV |
| FIRST AMER STR:AGG GRO | SEI ASST:DSFD GL GRO |
| FIRST AMER STR:GRO & INC | SEI ASST:DSFD GL MOD |
| FIRST AMER STR:GROWTH | SEI ASST:DSFD GL STK |
| FIRST AMER STR:INCOME | SEI ASST:DSFD MOD GR |
| FUNDMGR:AGGR GRO; FINL | SEI ASST:DSFD US STK |
| FUNDMGR:BOND | SIERRA ASSET:BAL |
| FUNDMGR:GROWTH | SIERRA ASSET:CAP GRO |
| FUNDMGR:GRO&INC | SIERRA ASSET:GROWTH |
| FUNDMGR:MGD T RET | SIERRA ASSET:INCOME |
| GMO:GL (US+) EQ ALL | SIERRA ASSET:VALUE |
| GMO:WORLD EQTY ALL | SM BARNEY CRT:BAL |
| GUARDIAN ASSET ALLOC | SM BARNEY CRT:CONSV |
| INTEGRITY FUND OF FDS | SM BARNEY CRT:GROWTH |
| MARKETVEST:INTL EQUITY | SM BARNEY CRT:HI GRO |
| MARKMAN MULTI:AGGR GRO | SM BARNEY CRT:INCOME |
| MARKMAN MULTI:CONSRV GRO | T ROWE PRICE SPCTRM:GRO |
| MARKMAN MULTI:MOD GRO | T ROWE PRICE SPCTRM:INCM |
| MAXUS LAUREATE FUND | T ROWE PRICE SPCTRM:INTL |
| MERRIMAN:ASSET ALLOC | VANGUARD LFSTR:CONSV GR |
| MERRIMAN:CAP APPREC | VANGUARD LFSTR:GROWTH |
| MERRIMAN:FLEXIBLE BOND | VANGUARD LFSTR:INCOME |
| MERRIMAN:GROWTH & INCOME | VANGUARD LFSTR:MOD GRO |
| MERRIMAN:LVGD GROWTH | VANGUARD LFSTR:STAR |
| MONTGOMERY:GL ASST ALLOC | VANGUARD STAR:TOTAL INTL |
| NATIONS LG:BL GR; INV | WESTON:NEW CENTURY CAP |
| NATIONS LG:GR; PRM A | WESTON:NEW CENTURY I |

Source: Lipper Analytical Services, Inc.

ing some aggressive small-cap positions and a fair representation in overseas markets. Sure, these carry above-average risk and volatility, but in the long haul they should grow faster than average, and this fund does have a few decades to see things work out. In those early years, only a small position in bonds will be held, to provide a degree of overall stability in the fund's value and to generate income to pay current fund expenses. Decades later, in our fund's twilight years, it will have flipped this mix to perhaps 80/20 in favor of fixed income and short-term treasuries. Then meeting the income and value-stability needs of its now-older investors, this fund will have gradually shifted its portfolio over time as its owners have been graying, coming to prefer reduced risk, and needing less exposure to possible home run or strikeout stocks.

Could you accomplish the same thing with individual stocks or with a carefully selected set of funds with varied investment objectives? Yes, of course. And much of this book has been devoted to showing you how. But some people prefer less involvement, finding it very appealing to select a single fund once and for all time, knowing that it intends to age gracefully while they do. This approach has great appeal to those who have difficulty making decisions (especially about when to sell and switch).

Life-cycle funds also might prove to have favorable tax effects. Doing it yourself, you'd own five or six funds to cover all major asset classes; you would periodically sell some of the aggressive ones, redirecting sale proceeds into the more conservative, income-producing funds—after taxes! Each sale probably would trigger capital gains taxes, assuming you make a point to follow contrarian principles and sell what is up and making you feel smart rather than down and temporarily worrying you! Your life-cycle fund manager very gradually shifts portfolio asset mix over time. Presumably, as the unrelenting march of years demands that some stocks be trimmed in favor of more bonds, the manager will prioritize holdings by keeping those with good prospects and shedding ones that have disappointed, possibly even showing paper losses. Thus, that dwindling equity component will consist of a few survivors such as Coca-Cola, Chase Manhattan, General Electric, Intel, McDonald's, and 3M—all with huge unrealized gains. Thus, a life-cycle fund could prove somewhat more tax efficient than a do-it-yourself process of periodically selling some aggressive funds and buying others with more conservative styles. By so doing, you will have in effect cashed in some of the paper gains on those great growth stocks by selling your growth-fund shares at a gain; you'll pay taxes en route sooner than owning and holding a single all-purpose life-cycle fund would force you to.

Be careful not to confuse life-*cycle* funds, described above, with life-*stage* funds, which are designed for multiyear but not lifetime ownership at different times in a person's life. An XYZ Earlylife Fund, for example, would be suitable for those in their 20s and 30s taking risks in pursuit of rapid growth. Such a fund would be merely an aggressive capital-appreciation or global-growth type in disguise, named for a life phase. The XYZ Autumn Fund would be an equity-income or conservatively slanted balanced fund for folks in their mid-50s, again a well-established type of fund living under an assumed (life-stage) name. XYZ's Winterfund, for octogenarians, would hold mainly high-quality government bonds with a small mix of short-term notes and T-bills to stabilize net asset value. Life-stage funds are not bad and are distinct from life-cycle funds, which truly are a new programmed approach to dynamic lifelong asset management.

# Hands Off That Rollover!

*J*ob security isn't what it once was. For that and other reasons, you may find yourself changing employers, probably several times. Each time, you must decide what to do with assets disgorged by your former employer's profit-sharing or 401(k) plan. Properly handling a rollover distribution can be one of your life's most crucial investment actions. Except for a large inheritance, you'll probably never have such a large sum to place with so little preparation. You must be ready for this contingency, because a job-change situation is a fast-moving, busy, and stressful time. Your rollover distribution cannot wait. Tax rules make it one of the few job-switching details imposing an absolute deadline. This strategy explains how to handle a rollover distribution— some dos, several don't-dos, and one absolutely never-do!

### How Do Rollovers Work?

The rules of many organizations' qualified profit-sharing or retirement plans require that when a person leaves a place of employment, that person's vested interest in the plan must be (in some cases, may be) distributed out, ending the relationship. The Internal Revenue Code imposes specific rules governing the timing and handling of such distributions. Of course, regulations may change, so make sure to consult your tax adviser and your old employer's benefits administrators. As of 1997, two key rules governed these so-called rollover distributions:

1. You must be certain that the plan you are leaving does not make a check for any assets payable to you personally. The check must be payable to some successor custodian, that is, an entity acting as a fiduciary for assets in some other qualified plan.
2. The transfer of assets, meaning acceptance of the check and your official enrollment in some successor plan, must be completed within 60 days of your being excluded from the old plan.

If you violate either of these conditions, two very bad things happen: Your entire distribution becomes subject to 20 percent withholding tax, and you'll get a Form 1099 reporting it as taxable income in the year received. Thus, a substantial chunk of your retirement plan assets will be taxed away. Upcoming pages will give you guidance on what to do when you face a rollover situation.

## Be Prepared and Proactive

Think of a rollover distribution as if it were an inheritance, but one available only on very strict conditions: that you put the money into a properly qualified retirement plan and invest it with reasonable care within 60 days. If such a legacy were coming your way, but strictly with those strings attached, surely you would follow the rules and do what you must to meet those conditions.

Do this now, even if there's no hint you might be leaving your job soon: Dust off your employee-benefits manual and look up your plan's rules. In many cases, you'll be able to find the applicable rules in your profit-sharing or retirement-plan guidebook. The key section will have a caption such as

"Distributions upon Separation Prior to Retirement Eligibility Date." If all key details are not clear, visit your personnel department and ask a "what if" question. Take good notes and accept any and all explanatory handouts they might offer. Most important to understand is the time sequence associated with any distribution. Many plans make disbursements exactly so many days or months after an employee leaves the company; some others give an employee some power to choose his or her preferred date of distribution within a defined time window. How does your plan handle these situations? The answer tells when your 60-day clock will start running.

## Self-Management versus Your New Employer's Plan

You might have two choices, although many people find they have only one path to follow. One definitely available choice will be to establish a rollover IRA account (which cannot be mingled with any contributory $2,000-a-year type of IRA account!). To open such an account, instruct the old plan to send a check for your vested assets to that IRA's designated custodian. If you move straight into a job with another organization offering a qualified plan, you might have a second choice: rolling the old-plan assets into the new-company plan. You should ask about those details as part of your interview process or your in-processing orientation. The key questions are, first, will the new plan accept assets poured over from another plan? And second, can you accomplish that transfer in a time window that satisfies both plans' rules and stays inside the 60-day IRS rule?

Even if given an option to roll into a new employer's plan, I personally would not do so. I would create a rollover IRA instead. My two reasons are diversification (having less than all my retirement plan assets managed under the same rules of one plan) and greater control and freedom. You may find your new plan offers a relatively limited range of investment options (perhaps no international stock fund, for example) or, even more important, limits when and how often you can make transfers among your investment choices. Similarly, your old employer's plan, even if it allows you to remain a member, will have such limitations, and they may be tighter for separated beneficiaries. Managing your own rollover IRA account within a large mutual funds family is an easy alternative that will eliminate such limitations. Before choosing my preferred route, however, consult an appropriate expert because taxation and distribution options may differ.

## Choices in Self-Management

Choices for placing a rollover independent of your new employer's plan are wide. You can go to a bank offering IRAs; they will gladly accept your deposits. That will feel safest, but it's a bad choice unless you're very near retirement and have large equity investments elsewhere. Bank accounts fail to provide acceptable growth potential after inflation adjustment. Another choice is to open a self-directed rollover IRA account with a brokerage firm, letting you buy and sell individual stocks and bonds. Many people will find such an arrangement burdens their time, would fear making mistakes in a relatively nondiversified account, would be paralyzed by the pressure of handling "serious money" so directly, or would find commissions too high. Others might be too confident of their stock-picking abilities or would be tempted to take too deep a plunge with a big chunk of assets in one investment, possibly with very unhappy results. These are both strong reasons not to pursue that self-directed choice unless you're a very experienced and cool-headed investor. Thus, the fund-family option seems a likely top choice.

### Dos, Don'ts, and One "Never"

**Never under any circumstances take possession of the rollover funds.**    Taking possession will subject you to taxation and 20 percent withholding tax. Don't yield to temptation by spending all or part of your retirement money on today, while you are still young and have good earning years ahead. Keep that pot of money for its intended purpose—retirement only! And do not let a third of it get taxed away. A corollary is to be sure your transfer to a qualified successor custodian is accomplished within the 60-day limit. That time frame is unbending; get the job done early so you can then relax.

If you're having trouble making an investment decision, choose any large mutual fund family (presumably, one that does not charge loads on your purchases) and for starters put the money into its money market fund, just to get the transfer done on time. (Do not, however, leave assets in that money fund for long or "forget" to finish your decisions; doing so will seriously reduce your long-term rate of return and retirement standard of living!) View this money fund gambit merely as a temporary legal crutch while you make better investment decisions.

**Do some self-educating.** You can do this any time, but it's best to take time before an actual job change triggers urgency. Spend time at your public library; attend some investment lectures or seminars; call or mail for several fund families' retirement kits and some fund prospectuses. Think about what you'd do "if"; as a result, you'll be well prepared in the not-unlikely event that "if" actually becomes "when." Think about diversified asset allocation and identify some mutual fund families that would allow you to accomplish it. The more such thinking you do before you're under a real time gun, the better off you'll be when an actual job change occurs. You'll face plenty of other details and pressures (new colleagues, new commuting routines, maybe real estate and moving details), so working out your retirement-related investment thinking in advance will spread out your overall load, thereby reducing stress.

**Don't jump at the first thing offered you.** If you are changing jobs due to a merger or downsizing, realize that sales professionals are highly aware of such events and use them as major marketing opportunities. You will be targeted by one or several sales campaigns; listen to the advice given and cheerfully accept any booklets and planning checklists offered. But reserve your right to read these over at your leisure. Refuse to be pressured into a quick decision. You surely will feel strong pressure from the sales community, where your retirement asset pool is an inviting source of large commissions. I find it unnecessary and unwise to pay as much as 7 percent or 8 percent of your precious retirement assets up front to someone for "help" in selecting investments that you could as readily and successfully choose with a little self-preparation.

Studies indicate that mutual funds sold with commissions do not systematically perform any better than those bought by consumers without incurring such costs. With more than 9,000 mutual funds available, it's virtually impossible to select the absolutely ideal combination of investments, with or without external guidance. Think of this as a decision about whether to cut someone else in on 7 percent of your eventual retirement nest egg, since commissions you pay now will compound into larger sums later on—sums in your asset pool, or someone else's!

**Never allow the vast array of choices, or your fear of making a suboptimal decision, to paralyze you into indecision.**   This is a very common problem for people, and for understandable reasons discussed in Strategy 10 on perfectionism. Now, since you're dealing with a major pool of assets whose importance is huge (your retirement living standard), those pressures mount. Come to terms with your own human fallibility and get on with your investing life. The unattractive alternative is a dysfunctionally neurotic life of mental and emotional paralysis, indecision, endless self-questioning, and unhappiness.

**Relax—your decisions are not once-for-a-lifetime in nature.** You can choose one mutual fund family now and, if you later decide another is better, simply switch. The whole exercise of changing might cost you in the range of $25 to $75, plus a little paperwork and telephoning time. That's a tiny price in contrast with your alternative cost of failing to make a decision within that unforgiving 60-day window. At a micro level, remember also that choices of individual funds within your fund family need not be permanent. Subject to typical fund-family rules prohibiting multiple switches in any 12-month period, you're free to move from fund to fund at will. Therefore, stop agonizing over each move as if it were a once-forever choice.

**Diversify (no surprise here!).**   You probably should choose a single family, since you will be moving assets from one fund to another and it is much too slow, cumbersome, and costly to keep moving IRA assets between custodians. Many fund families meet basic criteria of offering multiple options and selling on a no-load basis. Over time, expect product-line broadening and mergers of fund families. An example of the latter was the 1996 combination of Twentieth Century (strong in equity funds) and

Benham (focused on fixed-income investing), now called American Century Funds. A good alternative to limiting yourself to a single fund family is Schwab OneSource, a so-called funds supermarket that lets you mix favorite funds across several families in a single IRA account wrapping. This minimizes paperwork. Others are emerging, but Schwab is largest and relatively inexpensive; Fidelity was next largest as of mid-1997.

Figure 24.1 is a list of large mutual fund families, showing their numbers of funds and total fund assets under management as of early 1997. Some phone numbers may change over time; check current ads.

**FIGURE 24.1**   Large Fund Families: Primarily or Purely No-load

| Fund Family | 1/97 Assets ($ bill.) | Phone |
|---|---|---|
| Fidelity | 347.2 | 800-544-8888 |
| Vanguard | 121.4 | 800-662-2739 |
| Wellington | 63.5 | 800-662-2739 |
| T. Rowe Price | 61.8 | 800-225-5132 |
| American Century | 50.7 | 800-531-5575 |
| Charles Schwab | 42.8 | 800-435-4000 |
| Dreyfus | 41.7 | 800-782-6602 |
| Janus | 34.2 | 800-525-3713 |
| Scudder, Stevens & Clark | 22.2 | 800-225-2470 |
| Strong | 17.1 | 800-368-1030 |

# Improve Results
# by Containing
# Controllable Costs

*A*nything worth doing ought to be done as well as possible. No matter how well you allocate assets, whether your timing is excellent or just average, or how much good research you do, you can still better your personal bottom line if you control investing expenses. This strategy covers several areas where investors spend money either needlessly or excessively, and shows ways to improve your results at the margin by saving on such costs.

## A Penny Saved Is Much More

Make a habit of considering all alternatives before executing any decision. Proceeding strictly on the basis of habit may not always be smart. Once an investment move is decided upon, you may have some choices in how to implement it. Which route you choose has implications for net cost, which of course affects your eventual return on capital invested. What you don't spend needlessly is available to invest or to pay off debt. That raises a second point of perspective: Look at each cost (including lost opportunities) not just as spent in today's dollars but instead as a future sum, after the powerful effects of compound interest.

For example, suppose the difference in cost between clever versus lazy-habit execution of a decision is $100. From age 25 to 65, if assuming an average 9 percent return, $100 would compound to $3,141. That sum could then be invested (using interest rates prevailing in 1997) to produce $188 per year in tax-free income while keeping principal intact to pass on to your heirs. That's what $100 is worth, in long-term perspective. With such thinking in mind, let's examine ways to save while executing your investment plans.

## Ways to Capture Cost Savings

The balance of this strategy focuses on seven areas of investing costs that you can turn into savings. What you save can mount up to a great deal after investment over a lifetime. The ideas are covered in roughly declining order of dollars involved and numbers of investor to whom they apply.

### *Mutual Fund Loads*

As this is written, mutual fund ownership has essentially become the investment medium of choice. Millions of investors own funds in a variety of ways: directly, as gifts to children for future education costs, in their IRAs, and through employer-sponsored 401(k) plans. In many such cases, you have a choice of whether to pay a commission (or load, as defined in Strategy 17). About 9,500 different funds (not even counting classes of shares) exist, making seemingly every conceivable investment objective available. Except in a few arcane areas of investing, you can find a no-load fund with an investment objective identical to that of any load fund. Many load-based families of funds allow you to switch your investments to other funds with a common brand name; huge no-load families offer equal flexibility.

Performance will be the main determinant of your eventual wealth, but loads can slice off a major chunk, especially when you view load dollars in future, post-compounding terms. Here's one example: Assuming a 9 percent average return, a 6 percent load on a one-time $25,000 mutual fund purchase, "only" $1,500 now, means $48,000 in principal 40 years later. Who would you prefer to have that $48,000: your family or someone else's? Extensive unbiased studies fail to detect any systematic performance advantage in favor of either load or no-load funds. That's true across various investment objectives, although the more conservative your style (and thus the lower your gross return), the more deeply loads will bite into your net result.

Any commissioned salesperson can show you that a particular fund he or she wants to sell you has outperformed some specific no-load fund or funds. You will never be shown a full comparison of returns of all similar funds for multiple time periods. And even if past performance actually had been systematically better for load funds, that would not guarantee future results. For an investor doing his or her own homework and making intelligent asset-allocation decisions, the fund-selecting help provided by commissioned representatives of fund families, brokerage firms, banks, or life insurance companies is of questionable value. Its cost is considerable.

Of course, that lack of conclusive performance advantage cuts in both directions. Some individual funds that charge loads have had stellar performances. Fidelity's Magellan, with its 3 percent charge, is a premier example. If one had had the foresight to know what high returns it would earn over a long period, the 3 percent charge would have been well worth paying as cost of admission. But hindsight has identified such winners; foresight is clouded, especially as portfolio managers can change tomorrow and style can shift over time, with unpredictable effects on results.

To me, so much useful information is so readily available free or at nominal cost in magazines, the *Wall Street Journal,* and tracking services that paying loads makes sense only in such limited and unusual circumstances as a unique investment approach or an especially outstanding manager. And a second concern is that loads, although already sunk costs, carry undesirable psychological weight when you later consider, for whatever reason, a switch from one fund to another. A load paid years ago might deter you from making a good future reallocation decision.

### Brokerage Commissions

Again, the central question is whether you need assistance, and are willing and able to pay the considerable costs paid to full-service brokerage firms. If you do your own research, maintain your own discipline, and—most important—make your own decisions, you need not pay immensely higher commissions for services you don't use: advice, ideas, and hand-holding. Many investors retain an account with a full-commission house out of habit rather than because their individual registered representative is truly outstanding. If you are in that category, carefully examine brokerage advertisements in *Investors Business Daily* and *Barron's.* Several moderate discounters provide commission-comparison tables listing typical charges by major full-service houses. Compare those top-line charges against the flat rates offered by truly deep discounters. In summer of 1997, more than a dozen firms offered commissions of $15 to $29 per trade regardless of size. Cost differences, particularly if you're a fairly active investor, are simply phenomenal.

Another plus on the side of deep discounters is that most do not solicit business by phoning to offer you current ideas. Review Strategy 6 on being an intelligent buyer rather than a sold-to investor. Freedom from solicitation is potentially quite important. Any idea presented will be packaged to sound highly attractive. A sales professional's skills may persuade you to act in violation of your carefully conceived plans and your existing, deliberately chosen, asset-allocation balance. So, new ideas presented by an intruding force actually can upset your program. This observation applies to cold-calling brokers and those with whom you already do business. Too many sell the idea of the month in the hope it will catch on with some part of their audience.

To be fair, full-service brokerage firms clearly beat their low-cost, no-frills cousins in three areas. Discount brokers generally do not participate in underwriting initial public offerings, and deals to which they do gain access of course are never hot ones. Deep-discount brokers lack facilities to execute transactions in non-U.S. markets, since they focus on cookie-cutter activity that requires low infrastructure cost. Finally, you may well find it difficult to execute a short sale, if you are so inclined, through a deep discounter. Again, they try keeping operations streamlined, so they are unwilling to spend time and effort to borrow shares from another firm if necessary to allow your short sale. If any of these areas is important to you, making selective use of a full-service brokerage firm could be worthwhile.

### Unnecessary Charges for Routine Actions

Many investors make the mistake of paying large fees (usually $50 per transaction) to their brokerage firm or bank for carrying out Treasury bill purchases. Some may do so as a matter of convenience. More likely, most investors pay those fees to brokers and banks because they don't know they can do it themselves—or at least exactly how to do it. Costs of this mistake are extremely high when put in context. If you buy a $10,000, six-month T-bill with a 4 percent yield, your interest earned in six months will be $200. If you pay $50 in service charges to your broker, you've spent 25 percent of your already-low return unnecessarily. Your quoted 4 percent yield becomes 3 percent, which taxes and inflation reduce to below zero.

As an individual, you seldom or never should actually buy T-bills. If you own them, do it in a no-load money-market fund rather than directly. But if you must buy T-bills directly, at least do it without paying a service fee. Your bid can be submitted on a Form TB-12; bids are accepted on a competitive basis (in which the Treasury pays only the interest rate necessary to sell as much debt as it needs to); and on a noncompetitive basis, where you as buyer agree in advance to take the average rate paid on all accepted competitive bids. Auctions of 91-day and 182-day bills occur each Monday and the securities sold are issued on Thursday, to mature 13 and 26 weeks later. If your competitive bid misses the market, you will earn no interest until you make a later, successful bid.

Details of the whole process are available from two excellent sources: One is the book *The Handbook of Treasury Securities,* edited by Frank J. Fabozzi (New York: McGraw Hill, 1986). Another is a booklet titled "Buying Treasury Securities," available from the Federal Reserve Bank of Richmond (P.O. Box 27471, Richmond, VA 23261).

My advice is to avoid this process entirely. Let professionals do it for you and keep your temporary cash in a money market mutual fund. You thus avoid the service charges involved in Treasury auctions using a bank or broker, the uncertainty over whether your competitive bid will succeed, and the inconvenience of converting funds at your bank into good federal form. Money market funds, by contrast, allow you to buy and sell in any dollar amount you choose (rather than only in $5,000 multiples with a $10,000 minimum). Purchases in such funds can be made by telephone and redemptions are made by phone or by writing checks against your account.

### Charges to Transfer and Ship Certificates

Undeniably, there's some comfort in having a physical stock certificate in your hands (or, more properly, in your safe deposit box). An engraved document signed (albeit by machine) by a corporate officer seems more assuring than electronic blips stored in a computer, evidenced only by a monthly brokerage statement saying you do indeed own 500 shares of XYZ WidgetCorp stock. But, like it or not, taking physical delivery is becoming costly and in the near future seems headed for phasing out. Electronic, book-entry ownership will be the norm.

Already, bucking the trend has gotten costly. Major brokerage firms have recently added service charges in the range of $25 to $30 per certificate if you want your stocks and bonds transferred into your name and physically shipped out to you. Some discount firms, in an understandable effort to reduce the labor and telephone expense involved in chasing after late-delivered certificates, now refuse any sale order unless your stock is already in their possession. No matter where your brokerage account is (discounter or full-service firm), you could face a logistics problem if some certificate you have ordered to be delivered out is not yet received. Suppose you need or wish to sell—you'll be unable to make delivery in three days!

Holding your securities in "street name" rather than insisting they be delivered out really is a reasonable and safe choice; it saves you money as well as trips to the safe-deposit vault. Brokerage firms pay insurance premiums to the Securities Investors Protection Corporation (SIPC) to carry $500,000 insurance on the value of securities (and $100,000 on cash) held for your benefit in their name, in case the brokerage firm should fail.

This insurance does not protect anyone against investment loss, but merely against financial failure of the brokerage firm! Chance of failure is quite low, and in fact is lowest for established, profitable, large discounters, as they do not engage in risky position trading for their own accounts, as some full-service firms do.

Soon you will have no choice in the matter, so you might as well start saving these unnecessary costs now. Besides, if you own mutual funds, chances are better than 99 percent that you've seen how book-entry tracking of your holdings works. Almost no one requests physical delivery of fund shares these days. Have you ever lost shares in your fund?

### Multiple Charges for IRA Accounts

Here's a place where lots of investors shoulder excess costs that are not even tax-deductible. IRA accounts with brokerage firms and mutual fund companies often carry annual maintenance fees, and always involve close-out costs when transferred to another custodian. Fortunately, competitive pressures are starting to limit IRA fees, and several marketing organizations have eliminated them entirely. But where IRA fees exist, they can bite at two levels. First, you may pay at the account level to each of several organizations with whom you've invested some of your IRA assets. Second, if you invest your IRA money in mutual funds, you might also pay fees at the per-fund level. With some careful work here, you can sharply reduce and possibly eliminate such fees, which can exert a meaningful drag in early years when your IRA assets are smallest.

Suppose you've put $2,000 into an IRA with a mutual fund family. A not-unusual charge for account maintenance would be on the order of $30. That's 1.5 percent per year to be subtracted from your return on that first-year contribution. Suppose the next year you invest $2,000 with a different mutual fund family. Chances are, their service-charge cash register will jingle to the tune of about $30 annually too. Diversify across a few more fund families and not many years down the road you'll be spending $150 or more annually in duplicated account maintenance fees.

The right solution will feel painful, but is worth pursuing. When you transfer assets from one IRA custodian to another (by closing and moving your IRA account), you'll incur an account-closing charge. Typically it runs roughly twice your annual maintenance fee, around $50 to $75. There's a deterrent power in such pricing, of course. You would do well to identify which fund family offers you the broadest array of fund choices and consolidate your IRA accounts there. Paying the fees to close out and transfer (do it with a personal check rather than letting them be deducted from your IRA assets!) will be painful initially but your reward will be a high return. For example, if you pay a $60 transfer fee rather than your next annual $30 maintenance fee, your added cost of $30 will bear a 100 percent annual return starting the second year, since you'll start saving $30 per year then.

In a similar way, you can avoid multiple charges at the fund level. Suppose that within your $2,000 IRA with a given fund family (e.g., Fidelity) you also get charged a $10 or $12 fee per fund held on a specific anniversary date. If you've diversified your holdings into four funds, that means you will spend an extra $30 to $36 annually (for the three funds after your first one) for that privilege. That's 1.5 percent to 1.8 percent! Here, solutions range from moving all your IRA assets temporarily into just one fund each time the fee anniversary date recurs, to moving your account to another family not imposing such fees. I predict that in time such multiple fee structures will wither under competitive pressure. For now, you must proactively play smart shopper. Ask questions, read the fine print, and vote with your feet.

Mutual fund advisers and administrators earn annual fees as a percentage of the assets in each fund. These costs are assessed on a daily basis and already have reduced the net asset value and therefore your net return from your fund. What justification is there for adding another $10 annual charge to investors wishing to own more than one fund? Account-level charges are more clearly reasonable, because custodians do not work for nothing and because significant paperwork and government reporting are generated for each IRA account. (Some fund companies absorb such charges as an inducement to capture your retirement assets, knowing they'll earn substantial advisory fees over many years as a reward. In time, more will.)

Many fund families offer wide varieties of funds, making them reasonable choices for IRA money. Do some shopping among those with good performance, in search of low or zero fees. Their nearly daily advertisements in major newspapers will make your search fairly easy and very profitable. Remember how large just $100 saved can become over many years after compounding? Now we're talking about not a single $100 saved, but a comparable amount every year from now to retirement time! Over 40 years, again assuming an average 9 percent return, just $100 per year in fees saved would mount up to $33,788; over 20 years, it would be $5,116. These dollars are well worth your taking the time to nail down, I'd say!

### Needless Costs for Small Trades

As in shopping for detergent or canned soup, investing small amounts of money at a time can expose you to higher costs. Early in your investing life, this is a major argument for focusing on no-load mutual funds. Throughout your money-managing career, it's a reason to patronize discount brokers. There are several ways you can reduce or eliminate charges for small transactions, including dividend reinvestment plans and purchases of odd lots.

**Dividend reinvestment plans.**  Commonly referred to as DRIPs, such opportunities are offered by hundreds of publicly traded companies. True to their name, DRIPs allow your dividends to be reinvested automatically. Some such plans charge small fees such as $0.03 or $0.05 per share; others absorb any such costs, and a few even let you buy more shares at a discount. Most reinvestment plans also have optional cash investment features, allowing you to add money to your account in moderate amounts. When it is time to sell, your shares can be disposed of, again, either at a few cents each or at no charge. But you will lack control of timing and therefore selling price!

A growing number of companies now allow investors to make their initial stock purchase through direct investment plans, eliminating the usually onerous minimum commissions most brokerage firms charge. Among the large companies offering such plans are, for example, Texaco and Barnett Banks. These plans then allow dividend reinvestment as well as future voluntary cash contributions. You may find such plans have a couple of downsides: Limit price orders are not acceptable, and your ability to time (and thereby price) your transactions is sharply limited, since such plans make transactions either on the day of receipt or only on arbitrary dates once a month or quarter. Nevertheless, as a foot in the door they provide a no- or low-cost opportunity. A useful newsletter service entirely devoted to this phenomenon is the *Moneypaper*, edited by Vita Nelson (phone 914-381-5400). Some companies' direct investment plans are available only by using this source as a clearinghouse.

**Odd-lot purchases.** Another piece of surprisingly good news is available for odd-lot investors, courtesy of the deep-discount brokerage community. One firm with which I've done business (with total satisfaction) for over a decade offers to buy or sell any odd lot of stock (99 or fewer shares) for a flat $20 commission (plus a $3 postage and handling charge). Since computerized order-handling has eliminated the old odd-lot price differential of 1/8 or 1/4 point, this low commission is a true bargain. That same firm's round-lot minimum commission, as of early 1997, was $30 (plus $3 for postage and handling). Trading in higher-priced individual stocks for just $23 each way can be quite advantageous. If this has appeal, contact Kennedy, Cabot & Company (800-252-0090); they run frequent ads in major daily financial newspapers.

### Expensive Seminars

Some individual registered investment advisers, and many conferences presenting several well-known professionals, offer advice for between a half day and a long weekend, at an exotic destination, for fees ranging from several hundred to a few thousand dollars. As a sophisticated investor, you've learned that there are no magic, secret formulas or systems guaranteeing an easy road to wealth. Often the celebrities conducting or appearing at such seminars make a living from attendance fees and sales of tapes and workbooks at these meetings. For the most part, such meetings with gurus are of more psychological than financial value. You will mingle (although realistically, probably at some distance) with a famous expert; then you will go home and face the real world of investing again on a daily basis. You can learn what you need from well-selected books and perhaps from attending free local invest-ment seminars (remember that the latter are sales opportunities for their speakers). So I generally advise against paying hefty fees to attend the gurus' workshops, which often project an atmosphere like a religious revival meeting of the faithful groupies.

Two highly reputable national educational organizations are major exceptions, since their meetings prohibit pressured selling tactics and offer very useful content. These are the National Association of Investors Corporation (which conducts annual state and national conventions) and the American Association of Individual Investors (whose chapters present interesting speakers monthly and strong annual one-day state and two-day national convention programs). Their addresses are listed in Strategy 30.

## A Subtle but Important Reason Why Saving Is Important

These methods can help you save costs on the margin in your investment program; as you can see your available dollar savings can mount up considerably. But raw saved dollars and cents are not the only reason to pursue low-cost investment options. High transactions costs often set up a mental block that discourages investors from making a justified change in their holdings, particularly relating to sales.

If you believe some reallocation is in order or feel that one cur-rently held stock offers lower future potential than an attractive possible replacement, high commissions can do great damage. If the cost of conducting necessary transactions to effect such switches deters you from taking action, you've allowed a fairly small factor (the difference between high and low brokerage cost, or the difference between a load and no-load fund structure) to get in your way. If your judgment proves correct and that con-templated asset switch indeed works out positively, high switch-ing costs will have given you an excuse to skip a move that might have netted you thousands of dollars in profit or avoided losses. Compound that missed gain over many years to retirement, and you are talking about very serious money—all for want of a lower commission cost. Imagine several foregone profits (or avoidable losses that grew large) over the years: the cost of allowing high commissions to get in the way can be staggering.

Investors generally tend toward being too passive, perhaps overly patient in their asset management. Dead money and dying stocks stay buried in portfolios for years beyond their justified holding periods. Anything that will enable an investor to become more proactive in managing his or her affairs is a plus. Making arrangements to ensure low transactions costs is therefore an important step toward overcoming investment-management inertia.

# Be Tax-Smart, Not Tax-Obsessed

**W**hat the taxing authorities do not get from investors is a good thing in two ways—what you keep remains available to spend or to gain value for the future, and it cannot be spent on trying to control otherwise free people's lives. No one should pay any more in taxes than they legally must. However, investor aversion to taxes can become a counterproductive obsession. This strategy outlines circumstances where too much focus on taxes can actually prove damaging to your investment well-being, then it examines common areas where underawareness or carelessness regarding tax details can cost money needlessly.

## Perpetual Holding Due to Tax Phobia

Refusing to sell an investment when logic dictates a switch is often driven by tax phobia. (For more information on this topic, refer to my book, *It's When You Sell That Counts*, McGraw-Hill, 1997.) A consuming desire to avoid incurring tax liabilities can be triggered by either real or imagined problems. In many cases, refusal to sell "because of the taxes involved" actually is a way of rationalizing a preference for inertia over action.

A variety of factors may cause a subconscious desire not to sell. Some involve an emotional attachment, such as those shares grandfather left to you; those from a company you used to work for; and those stocks that really have treated you pretty well and feel like friends. For many people, selling raises the distasteful stress involved in making financial decisions. For others, coming to closure is difficult. Some feel (in a mildly paranoid way) that as soon as they sell it, a stock will skyrocket. Aversion to the taxes forced by a profitable sale thus is often a smoke screen for such hidden agendas.

Reality checking is the only prescription for this minor and largely unfounded tax phobia. When it is logically time to sell, you may need to think as follows:

> I bought this stock to make a gain. I knew when I bought it that all gains were taxable. The rules have not been changed; taxing gains is not a surprise. I have made a gain; it is time to accept my gain, so, it also is time to pay my tax. I should be happy to have gains on which to pay taxes. The alternative is worse for my wealth and my stress.

But, you ask, what about cases where I have a really major gain? Here, some preventive and palliative measures are available. A sensible approach is to sell off part of the highly profitable position each year. Simultaneously weed out one or two losing stocks to offset the gain entirely or in part. Weeding out losers or bad laggards frees up your capital for better uses. A side benefit is that dumping those troublesome holdings will remove nagging bad feelings and help focus your thinking 100 percent on future results, which are all you can affect at this point.

Even better is to prevent a major tax liability from mounting up by implementing a pay-as-you-go plan: Even with great growth stocks, periodically take moderate profits and pay the resulting taxes. This advice is not widely supported in the investment community, but I believe it cures more problems than it causes. If you own shares in a great company such as McDonald's, Merck, or Coca-Cola for many years, you can build up such a large paper gain that you see it as impossible ever to consider selling. You will mentally calculate how far your stock must fall before selling and paying your tax makes sense. The sheer size of the tax "nut" will make you resistant and resentful. You will have financially and psychologically locked yourself into those stocks forever. The problem is, many great growth stocks eventually become formerly great stocks of mature or troubled companies. A few recent examples include Apple Computer, Polaroid, IBM, and Kmart. People with huge paper gains in those trapped and rationalized themselves into holding all the way down just to avoid paying taxes.

Here is an alternative: Sell those great growth stocks occasionally and pay your taxes. Then go back in. Some would object that the stock may never decline enough to allow paying taxes and commissions and coming out whole. But if this strategy is executed properly, that is seldom actually true. The key is timing your profit-taking sales to periods when you have just enjoyed *unreasonably* rapid paper gains. Such gains are not sustainable. Taking a sale action in such pleasant circumstances requires a contrarian's self-discipline, as discussed in Strategy 9.

What is an unreasonable short-term profit? That is impossible to define precisely, since every stock has its own unique personality, changing volatility of price action, and no perfectly repeating patterns. But when a stock makes a normal year's gain or more in a couple of months or even faster, it is time to give it a rest. When the stock of a 15 percent long-term type growth company (e.g., a McDonald's or Colgate-Palmolive) has just rallied 15 percent or 20 percent, it has gotten ahead of itself. It will come back, or at best will move sideways for a while until it is no longer temporarily overvalued. Your sale should be made when it benefits from that rapid rise. Do not worry about capturing the exact top, since you cannot. But do capture a highly pleasant although unsustainable advance. Then wait for some pullback (again, having no fantasies about buying at the exact bottom) and buy in again. This exercise will accomplish two things: You will learn to sell with more skill and less fear; and you will have raised your cost basis in this great growth stock, reducing chances of some future self-imposed mental lock-in.

Allowing yourself to be mentally locked in due to big tax liability can cause a second, equally serious problem: Once you experience a fairly serious decline, you will refuse to sell for mourning over the paper profits you've given back. As price moves lower, stubbornness and refusal to admit a mistake take over: You could be locked in forever, at least in your own mind!

## Owning Things for Their Supposed Tax Virtues

Successive tax reforms since the 1970s have gradually reduced the chances of falling into this trap. But some areas still exist where investors place too much emphasis on tax savings or deferral and not enough on soundness of the basic concept. Examples include real estate in general, tax-subsidized housing in particular, and resource exploration and development plays.

Tax-oriented investments often involve three serious problems:

1. Their sales pitch excessively focuses an investor on tax consequences rather than underlying investment merit. Short of a 100 percent meltdown in value, the rationalization heard too commonly is, "Ah, yes, but think of all the taxes I'm saving."
2. Tax-oriented investments usually are illiquid by nature and often actually require minimum locked-in holding periods.
3. Tax laws may change. Pressure to eliminate the annual federal budget deficit makes some previously "untouchable" tax preferences potentially vulnerable. With a simple legislative stroke, what originally promised a good overall return because of a significant tax-saving component can become a mediocre or disastrous investment. Then, many other investors will want to exit, depressing market prices of the asset even further.

## Owning Tax-Free Bonds No Matter What

Some investors are so obsessed with paying little or nothing in taxes that they actually will reduce their own net investment returns unnecessarily just to spite or frustrate the tax collector. A major manifestation of this approach is to invest in nothing but municipal bonds. Some years ago I helped with the portfolio of a dear elderly couple who, unfortunately, delighted to the extreme in the idea of paying no income taxes if at all possible.

At that time, good-quality corporate bonds yielded 10 percent and municipal bonds were at 8 percent. Their marginal tax bracket was 15 percent, and they actually were quite close to a zero bracket because of a combination of modest income and heavy medical deductions. Despite many explanations that 10 percent taxable interest less a 15 percent tax yielded 8.5 percent in spendable income while municipal bonds would give them only 8 percent, they were unmovable. "We know, we know. But we'd just rather not give Washington any of our money. Then there's that awful governor of ours, too. . . . "

A single-minded focus on municipal bonds can cause even more problems than that. As detailed in earlier strategies, investing strictly for income will deprive you of capital growth and thus reduce your overall investment return. A dime of tax saved may result in a dollar or more of total gain forgone in the long run.

Incredible as it may sound, some investors actually make the tax-obsessive error of buying municipal bonds in tax-deferred accounts. Doing this in a Keogh or IRA account lowers your wealth twice. First, asset build-up is reduced, since you will earn a lower interest rate compared with that from taxable bonds. Second, you will turn a tax-free income stream into taxable distributions when you make later withdrawals! That's because any kind of gain in value by your account of whatever character (capital growth or dividend/interest income) will be taxed. So putting municipals into a tax-deferred account subjects their income to taxation—the money-losing alchemist's way of turning gold into lead.

As a general rule, don't focus on the tax-saving virtues of municipal bonds unless you are in a 28 percent or higher bracket. At 15 percent, there is no advantage. There are two minor exceptions to this rule:

1. Surprisingly, in a child's college account, after age 14 and as the need to avoid loss becomes paramount as tuition payments approach, municipal bonds can work well by keeping the total income from investments below the annual threshold ($1,300 in 1996) that would jump the child's income into the parent's bracket.
2. As described later in this strategy, sometimes taxes on Social Security benefits can be avoided by switching

from taxable to municipal bonds. This depends on your overall income level and your mix of income sources.

## Places to Be Careful

Just as overemphasis on taxes can be a mistake, ignoring tax consequences can be quite costly. Next we focus on some errors: annual pitfalls; big-picture tax-deferral omissions; and errors after retirement. One caution: Federal and state tax laws change over time, sometimes significantly. This strategy reflects the situation before the 1997 tax legislation was finalized. At least annually, consult your legal or tax professional, or both, for an individualized update.

### Annual Tax Pitfalls to Avoid

**Buying a dividend.** It is a mistake to buy a dividend. That may sound strange or illogical to investors significantly concerned with developing retirement incomes from stocks and mutual funds. But buying a dividend is a common mistake that takes money from your pocket and puts it into the federal and state treasuries not once but twice!

What is meant by "buying a dividend"? This is what Wall Street calls the practice of acquiring an income-producing stock just before its quarterly ex-dividend date rather than just afterward. The ex-dividend date is that trading day when the seller gets to receive one last dividend payment and therefore on which the buyer acquires that stock without (thus, *ex*) any right to receive its upcoming dividend. Here's a sequence of how a company's quarterly dividend might be declared and paid:

| | |
|---|---|
| Board of Directors meets and declares $0.75 per share | January 23 |
| "Record date" is established as | February 6 |
| This means the "ex-dividend" date is | February 3 |
| Dividend is actually paid on | March 10 |

The amount of time between the declaration and payment dates can be longer or shorter than that shown in the example.

By NYSE rules, at least two days must fall between the declaration and publication of the dividend and the ex-date (so investors have time to consider and act on the news). With the T+3 settlement time that was made effective on June 7, 1995, the number of trading days between *ex-* and *record* is fixed at three, of course excluding weekends and holidays. The *record date* is that day on which the company's stock transfer books will be temporarily frozen so a list can be made of stockholders entitled to the upcoming dividend and how many shares each holds. If you are not a shareholder of record on that date, you will not receive the dividend.

In this example, the company pays $3.00 per share annually as four quarterly dividends of $0.75. You can learn a company's key dates for dividends in several ways: consult the prior year's annual report, call the company's investor relations office, or look at the Moody's *Dividend Record* or S&P's *Daily Dividend Record* manuals, available at many libraries. The data can be found in an S&P's *Monthly Stock Guide,* on an S&P's *Individual Stock Report* (or "tear sheet"), and in *Barron's.* Calling your broker is an option, since most have such data available on their computerized news screens. Or consult Prodigy or another online system. Any of these routes is less time-consuming and frustrating than watching dividends-declared tables in your newspaper every day.

If you buy the stock before the ex-dividend date, you will pay a price for it that reflects your right to get the upcoming payment. If you buy this dividend and hold the stock for just over one year, you will be entitled to five quarterly dividends, just as you will celebrate two birthdays in 366 days. Suppose the stock yields about 5 percent and currently trades at $60. On the ex-date, sellers keep the dividend rights and buyers do not receive them. On that day, therefore, the price of the stock (holding aside any other reasons for market moves) will drop by the amount of the dividend, or about $0.75 at the day's opening. So your $60 stock predictably falls to $59.25. But your wealth is reduced even though your upcoming dividend will equal price decline. Why? Taxes! Figure 26.1 shows what happens depending upon how you time your purchase in this stock.

As shown, "buying a dividend" subjects you to taxation on that amount of dividend in the current tax year. That is just the first time you reduce wealth by following this approach. The second occurs when you sell.

**FIGURE 26.1**  Income Effects in Year of Purchasing a Dividend

| | Purchase Timing Strategy | |
| --- | --- | --- |
| | **Buy the Dividend** | **Buy after Ex-Date** |
| Stock Price upon Purchase | $60.00 | $59.25 |
| Dividend You Get | 0.75 | None |
| Stock Price after Ex-Date | 59.25 | 59.25 |
| Pretax Wealth | 59.25 | 59.25 |
| Taxable income event of Getting Dividend | 0.75 | None |
| Taxes Due (Assumes 28% Federal, 5% State) | 0.25 | None |
| Wealth after Taxes | 59.00 | 59.25 |
| Wealth Taxed Away | 0.25 | None |

Suppose you eventually sell the stock at $65 per share, for a capital gain. Figure 26.2 shows what happens under each of the

**FIGURE 26.2**  Capital Gain Effects of Buying or Avoiding a Dividend

| | Purchase Timing Strategy | |
| --- | --- | --- |
| | **Buy the Dividend** | **Buy after Ex-Date** |
| Cost Basis (Price upon Purchase) | $60.00 | $59.25 |
| Sale Price (Ignore Equal Commissions) | 65.00 | 65.00 |
| Taxable Capital Gain | 5.00 | 5.75 |

two scenarios. Because capital gains are taxed at a lower rate than ordinary income (or, at least, were when this was written!), you will pay fewer cents in taxes on the $0.75 of additional gain in the right column, as compared to the $0.25 tax on the dividend as regular income in the purchase year. Thus, by purchasing after the ex-date, you transform the tax on the immediately upcoming dividend from a regular to a capital-gain event, and you postpone payment of that tax itself for your entire holding period. Thus, you save twice by refusing to "buy a dividend."

A caution: Some brokers, knowing that particular clients are highly income sensitive, actually use the buy-a-dividend approach in urging clients to place purchase orders for stocks. "You can get five dividends in the first thirteen months," they point out. You now know why that is a bad idea to buy.

Waiting to buy until after the ex-date can be good for another reason. There appears some evidence that unsophisticated holders, planning to dispose of a stock anyway, tend to hold on for one last dividend and then sell. Their behavior exerts downward price pressure on a stock's price beyond the "automatic" drop of the actual ex-dividend amount. This being true, an astute buyer might wait several days beyond ex-date and perhaps see his or her cost per share drop a little further, creating a bargain as reward for patience and expertise.

**Mutual fund distribution errors.**  You can make the same type of error by failing to take into account mutual funds' and closed-end funds' annual income and capital gains payment cycles. Except for those designed to provide regular income, most funds pay both their net investment income (dividends and interest less fund expenses) and their net realized capital gains distributions once a year. In an average year, a growth-and-income fund might generate about 2 percent to 3 percent per year in income.

Capital gains distribution can be quite large, often dwarfing income distributions. That is most true in years when stocks generally have risen considerably, when some major change in economic outlook might have caused a big shift in the fund's portfolio holdings, or when major share redemptions forced the manager to liquidate stocks to pay departing holders. A perhaps slightly extreme recent example is First Financial Fund, which paid capital gains distributions of $6.625 for 1993 and $4.38 per share for 1994 to shareholders. These distributions represented 20 percent to 30 percent of the fund's value before the ex-dates. Of course the fund's shares fell in price to reflect the ex-date events. It would be foolish to purchase such a fund (in a taxable account) late in a fiscal year when a large capital gains distribution is approaching. You are literally buying a tax liability in doing so.

There is some evidence that, in cases of very large capital gains distributions, closed-end funds' share prices may drop by less than the full ex-amount. Why? When sophisticated investors know a large distribution is about to "go ex," they will hesitate to purchase shares before the ex-date, to avoid buying a tax liability. In effect, they refuse to "pay up" in market price for the full amount of a large upcoming distribution. Then, when ex-date arrives, the market price drop could well be less than the full dividend amount. That difference, theoretically, could be the marginal tax bracket multiplied by the full dividend, or about one-third its amount.

Some detail-oriented investors can take advantage of such market machinations by deliberately buying that dividend in a tax-deferred account such as a self-directed Keogh or IRA, probably capturing a net gain in wealth. Suppose a closed-end fund trading at $20 is about to pay a $6 year-end capital gains distribution. If our tax-avoidance effect operates as described, that fund's market price might drop only $5 (or even a bit less) rather than the full $6 ex-amount. Thus, a pre-ex-date tax-deferred purchaser would have a $6 dividend receivable plus a share now trading at $15, for a total value of $21 on a $20 purchase. Even after eventually paying taxes upon withdrawing assets from that retirement account, there would be a net gain in wealth, since taxes would be less than 100 percent. Thus, tax effects of distributions by funds can be both a pitfall for the unwary (in mutual funds) and a potential opportunity for the savvy (in closed-end funds).

**Forgetting foreign tax credits.**   One tax effect of owning funds is often carelessly overlooked. When a mutual fund or closed-end fund receives dividend or interest income from its portfolio securities, some nations in which it is investing may impose "source withholding," because the fund is considered a foreign person by local tax laws. Since the United States has tax treaties with most other nations, you as a holder of the fund shares are entitled to a flow-through, in the form of a credit equal to the tax you effectively paid to that other nation when your fund "lost" income in the form of source withholding.

How do you learn the details? You can telephone the fund or look at the "statement of operations" in its semiannual or annual report. If the fund invests in any securities overseas, some source withholding is likely, since most nations impose the practice. The very top of the statement of operations will tell you. Its first line or two will list "dividend income received," "interest income received," or both; the next item will be "less taxes withheld at the source" or similar words. Now you can expect a credit the next coming tax season unless the fund changes its investment style and no longer receives such foreign-source income.

How much will your exact credit be? Relax: The fund will figure it for you. Expect to get an IRS Form 2439 showing the amount of the credit due you. This form looks very much like the familiar 1099–DIV, but there is an important difference: You must attach a copy of the 2439 to your return in order to claim the credit, but you do not attach any 1099s. This credit is taken on the back side of the cover page of your Form 1040 under the section called "credits." (You must file a 1040 ("long form") and not a 1040A or 1040EZ to make this claim.) Hold your filing to receive all the 2439s due you, and by all means be sure to claim your credits on your annual income taxes.

If you own funds affected by source withholdings in your tax-deferred accounts such as a Keogh or IRA, the news is good, but with a delay. Since you do not file an annual income tax return for these accounts, you would have no tax against which to take any credit. Instead of sending you a useless Form 2439, the fund must report the credit due you to the U.S. Treasury, and furnish details of your plan account number. The U.S. Treasury, in turn, grinds out a check and sends it to your plan's custodian, which dutifully deposits the money into your account, but only in the fullness of time. My most recent experience with this process witnessed a credit appearing on my brokerage statement in late August. As they say, better late than never.

Like funds, American depository receipts (ADRs) for foreign-listed stocks can involve source withholding, setting in motion the same process.

## Big-Picture Tax-Savings Omissions

The next three items involve considerably more dollars than those just discussed: employer plan participation, employer matching, and double-barreled tax deferral.

**Bypassing a voluntary employer plan.** Resist the temptation! Increasingly, employers are abandoning pension plans that impose fixed future obligation on them. In their place are defined-contribution plans. These force employees to choose how to invest their company-related retirement assets. For many, that is a painful process requiring decisions and therefore creating stress. Try to view it as an opportunity to take control of your own future and as a useful learning experience. You can very likely earn higher total returns than a typical bond-heavy pension plan would have. In the process, you will gain a working lifetime's experience in money management and will arrive at retirement day much better prepared to fend for yourself thereafter.

Besides an educational benefit, employer-sponsored retirement or profit-sharing plans provide three other wonderful features. The first is so-called "forced saving," perhaps more positively called self-imposed discipline. Excepting those lucky enough to be born into money, most folks know this simple truth: You must pay yourself first (i.e., save) or there will be nothing left at the pay cycle's end that you can save. Periodic withholding by your employers ensures that "what you can't get your hands on, you won't spend." Back in the days of pension plans, you would not have told the company it's all right to skip it. Now you are responsible to contribute. Don't fail to do so!

**Employer matching on top of your voluntary contributions.** Each plan's details differ somewhat, but basically, if you put in a certain percentage of your earnings, under most plans the company must, as a result, contribute a defined amount as well. Often, this is in the form of a 100 percent ("dollar-for-dollar") match, or perhaps 50 percent. For example, if you set aside 4 percent of gross, the company would contribute another 4 percent if fully matching (or perhaps just a partially matched 2 percent). Many people see such a plan as a tax-deferred 4 percent raise. I view it in much more dramatic terms: This is the easiest and only sure way I know of to get an immediate 100 percent return (or 50 percent return) on your investment! (Put in 4 percent, and the company must add another 4 percent, immediately doubling your stake.) How can you pass that up? Don't!

**Double-barreled tax deferral.**    First, what you contribute to a qualified plan goes in without first being taxed. For example, if you earn $50,000 a year and contribute 4 percent or $2,000 to your qualified company-sponsored plan, your W-2 form will show $48,000 salary income for federal and (most) state tax purposes. (The full $50,000, alas, will be taxed for Social Security and Medicare purposes.) This is better than saving $2,000 in after-tax dollars, since you need about $3,000 in salary to leave you $2,000 available for after-tax savings. Because you originally paid no tax on the salary earnings by putting them into the plan, you will be taxed on the full amounts withdrawn later on. That is not only fair but actually is favorable. Tax on the salary contributed will be delayed, reducing its discounted present value; the eventual tax may also be at a lower rate, if you time and plan things carefully after retiring, than you now pay.

The up-front tax savings is only part of the benefit, however. All money in the qualified plan earns its income or capital gains on a tax-deferred basis. So the earnings themselves can earn more earnings without getting partly withdrawn to pay current taxes. This whole process lasts until you make withdrawals as eventually required by law, depending on your age.

Suppose you feel you cannot afford to make the full allowable contribution to your employer's plan, for example taking a 9 percent pay cut even to get a 6 percent match. Fortunately, it is never an all-or-none question. Start with the minimum contribution that gets the maximum match. Suppose the company will match 100 percent on the first 3 percent you put in, and then 50 cents on the dollar after that. Then start at 3 percent when you join the company. Each year as you get a salary review or cost-of-living increase, discipline yourself to raise your contribution rate immediately. Suppose you get a 3 percent or 4 percent increase after a year; raise your contribution rate then by at least 1 percent. Follow that same process each year, as aggressively as you can afford to, until you reach the allowable maximum contribution percentage. You'll be surprised at how pain-less this gradual process will be. And over a long period, your rewards will be huge!

**Ignoring IRA and Keogh opportunities.** Anyone with labor-derived income (or their nonworking spouse) can put aside money on a tax-advantaged basis for retirement in an individual retirement arrangement. Self-employed persons may in addition set up a "Keogh" (named for a New York legislator who sponsored the original legislation) or SEP plan. IRA deposits were expanded in 1997, to the lesser of $2,000 or labor-earned income annually, plus another $2,000 in a separate spousal account (formerly just $250) for a nonworking spouse. SEP contributions can go up to 20 percent of earnings, and can be 100 percent if self-employment income is $400 or less (again, these are 1996 rules, changeable whenever Congress convenes).

Many people felt that IRAs lost their luster when tax laws changed in 1986 to limit or eliminate tax deductibility of contributions. Statistics compiled by the Investment Company Institute show IRA contributions to mutual funds fell about 70 percent after that tax change. Failing to contribute to an IRA is a mistake, even if your income level makes contributions nondeductible. There are two reasons, parallel to benefits in company plans described above: disciplined savings and tax deferral on the asset growth. Even if IRAs offer just two of three possible goodies, take those gladly! Each year is an opportunity lost forever if not taken on time. All nondeducted contributions raise your cost basis, lowering the percentage of each future withdrawal that will be taxable.

The August 1997 tax law provides a potential bonanza for IRA investors. The newly created "Roth IRA" or "IRA Plus" allows nondeductible $2,000 annual contributions at most income levels, but all future returns earned will be *free of tax*, not tax deferred. All withdrawals will be free of tax burden! Existing IRAs may be partly or fully converted into the new form by paying tax on the gains over cost basis accrued to date. *The younger you are and/or the smaller your accrued gains, the more worthwhile it is to convert and pay the tax,* which for 1998 only may be spread over four years.

For example, suppose your old-type IRA has a current market value of $16,000, including $6,000 of gains over your basis (your basis is your nondeducted contributions). Paying approximately $2,000 of tax (28 percent federal bracket plus state at perhaps 5 percent) once will free you from all future federal income tax on further gains. If you are age 33 and project a 9 percent average annual return to age 65, your principal would double every eight years, or multiply 16-fold. Your projected $256,000 IRA nest egg ($16,000 times 16) will be totally free of tax when withdrawn. These figures assume you never contribute another dime! Paying the $2,000 tax now will eliminate taxes of who-knows-what bracket on $246,000 later. This is a tax-paid "investment" worth making even if it requires skipping one year's normal $2,000 contribution. (When the market takes a dip, that will be a great time to make the conversion, since your taxable gain will be lower at such a time.)

This change makes it all the more important that you get an updated copy of IRS Publication 590, "Individual Retirement Arrangements" every year or two, since it contains any recent changes in rules and also acts as a convenient reference source on basic questions. Local IRS phone numbers and addresses are in your telephone book; forms and publications can now be ordered via the Internet, too (www.irs.ustreas.gov)!

**Failing to consider variable annuities.** Company-sponsored plans and IRAs, in that order because of the matching aspects and the greater dollar limits, are first priorities, virtual "musts." Variable annuity opportunities also are worthy of your consideration, but only third and, for most people, below the "must-do" line. They involve no company matching, contributions are not tax deductible, and they incur higher expenses plus potential exit costs.

A variable annuity (or VA) is a contract with an insurance company. It is more complex than a straight or fixed annuity. With a VA, the amount you will receive as an income stream in retirement will depend on the investment performance of the assets owned inside the contract. You, the buyer, take the investment risk and reward; in a straight annuity the insurance company was in that position, since it promised a certain monthly income related to the amount of deposit(s) you put in.

You can think of a VA as a giant, nondeductible, self-managed IRA account with an added death benefit (under most contracts, your heirs get back at least what you put in even if you never live to collect any or many monthly income checks). Inside the annuity contract, which acts legally as an "insurance company wrapper" to qualify the plan under the IRS code, you have a variety of investment choices. These literally are mutual funds, each one available only through the VA contract itself. You could put all your assets into one fund, or spread things around over many. You can move assets back and forth from time to time. You can add more money as often as you wish, and in virtually unlimited amounts. When you move assets from one fund to another, just as within an IRA account, no tax liability is triggered. Also, there is no current tax paid on VA funds' interest or dividend income.

A VA contract imposes some costs above those of plain mutual funds inside an IRA. First, there is an insurance company mortality and expense (M&E) charge. This covers their general expenses and profit for handling the contract, and pays for the rather small risk that they will need to make your heirs whole if you die before receiving as much as you'd put in— assuming you lose money on the investments. There often is an additional annual administrative "policy fee" of about $35, which helps spread expenses of small plans fairly, since it is a lower percentage for bigger depositors. This charge covers accounting costs; expenses of producing and mailing statements and tax reports; and costs of maintaining telephone help lines and personnel. Those are the inescapable annual charges.

In addition, there are costs related to sales and redemptions. Most VA contracts involve penalties for withdrawal in the early years. Typical might be a 7 percent charge on amounts withdrawn in year one, declining to zero by 1 percent steps annually. Such costs are on top of any tax consequences for premature withdrawals from a VA contract. Finally, some (not all) VA contracts carry a front-end commission that immediately eats up as much as 7 percent of your assets.

If you understand VAs well enough, you may wish to avoid such costs by seeking a no-load contract. Consult the reasonably frequent articles on the subject in *Kiplinger's Personal Finance Magazine* or *Money* for lists of companies that offer such contracts. Good libraries subscribe to magazine subject-indexing databases that will help you find the right issue quickly.

## Tax Errors Made in Retirement Years

You invested successfully, planned for your big-picture tax aspects well, and remembered the annual details for limiting taxes as described above. Great! Now beware of some common potential blunders during retirement: not taking available tax breaks, not timing controllable decisions to low-bracket years, and under-evaluating the 85 percent Social Security earnings tax test.

**Not taking available tax breaks.** Technically, this is not strictly related to investments per se. But in a discussion of wealth maximization by investors through lawful tax minimization, it merits mention. Two points are of interest: one, almost impossible to miss, is a larger personal exemption amount for individuals and spouses aged 65 and over, than for younger taxpayers—take it. A second, the "Credit for The Elderly or Disabled," is available only depending upon your income level in combination with age and possible disability status. IRS Publication 524, available at no cost, gives the details. Generally, you can claim this credit if your income from all sources is under $12,500 to $20,000 (including specified maximums of untaxed Social Security benefits) in a year.

You might be able to time your recognition of income so you can qualify for this credit in at least some years. Generally, you would bunch higher and then lower income into alternating years. Here is just one example of how you might accomplish it. Suppose you retire at age 65 in, say, October of some year. Perhaps you have enough money in your own name (outside tax-deferred accounts) so you can live for most of a year without cashing in IRAs, company profit-sharing plans, or taking VA payouts. You do so, and then late in the year when you turn 66, take just enough income from such plans, on top of personal interest and dividends, to keep you under the credit threshold. This new sum of money can hold you through much of the next year. You continue to postpone collecting Social Security, assuming your health outlook is good, since this raises your benefits once you start drawing them. In year 66, you qualify for the elderly credit. Maybe in year 67, you draw down a fairly large amount from your IRA assets, disqualifying you for the credit that year. But then in year 68, you take down little or no such taxable-income-generating assets, and perhaps offset some income by realizing any paper losses you might have on personal investments. Perhaps late in that year you finally start accepting Social Security benefits (at an enhanced rate). Again you have created a year of qualification for the elderly credit.

All this is done simply by planning and timing. This was a general theoretical example, not a detailed action plan; consult your own advisers on specifics for your particular situation.

**Not timing controllable distributions to low-bracket years.** There are several types of income, many of them related to the event of retiring, whose timing you can control. By doing this carefully, you typically can place some of your money in the lower tax bracket rather than allowing it to be taxed at the upper-bracket rate. Here is another theoretical example (again note the caveat stated in the above paragraph): Suppose your company's profit-sharing plan will automatically pay you out a lump sum exactly six months after your official retirement date. And suppose you plan on stepping aside somewhere around midyear. What a tax difference you'll feel if you work through July 5 instead of June 21! That extra two weeks will postpone the plan distribution into the following calendar year, when it will not be piled atop your final six months' salary to determine your marginal tax bracket.

Beyond this major, one-time event, you have some other choices. Most of them are not constrained until you reach age 70½, when tax laws require you start taking out certain minimums from tax-deferred plans such as IRAs and Keoghs. Again, you can take an approach of alternating high- and low-income years. In a high-income year, you can draw out enough assets in December to live comfortably through the entire next year. You can postpone taking much or any controllable income until January, 13 months later, creating a low-income year that will reduce your marginal bracket. In that low year, realize available capital losses: Bunch charitable contributions, pay deferrable medical costs, and so on.

Your retirement assets will have come from hard personal work and shrewd investing. Why squander some of them on the margin by poor or careless execution of tax-oriented income recognition timing?

**Underevaluating the 85 percent Social Security earnings tax test.** This may not be relevant for you, depending on your income level. And again, tax laws may well have changed since 1997. Up to 85 percent of your monthly Social Security benefits may be subject to income taxes, depending on the level of your individual or joint income (here, deductions are not relevant). Sometimes you can control the outcome of that test, if in a given year you're close to the dividing line. Timely realization of a capital loss in December, or postponing a gain into January, could make the difference. Many people are familiar with such choices. Another, however, often is overlooked: Think carefully about the character of interest income you receive. It may be appropriate to shift some of your bond (or bond fund) holdings from corporates and taxable governments into municipals. An example will illustrate the possible importance of this exercise.

As of 1996, the thresholds for taxing Social Security benefits were a 50 percent inclusion above $25,000 or $32,000 for single or married taxpayers and an 85 percent inclusion of income above $34,000 or $44,000, depending on marital status. Suppose you are near one of those cutoff levels and have some bond holdings, perhaps $100,000 in U.S. government bonds (or such funds) generating 7 percent income, or $7,000 per year. You might be better to sell those bonds, assuming it would not generate a big taxable gain that undermined the whole plan, and move to an equal amount of municipals generating 6 percent income, or $6,000 per year. Not only would you save the income tax (either 15 percent or 28 percent, depending on your total income and deductions) on the taxable bond income, but your choice to accept gross income of $1,000 less (municipal bond income does count toward the Social Security test) will put you that much further below the 50 percent or 85 percent taxability threshold. If you're extremely close to the line, landing on the wrong side could literally mean an effective marginal tax rate above 100 percent on the extra dollars of gross bond-interest income.

Here is a best-case example of possible savings: Take a gross interest reduction of $1,000 by switching $100,000 of bonds from taxables to municipals. This saves as much as $2,000 in federal income tax, since $7,000 is removed from 28 percent bracket taxable income (plus a bit if you itemize medical expenses above the 7.5 percent threshold). If you are close to the line, the $1,000 interest forgone could leave you just below the 85 percent Social Security test threshold, which would protect 35 percent of your Social Security income (maybe as much as $7,000 out of $20,000?) from also being taxed, saving you another $2,000 in taxes. Thus, this deliberate $1,000 reduction in investment interest income could trigger $4,000 in tax savings. Looking at this in reverse, insisting on taking that $1,000 in income results in a $4,000 higher tax bill, or a 400 percent marginal rate. As they say, check with your tax adviser. This sort of thing is easier to do at the start of the year rather than at the end. And, if selling the taxable bonds at a gain, you probably need to make that sale in the prior year.

# Choose the Right Brokerage Firm for You

*T*his brief chapter makes a case for selecting your financial services providers individually rather than letting one try to serve all your needs. Among the resulting benefits are increased privacy, excellence from specialists, total freedom and breadth of selection, dollar savings, and sometimes speed and responsiveness.

## One-Stop Shopping: Is It a True Panacea?

Starting around 1960, bigger became almost automatically assumed to be better. Corporate conglomerates gobbled up as subsidiaries what once had been thriving, independent, and often unrelated businesses. These companies were run from a central corporate world headquarters, often under rigid policies. Neighborhood grocers were supplanted by superstores and "hypermarts" owned by national supermarket chains, with stores approaching four acres in size. You can buy many things there, but anything offbeat or sold in small volume is missing from their shelves. Similarly, investment organizations have promoted a financial-supermarket concept, as illustrated by such giants as Primerica, American Express, Sears, and Merrill Lynch.

Since the early 1990s, we've witnessed some evidence of a reversal in direction, a sea change in corporate strategy.

What happened? Conglomeration, that driving force behind the financial-supermarket idea, ran smack into several mega-trends that have proved too big to defeat. In an increasingly depersonalized world, people want to be treated as individuals. They want service; they value real expertise; and they highly prize personal privacy. Some problems demand intricate and exceptional attention to produce a proper, ideal solution. Cookie-cutter stores in shopping malls, run by relatively inexperienced clerks earning minimum wage, do not provide acceptable answers to every need. In metro Denver, a battery store has sprung up, selling literally hundreds of different types and sizes of specialty batteries. Why? Because places where you buy all those wonderful gadgets needing batteries often carry just an extremely narrow line of the most common batteries; to them, you see, it's a simple question of sales per square foot, inventory turns, and restocking labor hours. And those stores forget that old gadgets, no longer this year's hot sellers, are still used by consumers still needing new batteries!

Boutiques flourish everywhere, in the face of 24-hour hyper-marts. Why? Because you and I like special, personalized things offered and explained by credible experts. Where do you prefer to buy fine jewelry—at the mall? Where is the only merchant for miles around who carries your favorite wine or imported gourmet cheese? Odds are, not at the mall. Where do you find someone you could actually entrust to fix your great-grand-mother's watch?

### Good for Whom?

Financial conglomerate/supermarkets had a good idea, but primarily only when looked at from their perspective. They could cut costs by combining overhead. Perhaps most important from their viewpoint, they could capture and hold your assets no matter what you wanted to do. Take the case of Sears, Roebuck. Want to spend your money? They've been right there for a century. Want to buy on credit? No problem, forget your banker: use your Sears charge or your Discover card! While shopping for a washer or lawn mower, drop off your home insurance policy for a "friendly check-up" (and you'll very likely be shown something Allstate thinks is better). And speaking of insurance, how about a life insurance policy? And talking financial planning, you need some (of our InterCapital) mutual funds, don't you? Don't like mutual funds but prefer to trade individual stocks? No problem again: your Dean Witter broker is also available on-site. Speaking of brokers, if you invested well and could buy a new home, voilà!: Sears owned the Coldwell Banker real estate group from 1981 until divestiture in 1993. (Merrill Lynch had gone the same route a bit earlier, by acquiring Ticor Relocation Management in 1977 and selling it in 1989.) American Can? They got out of containers, changed their name a couple of times, and bought catalog retailers (some later sold) as well as both traditional insurance (Travelers), low-cost term (Primerica), and a stock brokerage firm (Smith Barney).

The central goal of financial supermarketeering is to capture your dollars and earn fees and commissions no matter what you want to do. That's great for a corporate supermarket, and they will tell you it's good for you—in the name of convenience. And convenience is certainly a strong, hot-button selling point in times of overly busy lives and crowded highways.

Following are some key questions to ask about whether that financial supermarket is appropriate for you:

- Does it do with excellence all the things you want?
- Does dealing with it give you a comfortable feeling about your privacy?
- In an age of electronic money and instant computerized transfers, isn't physical one-stop convenience becoming a moot point?
- Are you paying too much in commissions for the sake of having those other conveniences at hand?

**Excellence.**    In general, you select the people with whom you do business based on how well they serve your needs: There are municipal bond houses whose sole business and expertise is in that narrow area. Some brokerage firms have better access to overseas stock markets than do others. Your local bank offers a favorable service and fee arrangement with your employer if you accept payroll deposit of your salary checks. Major full-service brokerage firms will not offer certain mutual fund families (Fidelity and T. Rowe Price come to mind) because they are no-loads, but many of those funds are really excellent performers. Your credit card preference might be based on a 1 percent cash rebate, donations it makes to a favorite charity, frequent-flyer mileage, long-distance phone credits, or (how revolutionary!) a low interest rate or a zero annual fee or both. You may do all your own investment homework and wish to trade at the lowest possible commissions (recall from Strategy 25 how important such savings can become over the years). The bottom line is, you simply cannot find all, or even your most important cluster of a few, of these advantages at any single financial supermarket.

**Privacy.** How would you feel if your bank, knowing your CD is coming up for renewal, disclosed your name, telephone number, and your certificate balance to a mutual funds salesperson? Exactly that happens when you deal with banks that have adopted supermarket characteristics. Do you deal with both a full-commission broker (for her good advice) and with a deep-discount broker (when you generate your own ideas)? Wouldn't you prefer to keep both unaware of your double relationship? Do you want your commodities broker to know how big a home you just bought? Do you like the freedom to shop your auto insurance around for possibly better rates or truly personal service? Financial privacy, already sorely threatened, is at the root of your answers to such questions. Financial supermarkets, with their computers connecting all departments, actively want to know everything about you so they can sell you more of what they happen to have.

**Electronic convenience.** Moving money around is no longer the time-consuming, travel-intensive chore of past eras. Electronic bill paying; mortgage and auto-loan applications by telephone; automatic or ad hoc mutual fund purchases by deduction from your checking or savings account; getting information and even buying things (if you so choose) over the Internet; transferring money between savings and checking; switching from one mutual fund to another by telephone at midnight; moving from one fund family to another by touch-tone phone through Schwab OneSource; even buying mutual funds at an ATM machine—all are possible in our electronic-card, push-button, microchip age. You can even move money from one mutual fund family, via its money market fund's checking account, to another family the same day if that second family already knows you as a customer and accepts telephone instructions with a check to follow (many do!). With all this at your fingertips, who needs a financial supermarket that pushes its own line of proprietary products and does not want you to shop around for price, special features, or highly personalized service—and on top of it knows all your personal business?

**Cost.**    Strategy 6 laid out the case for making your own decisions rather than being sold currently featured financial products and fads. Given that you've developed the expertise and confidence to buy and sell on your agenda, it seems logical to save the considerable difference between commissions charged by full-service brokers and those of flat-rate discounters. Deep discounters are not affiliated with one-stop financial supermarkets. Strategy 25 noted the major long-term savings after compounding.

# Utilize the Necessary Experts

*P*rinted matter concerning investing has its limitations. So does today's increasingly handy personal computer software. You have individual needs and specific questions. These are best answered by experts in various fields, and definitely not by faceless would-be (and sometimes volunteer) experts on the Internet! Much in successful investing can be done with a library of crucial sources, and so a suggested reading list is incorporated into Strategy 30. But there's no substitute for real, live, personal expert guidance and custom tailoring where it is warranted. This strategy highlights areas where you should obtain expert assistance, and it offers tips on how to identify sales professionals posing as experts.

## Why You Need Some Experts

Alas, no book can be all necessary things to all people. Much as I love the printed word, bound forever handsomely, I admit it isn't enough. No single investment book, nor even a richly diverse collection, can do the entire job. With time's passage, the information in any book or old magazine can become incomplete and dangerously misleading. New investment concepts emerge and major technical details such as tax laws change, often considerably. Fewer than 20 years ago, such now-common terms as *junk bond, 401(k), 12b-1 fee,* or *life-cycle fund* were unknown. Today, they're important for any serious investor to understand. And each individual in today's increasingly diverse society is likely to have a unique combination of considerations in his or her life that make any one-size-fits-all investment formulas, even from the best of books, work imperfectly at best.

Recent developments in interactive personal computer software hold some, but not complete, promise for remedying such problems. They allow an investor or user chances to make exceptions, to define some individual differences, or to make a few not-unreasonable assumptions. Presently, however, such software accommodates only those possibilities its developers recognized, imagined, and programmed (we assume, accurately) to allow for. For those strongly oriented toward maximum self-education, interconnection to important libraries and original source documents via the Internet holds promise. Those with good research skills will be empowered to find much of what they believe they need in this exploding electronic-library world.

That environment's convenience, however, comes with hidden dangers attached. While 1994–1995 saw early Internet concerns center on privacy and 1997 became its year for a pornography-protection debate, one major problem appears insurmountable. In 1997, attention moved to it: The virus-like spread of dangerously misleading, even if sometimes well meant, "guidance" from undertrained, misinformed, or out-of-date amateur experts—or even from innocent correspondents whose main fault is that they either listen or write imprecisely. As so-called jailhouse lawyers or folk healers can provide some good but also some horribly bad advice, self-styled investment experts on the Internet can get their innocent adherents into messy and possibly irreparable trouble. Early 1997 brought two news items highlighting this issue: The SEC was developing artificial-intelligence software to detect online touting; and Motley Fool announced it would replace its volunteers with trained professional advice-givers. The bottom line: In this, as in any important matter, is that you should consult appropriate experts and expect to pay them for their expertise.

## What You *Must* Get from Experts

### Your Will

I am neither an attorney nor an estate-planning expert. Those matters are properly handled by an attorney skilled in preparing wills and, in increasing numbers of cases, personal trusts of various sorts. If you do not have your Last Will and Testament in place, properly drawn under the laws of your present state of legal residence, you're in major trouble. Don't spend the time to read any more investment books or attend any more get-rich seminars until your will is done. All the good advice and tips you can accumulate and practice after consulting such sources can easily be wiped out if your will is either nonexistent or poorly done.

Similarly, individual circumstances may argue for creation of certain types of trusts. Attorneys specializing in trust and estate matters should be consulted promptly. For probably not more than several hundred dollars, you can potentially save hundreds of thousands if your asset pool approaches seven digits by the time of your death. I deliberately omit naming specific circumstances or types of trusts so no reader can interpret such lists as all-inclusive: inevitably, they would not be. Identify an attorney who offers the following three core qualifications, and confide in her or him:

1. *Specialization in this legal field.* Do not choose a lawyer whose specialty is divorce, real estate, criminal matters, collision injury suits, or any other area.
2. *Full, open disclosure of fees in an initial free half-hour consultation.* The law holds mysteries for us laypersons, but no attorney should extend that veil to cover such mundane matters. Wills and trusts are not rocket science; they involve predictable amounts of time and energy per level of complexity. Avoid anyone who is vague on fee matters.
3. *Suitable personal comfort or intellectual chemistry.* You must have full confidence in an attorney, be willing to confide

all related personal details. Would you fail to tell a doctor about conditions or medications taken and expect a safe, useful treatment? No matter the reason, if you feel any discomfort with an attorney or get incomplete or condescending explanations, just go and find someone else.

Do-it-yourself will kits are widely available, usually priced in the $20 to $39 range. They might allow you to do the simplest of things by using their multiple-choice approach. But what if you make a crucial mistake and do not know it? One plus to such kits, as well as some books on self-written wills, is that they provide useful guidance and require you to make necessary checklists (thus saving delay and a lawyer's time on details). But they cannot adequately substitute for face-to-face discussion with an expert who will explore your specific needs knowledgeably. Pay the couple of hundred extra dollars and do it right!

How do you find the right attorney for you? You approach it in much the same way as you'd find a doctor. Personal recommendations from trusted friends or work colleagues may help, but ultimately this is a matter of proper fit and personal choice, of chemistry. Most local bar associations maintain telephone help lines that guide you to specialists. Phone numbers are found in the Yellow Pages or in special help sections in the front of major cities' directories. Expect to get several names, as they understandably will not recommend just one. Do some telephone screening and then make two or three actual half-hour visits.

### Tax Advice

I am in the narrowing minority of people who prepare their own tax returns. But I would not dare to undertake major transactions without qualified tax advice. Not all accountants, even CPAs, specialize in tax matters, particularly those related to retirement. Find one who does. Follow the steps noted earlier for screening attorneys.

With tax advisers, as with a physician or attorney, chemistry and trust are crucial. All such professionals are under well-defined, strict ethical and legal requirements to keep your personal revelations strictly private. So go ahead and confide fully in them. Only full disclosure will enable them to render the best advice. Some detail you consider inconsequential might be exactly the subject matter of an arcane exclusion or special provision in the federal or state tax code. So, tell all!

Here are some (just investing-related!) tax matters for which you should pay an expert:

- Titling of and transfers of securities
- Investment gifts
- Timing and realization of major capital gains
- Planning for, timing, and accepting retirement and profit-sharing plan distributions

We have a self-defeating tendency to plunge ahead into technically complex areas and, only after the fact, to seek affirmation from experts. This is extremely dangerous to your financial health. Always consult your chosen tax expert *in advance*, since some transactions are final and cannot be undone for repairs.

### Information from the Social Security Administration

You should obtain a "Request for Earnings and Benefit Estimate Statement" (Form 7004) from your nearby Social Security office. This does not even require a visit; telephone numbers appear under government listings in most telephone directories. With a touch-tone phone you can get a form sent by mail; filling it out requires less than five minutes. Predictably, the resulting response from the government will take about eight weeks to arrive.

This information is very important to you. You have a right to see it in advance and to be sure it is correct. Retirement experts recommend that you ask for an updated report about every 24 to 36 months. Waiting until about July will help ensure that the prior calendar year's earnings are reflected when your statement arrives. These output reports are computer-generated and are reliable in most circumstances (disability, blindness, unusual divorce/remarriage, and similar exceptions do apply). Assuming your situation is fairly standard, your report will show the latest revised version of what your Social Security benefits will be in the future, in response to the chosen "what if" retirement year you name when filling out the form. Don't be afraid: This is not a request for benefits and does not keep you from changing your mind later.

Knowing your likely level of monthly Social Security benefits starting at a probable age for retiring is central to discovering what assets you'll need to accumulate on your own. Learning your benefit entitlement will cost you a first-class postage stamp. Do not put off getting your first information until you're 61. And update yourself every two or three years until you actually do begin drawing benefits. Make sure the Social Security Administration has credited all your employment income to your record.

### Your Benefits Department

If your employer has one or more retirement-oriented benefits plans in place, find out all you can about them. While this book's focus has been on your investments, the financial security equation has an outgo as well as an income component. One very important aspect of your personal retirement situation is medical expense coverage. Legislation in the early 1990s mandated that employers make continuing medical coverage available to retiring employees desiring it; costs and the burden of those costs vary widely and are controlled in part by such factors as union agreements. As you come closer to an anticipated retirement date, start querying your personnel or benefits office on then-current laws and regulations on health coverage; undoubtedly they will have changed since 1997, and they could change additional times late in your working career. This is an area where developments are becoming more fluid. With political winds likely to change often, the advice with most lasting value is to "stay tuned for further developments."

Health care issues are only part of the picture. Pension and profit-sharing plans and your company-sponsored voluntary savings or investment plan are significant pieces of your equation. Begin periodically asking your personnel and benefits specialists about changes in plan rules, new entitlements available, and choices required as you reach certain age and years-in-service milestones. Also inquire about any other matters they know about which you might not know to ask.

All qualified plans require distribution of at least an annual summary of plan assets and benefits to participants. You should retain these papers for reference at any time and be sure to inform your spouse or other partner, and heirs of their location. You can befriend your personnel and benefits specialists by *not* being among those who discard or report losing those documents and casually ask for replacements. It is smart to be on friendly terms with those people rather than to have them be impatient with you and treat you curtly.

About ten years before your planned retirement date, start paying very close attention to the size of your plan assets, your vesting schedule (if you are not already at 100 percent), and your asset allocation. Over time, your allocation should shift toward a more conservative, but never a 100 percent-income posture (as discussed in Strategy 22). Your choices of vehicles within your employer's plan(s) should be made in an overall context, looking at all your assets and all your options. For example, if that plan has a terrific aggressive equity fund, you would heavily weight your equity assets there but do bonds and conservative funds in your IRA and personal accounts. Likewise, if you personally hold lots of municipal bonds, you could go light on bonds within the company plan.

Commonly, employee retirement plans offer only limited frequency of dates to switch among funds. As you reach 50, 55, and older, you need to know those rules by heart or have them on a 3×5 card in case contrarian market opportunities arise. Sometimes after 55 you have more freedom to make switches; plans recognize a need to allow flexibility as time horizons shorten. Know the rules, and keep asking every couple of years whether any of them have changed. Read and save all the information bulletins and periodic reports distributed. Knowing what's there will help you ask necessary but intelligent questions, not one showing you never read anything! You also need to know this information so you can work intelligently with your attorney and tax planner, as discussed earlier. You'll be wasting your time and theirs (for which they charge hourly fees!) by arriving without such information in hand.

## Other Help from Experts You *Should* Use

### *Seminars*

Your Sunday newspaper will almost always contain numerous advertisements for seminars on financial topics. You can use these as learning tools. Following are some points of observation and advice.

- *Don't inhale too deeply.* Most such seminars are sales presentations or are designed to identify and qualify sales prospects. One excellent test of a presenter's credentials and intentions is to request a list of outside reading materials you can study. That will reveal your instructor's knowledge beyond a prepared sales script and will identify you as a thinking, demanding consumer.
- *Maintain a healthy skepticism.* Most seminars are taught by sales personnel (with or without help from truly qualified outside experts). The subject matter is whatever the sales professional is most comfortable selling, and makes a good living selling. Living wills, annuities, single-deposit life insurance, universal life, subsidized-housing partnerships, and similar products come to mind. You'll leave that seminar feeling you've been to a tent-meeting revival if you don't keep your guard up.
- *Never buy on the first contact.* Never continue any contacts where you are not willingly supplied with detailed written materials. Have outside experts study those materials before you sign or buy anything.
- *Place more trust in seminars wherein you pay a reasonable fee in advance for materials.* Such sessions tend to be more informative and involve less (or no) selling pressure because costs of the event have already been absorbed.
- *You can learn much about various financial products from these seminars but are under no obligation to buy.* Do not buy out of a sense of owing someone anything in return for their time or the meal they served. Always ask for references, and always check them out.

## Night School Classes

Many high school districts, adult continuing education programs, and colleges offer instruction in personal finance matters for modest enrollment fees. These usually are worth paying for, but only if they cover material you haven't already mastered. Ask for some detail of the topics covered in advance of signing up. Don't become a seminar groupie, attending everything available.

You might even consider attending a local university's night finance or investing courses on a noncredit basis. These will be more challenging and commensurately more rewarding than seminars. The educational community will cater increasingly to needs of baby boomers in their mature years because they are numerous, and because schools need both added revenue and community support. If such programs are not yet available, ask for them. Publicly supported entities do respond to taxpayer needs, but they will continue to teach classes only on art appreciation, exercise, travel, minority cultures, and poetry if you do not request other subject matters. Speak up!

## Libraries and Librarians

Public library systems are very responsive to their taxpayer-patrons' needs. Libraries depend almost entirely on taxes for continued operation, which means the continued employment of their staff. As baby boomers age, less money should be spent on children's programs and VCR movie-lending collections and more on the wants of seniors. But like educators, libraries will need to be informed of your needs and nudged to serve them.

Library professional staff members are amazingly helpful resources. Almost unanimously, they'd prefer to help a library customer get some useful information over shelving, cataloging, or dusting. But they have no idea what you need or whether you're frustrated in your search until you ask for assistance. Try to frame your questions fairly specifically. "Anything about retirement" can mean health and travel unless you specify "tax aspects of receiving my 401(k) distributions in this state versus in Hawaii," or something similarly clear. Do not ask librarians for investment advice; ask instead about strategies for finding this information.

Don't overlook, as many citizens do, your local university libraries. Public colleges and universities are tax-supported and are open to nonstudents by law, providing such guests comport themselves nicely. Collections are usually very good, especially where the university has a business degree program. Librarians will prove very helpful, although you may need to steer past student assistants for greatest benefit in research matters. Your borrowing privileges might be restricted or made subject to needs of active students (in which case try an interlibrary loan through your local public library). But generally you are free to enter and to study materials in the collections, usually only on no more condition than showing ID as a state resident.

Some private universities grant (typically more limited) privileges to the general citizenry, or in many cases on a reciprocal basis to alumni. Here you'll need to inquire a bit more politely and remember your status as an uninvited guest. Again, the infrastructure and collection usually are extensive and the staff is often highly knowledgeable and resourceful. If access is denied to the general public, consider asking an employee you know well (a neighbor who is a faculty member would be best) to see if they can arrange special visitor credentials for you. Asking never hurts.

## Another Option You *Might* Consider

A major objective of this book has been to empower you to take charge of your own financial future. By now, there are several areas where you're a virtual master; in some others you may feel still a bit inadequate. While mathematics definitely is required, never cower in the belief that investing is an advanced science; in reality, it is an art. But you may sense some places where your greatest needs still lie. Readings suggested in Strategy 30 can open your thinking even further.

Despite all efforts, you may yet conclude that doing all this for yourself is just not for you. You may still feel afraid, or too inexpert. You may not really enjoy cranking the numbers and doing investment work at an effort level needed to succeed in this important quest for financial security and comfort in retirement. You may prefer to spend your free time with hobbies, social or service activities, or the children or grandchildren. Thus, professional investment help may be your best choice.

If you decide to use professional help, I strongly urge that you confine your choices to *fee-only* financial planners. These professionals study your situation and needs, prepare a written report outlining recommended actions, and are then fully prepared to part company. You pay them a few hundred, to a few thousand, dollars up front to tell you what to do; they do not live on commissions from selling products. If you wish, and if you match their client profile on asset size and risk tolerance, you might then also hire such a planner to manage your investments for an annual fee. Such fees are based on assets managed and generally cluster around 1 percent annually.

Choosing a fee-only planner is crucial. Many financial salespersons have various degrees or professional designations but are compensated by commissions. By putting yourself in their hands you enter the potential conflict-of-interests zone: Will they be tempted to move your assets to earn commissions? Undoubtedly some planners who work on commission do excellent jobs and can provide strong investment results for their clients. Your problem is being unable to identify or differentiate them in advance.

By contrast, fee-only planners charge you fees for advice, full-time asset management, or both. In many cases, they specialize in using no-load mutual funds or discount stock brokers to execute investment moves. If they do not, or if they insist you place your account with a specific broker or fund family to stay under their management, I advise choosing another planner. Tied arrangements could imply sharing of fees or other incentives that do not always unquestionably place your interests first.

# Pull It All Together

$Y$ou've come a long way and have absorbed a lot of new ideas. You discovered how important investor psychology is to success in the markets, perhaps contradicting your earlier thinking that fundamentals are the whole issue. Then you picked up a lot of insights about the subtleties of specific investment media, including the potentials they offer if you understand and sidestep the potholes involved. You've gotten a practical taste of the need for, and details of, disciplined asset allocation in the context of lifelong investment planning. Recent pages provided you with specific new ideas about better, more cost-effective execution of the details, all the way from good tax-wise (but not taxobsessed) investing to choosing the right kind of broker for your specific needs.

At this point, particularly if you read along faster than a couple of chapters per day, a lot of ideas are probably spinning in (or around) your brain, needing some connection. Before the final strategy which provides an inventory of resources you will need for staying informed and current, these next few pages will pull together in one place the major ideas and themes of this book. The goal is to help you pull together your own investing life and get it firmly onto a positive track.

## Learning to Do What Is Uncomfortable

The central theme woven throughout this volume has been the need to look at the investment world in counterintuitive ways. That in itself is an unusual thought, since most investors act in a series of isolated episodes and usually do not view the whole when working on the parts. Counterintuitive behavior of course is the essence of contrary thinking.

Contrary investing, discussed in Strategy 9, in a nutshell means not going along with the crowd. That is most crucial either when a certain trend has been in force for a long time or when the crowd is acting emotionally. Greed drives undisciplined buying near market tops, and then fear pushes investors to panic and sell at just the wrong time; when large numbers act the same way at once, they create a classic selling climax. You must fight the fear that would draw you into that crowd stampede. Resisting selling from fear is half the battle; the even tougher challenge is to buy during a panic, when it really seems scary (or counterintuitive).

The opposite of a panic is a period of euphoria. That is when risk is no longer discussed, when millions of first-time investors flock to a concept, and when a simple road to riches seems to have finally been discovered. Such situations require a passage of time so that memories of past periods of pain are forgotten. As a bull market becomes longer and taller, it is easy to get increasingly comfortable with higher price-earnings ratios, historically low yields, the concept that "this time it will be different," or the false hope that Washington has figured out how to repeal business cycles.

At a micro level, you have been watching an individual stock rise, wishing you'd had the courage to buy it a few years ago at a fraction of today's quote. Quarter after quarter, earnings hum along at a nice steady growth rate. Finally, you cannot abide looking in from the outside: you must buy (now, at "any price," even though you do not think those words). You have allowed your long-developing comfort zone to draw you in late in the game. What seems so intuitively obvious (that this company seemingly can do no wrong) draws you and other buyers in late, at very high prices. You have paid the price of higher cost and higher risk for the added information that you needed to build your courage. The market will not pay you well for doing what is now so obvious to everyone. It will pay well (and already has) those investors who acted before everything seemed to be obviously perfect.

Comfort zones also cause problems with stocks you have owned for a long time, especially if they've treated you well. It seems inconceivable ever to part company with a stock that has been so kind, that represents a company so obviously strong and solid. Your comfort zone, here, has let you confuse the stock with the underlying company. A perfectly wonderful company can be underpriced, properly valued in the market, or grossly overpriced. You of course are most comfortable and most in love with both the stock and your own brilliance when the stock is highest—and when your risk from not selling is highest. What seems so comfortable is again the wrong thing to do. Stocks do not rise forever; there are seasons for everything.

In bonds every bit as much as in stocks, investors tend to follow trends. Few investors think in terms of psychology when handling bonds and bond funds, and yet the comfort zone operates here as well, prompting wrong moves late in a well-established trend. As with stocks, where the huge mistakes take place around the extremes, income investors run amok either when rates are extremely high or when they're quite low.

Three big mistakes in a high-rate environment are:

1. Moving all your assets into income investments.
2. Paradoxically, doing the exact opposite by panicking because bond prices have fallen, and selling out at low prices.
3. Buying bank CDs at seemingly irresistible interest rates. Recall how Strategy 5 demonstrated that you must invest for total return rather than purely for current income (to grow your assets and thus protect future purchasing power against inflation). So remember that terribly high interest rates are unsustainable (economically or politically) and will drive a rally in stocks as well as

bonds when they start to recede. And keep in mind that CDs are never a good buy. When rates are high, if you are right that rates are near a top, you should buy high-quality, long-term bonds instead. Not only will they give you a good yield, but their prices will rise considerably, which CDs are guaranteed not to do!

When available interest rates are painfully low, you again must do what's counterintuitive: Accept those rates with at least a portion of your assets, because this approach will reduce your risk. You must guard against four traps that ensnare investors when rates are low:

1. Bond, T-bill, or money market fund rates are so low you are turned off and grab for the gusto of a bubbly stock market. Comfort zone again! When rates start going higher, stocks will tumble.
2. You reject low short-term rates in favor of the higher rates on long bonds—again late in the rate cycle, when the next rate move is up and long-bond prices are at great risk of falling.
3. You reach for the highest available yields by buying junk bonds or funds, or international bonds or funds. Here, you're taking a quality risk at exactly the wrong time. As rates rise and a recession sets in, low-quality bonds will be at risk of default; the dollar will rise, cutting the value of your foreign bonds.
4. You grab for gadget bonds—items that seem to promise a high return without risk—or funds that invest in them. Wall Street finance engineers keep inventing new kinds of instruments to attract new money. What is untried by a couple of full economic cycles has no place in your serious-money portfolio sector.

True to contrarian principles, do in bonds what seems counterintuitive, both when interest rates are unsustainably high and when they are intolerably low. When rates are low, this means not doing the obvious by reaching for a higher yield. Instead, accept low yield in short-term instruments and thus insulate yourself from losses as longer-term bond prices and stocks wilt from rising rates. Exercise patience instead of insisting on high returns every quarter or every year. A dollar of investment principal preserved is not as exciting, but is every bit as valuable, as a dollar of capital gains. One way to avoid low-yield traps, although it will not feel obviously comfortable nor will it ever maximize return, since it is designed to limit overall risk, is to "ladder" your maturities. Again, CDs are a bad idea. Not because they obviously offer unattractively low rates, but because buying them will lock you in (subject to penalty for withdrawal, remember?) at a future time when you need to take immediate advantage of bond and stock panics and buy those instruments aggressively.

And speaking of yields, you also learned that utility stocks and REITs present a huge paradox: Investors looking for yield in those industries *should not* go for high yield (which comes with zero dividend growth and accompanying risk of a cut or omission). Instead, counterintuitively, you should buy low-yielding utilities or REITs with strong dividend growth rates. Again, this is a formula for total return rather than income now.

You picked up two other ideas about investing in bonds that run counter to old conventional popular folklore. First, bonds should not be bought to hold to maturity. That is a mistaken concept likely born in the experience of bank CD buyers. Bond prices will always fluctuate opposite the trend of interest rates. If you fail to sell, you are destined to give back excess gains beyond the coupon rate. Bonds that have risen above par due to falling rates will either be called away or mature at par, in either case taking back your paper gains. So standing pat dooms you to lower-than-acceptable returns for the balance of the bonds' life. The other seeming paradox about bonds is their major difference from bond funds. Except for the relatively rare term trusts, bond funds never "mature" as do the individual bonds they hold inside their portfolios. So a fund investing in long bonds will always be subject to major fluctuation risk. That is not something you want as you near retirement; at least individual bonds with laddered maturities will always have declining price volatility.

## Learning to Have an Overriding Plan and to Stick to It

This is not another of the many books on financial planning that help you figure out what you need to save to arrive in good shape on retirement day. While we touched on that very lightly and named some good sources of guidance, the focus has been on having a properly balanced asset mix and then keeping that balance on track over time. You learned that going entirely for income at age 60 and above involves highly significant risks: that inflation will slice into your fixed purchasing power and that medical science will let many of us outlive our assets. So you will be adopting the recommended "rule of 105," subtracting your age in years from the number 105 and always having at least the resulting percentage in equities so your asset pool will keep growing. Yes, that means 30 percent in stocks when you're 75! They don't need then to be emerging country small-cap stocks or domestic high-tech software companies, but solid companies that pay rising dividends and whose businesses (food, retailing, oil, or consumer small-ticket items) will probably always be around and keep growing as our spendable incomes and population do.

Asset class allocation is a major factor in overall investment success. You must be diversified among several classes, as discussed in Strategy 21. You learned in Strategy 22 that you should gradually adjust that mix in a more conservative direction—perhaps not less than each three to five years. But you also saw that temporary moves in various markets will take your mix several percentage points offtrack, and these should prompt you to rebalance. That discipline will have you profitably (but counter-intuitively) selling stocks when they've been exceptionally strong, and buying more when they (or any other major asset class) have been major laggards for a while. Thus you will automatically buy low and sell high.

Sticking with your plan also will help you by providing a defense against unwanted intrusion. You can tell the high-pressure salespeople and the telephone cold-callers, "Sorry, what you want to sell me does not fit into my overall plan," and hang up. What they want to sell will almost always be what works well for them (since it sells easily) rather than what you need. They usually sell excitement or try to guarantee high returns. You now know why such pitches are red flags and you will run the other way rather than let greed prompt you to write a check.

## Learning to Sell as Well as Buy

One of the more difficult prescriptions to take will be in the area of selling. We are pounded by advice (mainly from asset gatherers who collect fees if we keep our money in their product family) to "hold for the long term." Mutual funds, except the index type, almost all trade actively, with typical turnover rates of 50 percent per year or higher.

At the most macro of levels, you will need to sell some assets to stay on your allocation course. Perhaps that exercise will cause you to be slightly more comfortable saying sell as well as buy. It will not be enough, however. You learned how societal pressures and internal personal defense mechanisms subtly but very strongly prompt us to try to be perfect. Perfectionism (discussed in Strategy 10) has us resisting selling because we know we'll never get the exact high price. It has us refusing to come to closure because we prefer possibilities to a final verdict. It allows our ego to overrule logic, as our ego wants to be right all the time so it can feel better. You now know you must always battle perfectionism (in selling as well as buying).

The major reason you must learn to sell is that the world is changing (ever faster!) and therefore your previously established investment ideas are always in process of becoming outmoded. So you have accepted the challenge to become more nimble, especially where the factors creating high risk are present: high growth, high technology, high expectations, high price-earnings ratios, and high institutional holdings. You've come to realize that major institutional presence in a stock is often a danger rather than the comfort you formerly perceived: Institutions destabilize the market in the short run, creating major opportunities for those who move counter to the herd, but posing major price danger for many unsophisticated individual holders.

One of the ways you've discovered that will make your selling more feasible is the highly counterintuitive idea of clearly separating the company from its stock. Companies change relatively little in the short term, but their stock prices bounce around significantly. You now know that today's market price is not value. Price is just the current moment's barometer reading that reflects the state of investors' and particularly traders' emotions about and hopes for a company. And you know that perceptions and expectations are more often than not at odds with fundamental long-term realities. The differences are what people call low and high markets, and you are learning about becoming an independent thinker, able to resist the pressure of crowd noise and to do what currently feels lonely but is correct in terms of value versus current price.

## Learning to Keep the Total Picture in Mind

One of the more novel insights you should have acquired exists in the highly important area of asset allocation. Of course you already knew you should think of your personal (taxable) portfolio, your IRA, and your employer's 401(k) or similar plan in a single combined, integrated way. Each one need not be internally balanced in line with your now-proper asset allocation mix, but taken together they should. You probably are now thinking a little more sharply about the matching of tax status with an investment medium's inherent characteristics. For example, you are likely to put your taxable-bond holdings into your IRA or 401(k) and keep growth stocks in all asset piles. Index funds, because of their tax efficiency, you now know, fit better in your taxable holdings than in the already sheltered structures.

Probably the most novel thought presented in the asset-allocation area was that some items not often thought of as assets per se should be factored into the overall mix. You learned that Social Security benefits, your company or government pension entitlement, any fixed annuities, and trust fund income should be capitalized as if they were bonds. They provide fixed income, and their presence effectively shifts your overall allocation more toward income and less toward growth than you ever previously realized. Their only difference from bonds is that they do not provide a terminal principal sum you could reallocate elsewhere.

## More Information

Along the way, you have learned of several useful information sources. Those just scratch the surface. In Strategy 30 are more resources you should strongly consider. But one caution, again with a bit of an ironic twist: More information is a good thing, but total information is impossible to acquire and would lead to paralysis. You need to keep reading and thinking, but always with a practical goal in mind: toward becoming more able to make and execute decisions.

STRATEGY **30**

# Use These
# Outstanding Resources

*M*any good resources are available to self-educating individual investors. My purpose here is to name those from which I believe you will derive the most benefit for time and money expended.

### Financial Planning

Social Security Administration Form 7004, detailing your future benefits: 800-772-1213.

### Personal Computer Software:

- Dow Jones' "Plan Ahead for Your Financial Future"
- Fidelity's "Thinkware"
- T. Rowe Price's "Retirement Planning Kit"
- Price Waterhouse LLP's "Secure Your Future"
- *The Wall Street Journal*'s "Getting Going" by Jonathan Clements

## Public Agencies

The following agencies track disciplinary history of brokers and financial advisers.

To learn about complaints or proceedings, contact the National Association of Securities Dealers (NASD), 800-289-9999 or www.nasdr.com.

For a single source leading to state agencies, contact the North American Securities Administrators' Association, 202-737-0900.

## Self-Education Sources

American Association of Individual Investors (AAII), 312-280-0170. This not-for-profit has chapters in most states, offering monthly meetings; its *AAII Journal* is a fine value at $45/year.

Investment Company Institute (ICI), 202-326-5800, 1401 H Street NW, Suite 1200, Washington DC 20005–2148. The mutual fund business' own self-regulatory watchdog, ICI, provides useful, unbiased educational materials on funds.

National Endowment for Financial Education, 303-220-1200. Popularly known as the College for Financial Planning, NEFE offers detailed self-study courses for individuals and also leading to the Certified Financial Planner designation.

National Association of Investors Corporation (NAIC), 810-583-6242. The NAIC is the national umbrella organization for voluntarily affiliated local investment clubs; it provides a useful "Stock Selection Guide" for fundamental analysis and can help those wishing to locate or start a club.

*The Internet:* An assortment of investor "chat rooms" has emerged. Some are quite newsy, while others offer a platform for strident views, and the worst are concerted tout efforts. News referring to corporate news releases is the most helpful. Much more reliable on average are Web sites maintained by public companies and mutual funds families.

"The Club," 800-654-CLUB. Several hundred traded companies and closed-end funds use a single clearinghouse to offer rapid delivery of annual reports free to inquiring investors. Participating companies are highlighted with a clover-shaped symbol in the stock listings of the *Wall Street Journal* and in *Barron's*.

## Evaluative Guides

The Hulbert Guide to Financial Newsletters, 703-683-5905. Annually produced in softcover by Mark Hulbert, who also publishes a periodic advisory service.

Spencer McGowan's *Individual Investor's Guide to Financial Information*, 972-788-3911 (Simon & Schuster, 1991). This book reviews other investment books as well as advisory services and newsletters. It is valuable for the addresses and phone numbers alone, and is even better as a time- and money-saver!

## Discount Brokerage Firms

Rate schedules and phone numbers are compiled annually in the January issue of the *AAII Journal*. (*See* Self-Education.)

## Chart Services

*Blue Book of Five-Trend Cycligraphs,* a quarterly offering of Securities Research Co., 617-235-0900. Provides 13 years' perspective on fundamentals and prices, also offers useful wall charts.

*Long-Term Values* (15-year monthly graphs) and *Daily Graphs* (one-year windows published weekly) by William O'Neil & Co., Inc., 213-472-7479. Trials available.

*Value Line Investment Survey,* 212-907-1500. Now expanded well beyond its original coverage of 1,800 companies.

Each of the above includes a wealth of fundamental data as well as price charts, creating one-stop information sources.

A rising number of sources provide stock charts on the Internet. Some are free, while others require subscriptions or opening a brokerage account. Two free favorites are bigcharts.com and quote.yahoo.com.

## Major No-Load Fund Groups

Following are the ten largest fund families (assets at December 31, 1996) offering either entirely or predominantly no-load funds:

1. Fidelity, 800-544-8888; features a very broad product line
2. Vanguard, 800-662-2739; the leader in index investing
3. Wellington, 800-662-2739; affiliated with Vanguard
4. T. Rowe Price, 800-225-5132; strong in equities and overseas
5. American Century, 800-531-5575; merger of 20th Century and Benham
6. Schwab, 800-435-4000; principal emphasis in equity funds
7. Dreyfus, 800-782-6620; stronger at fixed income
8. Janus, 800-525-3713; aggressive, smaller caps
9. Scudder, 800-225-2470; international strength
10. Strong , 800-368-1030; narrower product line than some

## Mutual Fund Supermarkets

These allow the convenience of shopping across many fund families in a single-statement account:

- Schwab One-Source, 800-435-4000; the most funds
- Fidelity, 800-544-8888; own funds plus others
- Jack White & Co., 800-233-3411; allows limited shorting

## Libraries

Public and university libraries have powerful retrieval systems for books, which in some cases can be borrowed from far outside the local collection. They also have electronic catalogs of articles in business periodicals and multiple newspapers that provide very valuable information and insights for investors. Spend some time getting to know how these institutions' tools can help you.

## Suggested Reading

Of necessity, this list is extremely brief to prevent overwhelming the investor/reader. Items are listed under each heading in order of my judgment of priority.

## Contrarianism

Neill, Humphrey B. *The Art of Contrary Thinking.* Caldwell, Idaho: Caxton, 1967.

Dreman, David. *The New Contrarian Investment Strategy.* New York: Random House, 1982.

## Historical Perspective

Galbraith, John K. *A Short History of Financial Euphoria.* Nashville, Tenn.: Whittle Direct Books, 1990. Parallels of major bubble/fad tops.

Hirsch, Yale. *The Stock Trader's Almanac.* The Hirsch Organization, Inc., Box 2069, River Vale NJ 07675-9988, 201-767-4100. Annual desk calendar with a wealth of fascinating and useful market history and patterns.

## Fundamental Analysis

Graham, Benjamin, et al. *Security Analysis: Principles and Technique.* New York: McGraw-Hill, 1962. A college-level text for any serious investor.

Sharp, Richard. *Calculated Risk.* New York: McGraw-Hill, 1986. A solid volume on measuring and understanding risk.

## Technical Analysis

Edwards, Robert, and John Magee. *Technical Analysis of Stock Trends.* Boston: John Magee Inc., 1979. Extremely comprehensive; printings since 1948.

Plummer, Tony. *The Psychology of Technical Analysis.* New York: McGraw-Hill, 1993. Explains why technical analysis works.

## Investor Psychology

Mamis, Justin. *The Nature of Risk; Stock Market Survival and the Meaning of Life.* Reading, Mass.: Addison-Wesley, 1991. A deep exploration of why we feel the way we do about risk and loss and gain. Know thyself!

Wycoff, Peter. *The Psychology of Stock Market Timing.* Englewood Cliffs, N.J.: Prentice-Hall, 1969. Again, what makes markets move as they do.

Weiner, Elliot. *The Ostrich Complex.* New York: Warner Books, 1986. Not about investing, but about human tendency to avoid problems and pain.

## Other Books by the Author

*It's When You Sell That Counts.* New York: McGraw-Hill, 1997. Treats the tricky and largely neglected area of what to do after you buy. Available in bookstores and from clubs.

*Plugging into Utilities.* New York: McGraw-Hill, 1993. Easy set of dividend-growth signals for when to buy/hold/sell/avoid phone, water, power, and gas utility stocks. Total return clearly beats high current yield. Available at 303-988-2296.

# INDEX

## A

Acceleration, 92
Accrued interest, 142
Accumulation, tables, 45
Agility required by rapid change, 32, 125, 304
American Association of Individual Investors, 260, 308
American Depository Receipts (ADRs), 272
angle of price movement, 91–92
Annual returns of mutual funds, 181
Art, not science, investing as, 87, 89, 92
Asset allocation
and funds families, 247
or mix, 20, 22, 38, 48, 64, 76, 100, 187, 303
Asset class diversification, minimum, 222
Asset classes
past returns on, 36
diversification across, 218, 220–21
Asset mix
adjust with age, 184, 225, 241
shifts toward income, 151, 225, 228, 241
table, 228
unplanned, 63, 218
Asset separation, business vs. portfolio, 114
Author, other books by, 312

## B

Baby boomers, savings habits of, 1
Balanced funds, 186–87
Balloon events, 21, 29

Bank accounts, bank CDs, bank deposits, 33, 41, 93–94, 105, 124
Bank IRAs, bad choice, 246
Bank-sold mutual funds, 153
Banks
bonds, CDs, connection of, 135–36
low returns at, 2
Bear markets, 123, 134
in bonds, 1994, 147, 151–52, 153, 155, 161, 192
Benefits department at work, 4, 245, 292–93
Blackout or trading embargo period, 21, 24
Bond funds
vs. bonds, 150, 187
misconceptions of, 152
Bond market, percent of years up, 37
Bonds
vs. bond funds, 150, 187
holding to maturity, 135, 147
inflation-indexed, 33
not single-decision vehicles, 145–46
priced to call, 145
prices fluctuate, 142
quality ratings, 139
viewed passively, 135
Borrow short/invest long risk, 209–10
Brokerage firm, choosing a, 282
Brokers
hand-holding function, 253
skills, 72
Bull market
starting 1982, 37, 104, 134
signs of aging, 90
Bunching income into alternate years, 278
Business cycles, 163

**313**